Frederic George Stephens

Flemish Relics

Architectural, Legendary, and Pictorial, as Connected with Public Buildings in

Belgium

Frederic George Stephens

Flemish Relics

Architectural, Legendary, and Pictorial, as Connected with Public Buildings in Belgium

ISBN/EAN: 9783337155490

Printed in Europe, USA, Canada, Australia, Japan

Cover: Foto ©ninafisch / pixelio.de

More available books at **www.hansebooks.com**

FLEMISH RELICS;

Architectural, Legendary, and Pictorial,

AS CONNECTED WITH

PUBLIC BUILDINGS IN BELGIUM.

GATHERED BY

FREDERIC G. STEPHENS,

AUTHOR OF "NORMANDY, A SKETCH," ETC.

Illustrated with Photographs by Cundall and Fleming.

LONDON:
ALFRED W. BENNETT, 5, BISHOPSGATE WITHOUT.

1866.

To W. M. ROSSETTI.

Dear William,

The title of this Book indicates that its concern is with the past, and that its nature is fragmentary. The text describes the most famous buildings in the Low Countries, details much of their history and that of those who used them, and contains remarks upon pictures by Memline and the Van Eycks.

In acknowledgment of tried affection and abundant kindness, I offer to you the materials I have gathered and the opinions I have expressed,

And remain,

Your old friend,

FREDERIC G. STEPHENS.

September 12th, 1865.

Contents.

	PAGE
THE CATHEDRAL OF NOTRE DAME AT TOURNAY	41
THE ABBEY OF VILLERS	61
CHURCH OF ST. NICHOLAS, AND BELFRY AT GHENT	77
THE BELFRY OF GHENT	83
MAISON DES BATELIERS, GHENT	89
THE CATHEDRAL OF ST. BAVON, GHENT	90
THE HOTEL DE VILLE AT YPRES	103
THE BELFRY AT BRUGES, GRANDE PLACE	110
THE HOSPITAL OF ST. JOHN AT BRUGES	117
THE HOTEL DE VILLE, BRUSSELS	141
THE CHURCH OF ST. MICHAEL AND ST. GUDULE, BRUSSELS	147
THE HOTEL DE VILLE AT LOUVAIN	151
THE CATHEDRAL OF MECHLIN	156
THE CATHEDRAL OF NOTRE DAME AT ANTWERP	164
THE CHURCH OF ST. JACQUES, ANTWERP	170
CLOISTERS IN THE PALACE AT LIEGE	174
THE HOTEL DE VILLE AT AUDENAERDE	179

ILLUSTRATIONS.

HOTEL DE VILLE, BRUSSELS. … …	*Frontispiece*
INTERIOR OF THE CATHEDRAL, TOURNAY. …	41
RUINS OF THE ABBEY, VILLERS LA VILLE.	61
CHURCH OF ST. NICHOLAS AND BELFRY, GHENT. …	77
MAISON DES BATELIERS, GHENT. …	… 89
HOTEL DE VILLE, YPRES.	103
TOUR DES HALLES, BRUGES.	112
GRANDE PLACE, BRUSSELS. …	144
HOTEL DE VILLE, LOUVAIN.	… 151
THE CATHEDRAL, MECHLIN. … … …	… 156
INTERIOR OF THE CATHEDRAL, ANTWERP. …	… 164
THE AISLES, SOUTH-SIDE, ANTWERP CATHEDRAL.	165
THE CHURCH OF ST. JACQUES, ANTWERP. …	… 170
COURT OF THE BISHOP'S PALACE, LIEGE. …	174
HOTEL DE VILLE, AUDENAERDE. …	… 179

FLEMISH RELICS,

ETC.

HE Frankish race, which crossed the Rhine in the third century, occupied in the first instance the district known as Toxandria, which extended from near Maestricht for twenty leagues along the Meuse, where now are Antwerp, Breda, and Bois-le-Duc. Julian, when he defeated the main body of the invaders of those provinces which the Romans styled the Belgicæ, permitted the Salian branch of the Franks still to retain this district, on condition that its people became allies of the empire, a condition which—it is needless to remark to those who are acquainted with the antipathy so often exhibited between the Frankish and Germanic races—was fulfilled in many a battle fought against the tribes which followed in the footsteps of the imperial allies. In less ancient times the Franks appear more as the masters than the servants of the Romans; this was said especially of Merobaudes, one of their kings; the authority of Arbogastes, who succeeded him, was so great that when Valentinian II. desired to be independent of his general and to depose him, the troops obeyed their chief—as the poor emperor found to his cost, when they strangled him at Vienne. In the time of Honorius, the Franks were firmly established in Gaul, so that that hapless province, from the Mediterranean to the Meuse and Rhine, became a mere battle-field and stall of plunder. The best thing that Ætius, the imperial general, could do was to employ one mass of barbarians against another. As if to make the confusion of this period complete, and display what a wilderness of slaughter the once peaceful but long emasculated province had become, it is evident that the Franks themselves fought on opposite sides at the horrible day of Châlons (451), while it was debated whether Cæsar's conquest—which he "pacified" at the cost of a million of its fighting men and a million sold into slavery —should belong to the Huns or to tribes less barbarous than they. On the side of Attila was a brother of Meroveus, of the long-haired race, probably descended from the Merobaudes before-named, who now contested for pre-eminence with a Meroveus who followed Ætius, and was one of the sons of that Chlodion whom this general had defeated near Rheims in 428. At Châlons the son of Alaric the Visigoth fought with his people on the side of the Romans and was slain. Jornandes says, one hundred and sixty-two thousand men were killed in this fight; it was the last of the Roman victories.

Exhausted by its triumph and mastered by its own allies, the empire fell from bad to worse, so that, in effect, the ruling power in Gaul was that of the Visigoths, who, seated in Toulouse, held the southern part. The Burgundians had the eastern portion, while that in the north was in the hands of the Franks, who ultimately conquered the other tribes and divided the entire province between the sons of their king. We shall confine ourselves to a sketch of the history of the latter, because the people of the provinces which the Romans styled the Belgicæ, came in for the inheritance of Cæsar, founded the political power of the *Frankenric*, or Freeland, and gave the impetus which produced France, to which, for many ages, Flanders was attached.

So confused is the history of these times that Gregory of Tours, one of the best of the ancient writers (539–595), says not a word about the Pharamond of whom the French historians have made so much, and who plays so distinguished a part in the historical romances which were in vogue a few years since. The authorities for the existence of Chlodion and even of Meroveus are not beyond suspicion when they represent them as sole rulers of the people from 420 until 448. The historian of Tours, although living so near in time to this period, is uncertain about them. The Childeric, who is, after all, the earliest known ruler of that branch of the Franks which settled itself at Tournay, was a remarkable man, remarkable in his wife, and still more so in his son Clovis. Childeric carried his youthful gallantries to such an extent that the tribe banished him; he found refuge with Basinus, king of the Thuringians, whose queen, Basina, received him with even greater kindness than that of her husband.* His tribe during his absence was governed by Egidius, the so-called Roman General at Soissons. At the end of eight years Childeric was re-invested with power at home. Hardly was this affair settled, when, to the astonishment of the Frank, Basina presented herself with the avowed intention of marrying him. The amazed Childeric asked the "reason" for her journey and this resolve. She replied that he was the most valiant, strongest, and handsomest man she had heard of, and that if she knew another who surpassed him in those qualities, not even the sea should keep her from him. The king could not resist such vigorous courtship, and married this self-willed lady, who had formerly been his mistress.† Such was the mother of Clovis. Childeric died and was buried at Tournay, in 481. Of the singular discovery of his grave and its treasures, we shall speak further on.

Clovis became king when he was fifteen years of age, but did nothing to distinguish himself until five years later, when he led the whole force of the Salian Franks, which was not more than five thousand warriors, to unite with Ragnacar, the Frankish king of Cambray, in an attack on Siagrius, the *quasi*-Roman chief of the militia at Soissons, and defeated him.‡ The place of battle was at

* It was strange that he should find a refuge among the Thuringians, because this very people had, when defeated on the side of Attila, at the battle of Châlons, retreated through the country of the Franks, and exercised the most atrocious cruelties upon those who fell into their hands. "They murdered the hostages and the captives, slew two hundred young women by exquisite tortures, cast their limbs beneath the heavy waggons, and left them in the road." To them, nevertheless, Childeric went, and was doubly well received.

† If Gregory of Tours is to be believed, this lady must have practised magical arts. On the night of their nuptials she persuaded Childeric to go into the courtyard of the palace at Tournay, where they were lodged, in order that he might see the wonderful appearances which would present themselves. He went thrice. On the first occasion there came before him a long rout of *unicorns*, lions, and leopards, tumbling and wrangling with each other, but all without a sound, and shadowless. The second time produced bears and wolves; the first shambled across the courtyard and vanished while the king looked at them; the others ran in circles and leapt, but quite silently. On the third visit there appeared multitudes of dogs of great size and many colours, and innumerable cats, that always looked behind them. From the diversity and characteristics of these apparitions, Childeric was instructed to learn what were the qualities of the races which would arise from his union with Basina.

‡ "He sent him a challenge, almost in the language of chivalry," says Gibbon, "to fight, and name the place of battle."

Nogent, near Soissons, which, being inclosed by a circle of Roman tombs, not inaptly marked the spot where the last pretender to the imperial authority in Gaul was ruined. In the neighbouring city the spoil was divided, and the heaps of treasures which the Franks and their allies had gathered were placed in public while the process went on. A certain precious vase had been taken from the cathedral of Rheims, and for its return no less a person than St. Remi applied to Clovis (who was still a pagan). The Frankish leader—no impolitic person, nor one who was disinclined to please the Christians—desired this vessel should be set aside, in order that he might present it to the bishop. One of the soldiers, resenting this interference with the laws of prize, dashed the vase to atoms with his axe, and declared that no one should interfere with spoil, nor claim it ere it had fallen to his lot. Clovis, who had felt himself in the wrong, and probably feared to go further in the matter, commanded his anger for the time; but, about a year afterwards, and while holding a review of his warriors, he saw the vase-breaker standing before him in the rank. Going to the man, he snatched the axe from his hands, reproved him loudly for his slovenly appearance, and threw the weapon on the earth: as the soldier stooped to recover it, Clovis smote him on the head, killing him, and cried, " Thus didst thou break the vase at Soissons ! "

This king had very good reasons for keeping on good terms with the bishops or Christian leaders, who were, in effect, the most powerful persons in Gaul, and could be dangerous enemies even to such chieftains as himself. It is evident that he owed no small part of his success to the craft which led him to become their *protégé*. He was but an unimportant person until he became an orthodox Christian, and the representative of the Church militant against those Arian heretics whom the orthodox clergy hated more than they hated the Pagans. Although professing the same belief as the mass of his tribe, Clovis always treated the Christians with consideration, and married no less distinguished a Christian than St. Clotildis,* the first of the many saints of the blood royal of

---

* Clotildis, or Clotilda, was one of the daughters of Chilperic, younger brother of Gundobald of Burgundy; the latter slew Chilperic and his sons, and banished his daughters. Clovis, hearing of the extraordinary beauty of Clotildis, sent Aurelian to see if she was really so fair as men averred. The

France, who had been "fortunately," say the historians, brought up in the true faith, although in the midst of Arians. Mainly by means of the clergy Clovis established the Frankish dominion in Gaul. Clotildis incessantly urged him to join her Church; but, although indulgent to his wife in all other respects, he did not make public profession of the Christian faith until after the battle of Tolbiac, in 496. In the heat of this fight—so we learn from the historians, who relate events of the sort with a dramatic effectiveness which rouses the strongest suspicions—the king raised his hands to heaven, and invoking to his aid the god of Clotildis, vowed in

---

messenger disguised himself as a beggar, and on a Sunday morning went with others of that class to receive alms at a church door where, as she issued forth, the lady was wont to give to all who asked. Overcome by her beauty and noble appearance, the ambassador, as she extended the pittance towards him, seized her hand, turned back the sleeve which partly covered it and kissed the bare wrist with an ardour that had more than gratitude in it. Returning home, Clotildis, who was, it must be owned, ever on the look-out for something portentous, sent for the daring man who had saluted her, and inquired the cause of his very unconventional action. Aurelian declared himself to be the ambassador of Clovis, and produced the royal and golden ornaments which were in his charge, and intended for the adornment of the lady of Burgundy should she turn out to be beautiful. Although the position of the suitor was by no means equal to that of the family of Clotildis, yet he had something of a reputation, which made men believe it better to have him for a friend than for an enemy. Moreover, Clotildis' own position was, to say the best of it, precarious, because she was rather in the way of Chilperic; so, with some little pretended demur, the latter, who was himself an Arian, consented to his niece's marriage with the pagan. That Clovis was a pagan, and therefore convertible, a man much talked about and handsome, were inducements enough for Clotildis. She stipulated for freedom in religious matters, and the marriage took place at Soissons, in 493. She was an admirable queen, "her charity to the poor seemed a sea that could never be drained." After the death of Clovis, in 511, she lived to see the eldest born son of her husband by a concubine, who was begotten before his marriage to herself, and named Thierry, reigning at Rheims over Austrasia. Her own sons were Chlodomir, Childebert, and Chlotaire, who governed at Orleans, Paris, and Soissons respectively. She learnt the murder of the sons of Chlodomir by their uncles. She saw Chilperic, her own uncle's kingdom of Burgundy united to France by Childebert and Chlotaire, whose enormous wickedness to their brother's children so horrified her that she retired from them and spent the rest of her life at Tours, near the tomb of St Martin, and in doing all the good in her power, seemed to forget that she was queen and that her sons were kings. She foretold her death thirty days before it came about, and sending for Childebert and Chlotaire, admonished them in the most earnest manner to honour God and keep his commandments. She ordered her remaining property to be given to the poor, "*though of this there was little, for she had been careful to send it before her by their hands.*" She prayed until the last moment, and died June 3rd, 545. The Roman Catholic Church still keeps her festival on that day.

return for victory to become a Christian. He conquered, and kept his word by receiving the instructions of St. Remi, and allowed himself to be baptized in the cathedral at Rheims. On this auspicious occasion, which happened at Christmas, 496, nothing less extraordinary than the holy oil of anointment * was vouchsafed by special gift of heaven; a dove brought the marvellous liquid to the hands of St. Remi at the moment of baptism, and while, with pardonable dogmatism, he cried to the convert, "*Bow thy head, Sicambrian, adore that which thou hast burnt, burn that which thou hast adored!*" Three thousand Frankish warriors followed the example of their chief.

Clovis led an army against Gundobald, the uncle of Clotildis; defeated him near Dijon, accepted tribute, and allowed him to retain his dominions, much, no doubt, to the satisfaction of Clotildis, who was less than a saint in respect to the forgiveness of injuries. Fighting in the interests of the faith, Clovis next came in opposition to the Visigothic king of Toulouse, Alaric II. Before going against him, the Frank sent to seek a sign of his fortune at the shrine of St. Martin, at Tours. As his messengers entered the choir of that famous church, where neither by day nor night was the sound of chanting unheard, for the priests relieved one another perpetually, these auspicious words rose to the roof:—

"Thou hast girded me with strength unto the battle; thou hast subdued under me those that rose up against me. Thou hast given me the necks of mine enemies, that I might destroy them that hate me."

No wonder this presage was accepted with enthusiasm by Clovis, who heeded little that this method of making the house of God the residence of an oracle of almost Pagan sort had been pronounced sacrilegious by several councils.† As he proceeded with the

---

* This miraculously produced oil was long preserved at Rheims in a golden vessel styled the *ampulla*. It had the wonderful power of producing itself when needed for the coronation of a French king. A fragment of a vessel said to have been the *ampulla*, was produced at the coronation of Charles X. Hincmar, St. Remi's successor at Rheims, seems to have invented in the ninth century the whole story of this miraculous appearance of the fifth century. It is worth while to note that another vase of holy oil was kept in the church of St. Martin, at Tours; both were believed to be miraculously replenished.

† This method of consulting the oracles, as they were assumed to be, of certain martyrs and saints—among which St. Martin established an unrivalled

campaign more favourable signs presented themselves; a white doe showed a new ford by which his army passed a swollen river, meteors followed that army from the tower of the cathedral of Poictiers, near to which city Alaric was defeated and slain. The Frank pursued his advantage so far as Carcassonne, and seemed sure of the whole Visigothic kingdom; but Theodoric, the Ostrogothic master of Spain, aided his ally, and the invader was beaten

---

reputation by the event above described—was very common in that and later ages. Of the allied experiment which is known by the name of *sortes Virgilianæ*, take the following from Welwood about Charles I. of England:— "The king, being at Oxford during the civil wars, went one day to see the public library, where he was showed among other books a Virgil nobly printed and exquisitely bound. The Lord Falkland, to divert the king, would have his majesty make a trial of his fortune by the *sortes Virgilianæ*, which everybody knows was a usual kind of augury some ages past. Whereupon the king opening the book, the period which happened to turn up was that part of Dido's imprecation against Æneas, which Mr. Dryden translates thus:—

> "'Yet let a race untamed, and haughty foes,
> His peaceful entrance with dire arms oppose;
> Oppressed with numbers in th' unequal field,
> His men discouraged and himself expell'd,
> Let him for succour sue from place to place,
> Torn from his subjects' and his son's embrace;
> First let him see his friends in battle slain,
> And their untimely fate lament in vain:
> And when, at length, the cruel war shall cease,
> On hard conditions may he buy his peace;
> Nor let him then enjoy supreme command,
> But fall untimely by some hostile hand,
> And lie unburied in the common sand.'

It is said that Charles seemed concerned at this accident, and that Lord Falkland, observing it, would likewise try his own fortune in the same manner, hoping that he might fall upon some passage that could have no relation to his case, and thereby divert the king's thoughts from any impressions that the other might have made upon him. But the place that Falkland stumbled upon was yet more suited to his destiny than the other had been to the king's; being the following expressions of Evander upon the untimely death of his son Pallas, as they are translated by the same hand:—

> "'O, Pallas! thou hast failed thy plighted word
> To fight with reason, not to tempt the sword.
> I warn'd thee, but in vain, for well I knew
> What perils youthful ardour would pursue;
> That boiling blood would carry thee too far,
> Young as thou wert in dangers, raw to war.
> O, curst essay of arms, disastrous doom,
> Prelude of bloody fields and fights to come!'"

To return to Clovis; what sort of idea he had of St. Martin may be guessed from the fact that, after the victory over the Visigoths, to obtain which he vowed all his arms and his war-horse to the saint, he desired to redeem them with gold. Upon this so startling a price was named as that demanded by the saint for a release, that Clovis declared St. Martin was *nearly as good at a bargain as in a battle!*

from before Arles with considerable loss. He, nevertheless, retained the whole of the Visigothic possessions in France, except Septimania, and settled his son Thierry as ruler in them. Clovis returned to Tours, where he met ambassadors from the emperor of the East, Anastasius I., who sent him a crown, and robe of the consular order. The former Clovis deposited in the basilica of St. Peter's at Rome, where it remained for many centuries. He does not appear to have been named consul.* From this time Clovis spared no means and hesitated at no crime which could insure his family the royal seat of the Franks. He had no right beyond a personal one to pre-eminence, which on his death might accrue to any one strong enough to seize it. He induced Chloderic, son of Sigebert, the Ripuarian, to murder his father, under a promise of aid in securing the succession.† The parricide committed, he caused the guilty son to be slain, and appearing before the Ripuarians he demanded to be elected their king, averring that he knew nothing of the deaths of the princes. They accepted him with acclamations. He caused the king of Terouanne, a Frankish city in the north-west of Gaul, to become a monk, and afterwards decapitated him and his son. Ragnacar, the same who had helped him against Siagrius, came next into the hands of this ruthless chieftain. He bribed some of the people of this prince with gifts of collars of gilded brass, probably torques or carcanets of honour, to be privy to an attack of the soldiers of Clovis. The traitors tied the hands of their own prince behind his back and rendered him up to Clovis, who reproached the captive with weakness in submitting to be thus bound, and killed him with an axe. When the betrayers demanded their reward and complained that the bribes were spurious, Clovis

---

* See on this point, which is assumed to be an important one, the opinion of Sismondi, "Merovingians, A.D. 510," Hallam's "Middle Ages," Supplement 5, and Gibbon's "Decline, etc."

† After the deed was done, Chloderic sent to Clovis, and said to him, " My father is dead, and I hold his treasure and his kingdom ; aid me now, and you shall have what you choose of the gold." The answer of Clovis thanked him for goodwill, and begged that he would show the treasure to the messengers, when the whole should be his. Chloderic then displayed the treasures of Sigebert to the messengers, and pointing to a coffer, said, "In this my father kept all the gold coin he gathered." One of them replied, "Dip your arm to the bottom of the chest, in order to show us how deep it is." While he stooped, and his arm was buried in the mass of coin, they smote him on the head with the inevitable Frankish axe—*Francisca*, as it seems to have been called. —*Gregory of Tours*, 1, 2, 40.

bade them think themselves fortunate that, as traitors, he permitted them to live. One by one the descendants of the long-haired race of Meroveus were put to death, the Frankish power united in a single person, and the realm of France constructed, so that it stretched far beyond its present limits. It was broken up at the death of Clovis, who, however, settled many things and gave with unbounded liberality to the clergy. They in return reckoned him amongst the saints. He died on the 27th November, 511, at Paris, where he was buried in the church of St. Peter and St. Paul, now St. Geneviève, which he and Clotildis had founded shortly after the transference of the seat of his power to that city.

At the division of the Frankish realm among the sons of Clovis, Chlotaire took the northern portion ; this included nearly all modern Belgium, except the province of Liège, which fell to Thierry, the eldest brother. In course of time and crime, however, the whole realm came to Chlotaire, who murdered his nephews* with as little remorse as one can conceive. It seems as if Nemesis wrought by the hands of this sovereign, he was the most guilty of all his horrible family ; his son Chramna rebelled against him, got assistance from the Bretons, and was defeated. "Then," says Gregory of Tours, "he took to flight, having had ships made ready for him-

---

* One of these, Chlodowald (St. Cloud) was youngest son of Chlodomir of Orleans. Clotildis, who, saint as she might have been, had a savage love of vengeance, instigated her sons to attack the Burgundians. Chlodomir took Sigismund, one of their kings, and murdered him and all his people, but falling himself into an ambuscade, was slain in turn. His children were in the hands of Clotildis until Chlodomir and Childebert of Paris sent her a pair of scissors and a sword, by way of hinting that they must have their hair cut off, *i. e*, become monks, or die. On her answering that she preferred to have them slain than degraded with cropped locks, Chlotaire killed two of them with his own hands ; the third, named Chlodowald, or Cloud, sheared himself, and thus sacrificed his right to reign. When Thierry of Metz died (534), and was succeeded by his son Theodobert, who (548) left that realm in turn to Theodobald, and the last perished of plague in 553. Cloud made not a sign, but left all to Chlotaire, his father's younger brother. He took the monastic habit from St. Saverinus and retired to a hermitage in Provence, where it is said he wrought many miracles. Returning to Paris he was welcomed with joy, and built a monastery at Nogent-sur-Seine, now styled St. Cloud. He died September 7th, 560 ; this day is appropriated to him in the calendar of French saints. He is the tutelar of nailmakers; they keep him in honour, we suppose, by the name of clouts—a sort of nail, in French, *clou*. He is represented in pictures in the Benedictine habit, with royal insignia. (See *Die Heiligenbilder*, of Dr. Alt, Berlin, 1845.) The relics of St. Cloud were preserved at the monastery until the Revolution.

self and his family. Being compelled to wait for them, he was made prisoner and brought before Chlotaire, who ordered him to be burned alive, with his wife and daughters. In pursuance of this command, they tied him on a bench by means of a piece of linen taken from an altar, and shut him into a poor man's cottage with his family, after which they set fire to the house, in which all perished." Anything was better as a king than a ruffian of this sort; he reigned as sole king not more than two years, and when he died, just a year and a day after the burning of Chramna, it was while shrieking, "*What must the king of all the heavens be, who thus kills the great kings of the earth?*" He was buried in the basilica of St. Médard at Soissons, 561. A state of society such as that which is indicated by the narratives we have given, must, to be endurable, have had circumstances complementary to these and serving to set off their blackness with something which suggested light. Institutions where safety and freedom from horror and suffering could be experienced flourished under the monastic rule. Accordingly, the Frankish dominions swarmed with convents, where men might enjoy that which must have seemed heavenly repose when compared with the external turmoil of the Merovingian rule. By way of illustration and contrast here is a little verse, the simplicity and pious tone of which express more than its words. It relates to the Bishop of Tournay, the same St. Médard* to whom Chlotaire's tomb-ground was dedicated, who entered the see

---

* St. Médard succeeded St. Eleutherius as bishop of Tournay in 532. He was originally consecrated to St. Vermond, near Peronne, by St Remi in 530; he removed his see to Noyon in consequence of the cruelties of the barbarians, until he was appointed to the see of Tournay, whence he laboured with great effect upon the ruder inhabitants of that diocese. He bestowed the veil on Radegonda the Thuringian, first wife of Chlotaire, when that monarch repudiated her in order to marry Chamsena, the mother of Chramna, and second of his numerous wives. Médard was a constant friend to Chlotaire, who came in haste to his death-bed at Noyon. At the tomb of this saint so many miracles were wrought, and so great was the love of the king for him, that Chlotaire erected an abbey at Soissons in his honour, and caused his relics to be translated thither in a shrine which was covered with the most precious stuffs, seeded with diamonds and adorned with plates of gold. At the translation the king sometimes bore this *châsse* on his own shoulders, and thought himself honoured by the office. Such was the contradictory nature of this savage. St. Godard was bishop of Rouen, 511 to 529. (See *Pommeraye, Hist. de la Cath. de Rouen.*) At this time Chlotaire founded the famous church of St. Ouen, then dedicated to St. Peter, at Rouen.

of Soissons in 545. It was composed by St. Ouen, so says Vitalis, who preserved it for us :—

> "Godard of Rouen, Médard of Soissons, twins,
> Together issued from their mother's womb;
> White-robed, were washed together from their sins,
> Both went together, bishops, to the tomb."

The kingdom was again divided between the children of Chlotaire. Charibert became king of Paris; Gonthran, king of Orleans and Burgundy; Sigebert I., king of Austrasia. Chilperic I. succeeded to his father's dominions at Soissons, which included the greater part of Belgium. Charibert had for one of his daughters the Bertha who married Ethelbert, king of Kent, and brought Christianity for the second time into England. Chilperic was a jovial, incontinent sort of fellow, who exasperated the clergy by contriving to annul bequests to them, and incessantly grumbled that "no one rules but these bishops; see how all goes to the churches!" It was his wife, the monstrous Fredegonda, whose jealousy of Galeswintha, the fair daughter of Athanagild, the Visigothic king of Spain, caused some frightful tragedies and broke up several kingdoms. She contrived so that the sweet Galeswintha—whose history is as full of tenderness as those of others about her is harsh and dark—should be slain. In revenge for this, the victim's sister, Brunehault, whom Sigebert had wedded, urged her husband against his brother, and caused him to unite with Gonthran of Burgundy, so that such a whirl of war, false-swearing, and cruelty, began, that one sickens to write about it. Chilperic was besieged in Tournay, in 575, by Sigebert. During this siege, while the latter was at Vitry-on-the-Scarfe, near Tournay, he was proclaimed king of Austrasia and Neustria, and despite the warnings of St. Germain, who came before him wan and worn by sickness, marched to the destruction of his brother. St. Germain implored him thus: "O, king Sigebert, if you go, lay aside the thought of killing your brother and you will return alive and victorious, but if you go on full of vengeance, you will die, for the Lord hath said by the mouth of Solomon, 'Whoso diggeth a pit for his brother, shall fall into it himself.'" The king paid no attention, but went on. Chilperic and Fredegonda were shut up in Tournay; the former was placid after his fashion, but the latter was characteristically like a wild beast with rage and fear. She was then *enceinte*; the child was born during the siege, and she named it Samson, as an omen of deliverance. She sought safety in a characteristic fashion, by giving daggers to two devoted youths, sending them to murder Sigebert; going to his camp they effected this, and were cut to pieces. At this, the army of the murdered man dispersed; Chilperic came forth from Tournay, went to Vitry, saw his brother's body without any emotion, and ordered it to be splendidly interred at Lambres-on-the-Scarfe. These incidents are depicted on the stained glass of the cathedral at Tournay.

What remains of the furious Fredegonda, the bondsman's daughter, famous and magnificent beauty, mistress of many nations, queen and regent, implacable, ruthless, traitress, assassin, poisoner, who hunted Meroveus, her husband's son, like a wild beast, so that his best friend's last act was in putting him to death; antagonist of the equally magnificent Brunehault, who was a king's daughter, an outraged sister, and a king's wife, but who nevertheless was brought to the heels of a wild horse? The answer may be obtained in the crypt of St. Denis, which now contains the bare cover of her tomb: her bones were long ago dispersed. Take what M. de Caumont tells us about its chief modern interest: "Cette mosaïque se compose d'une infinité de fragments d'émaux de différentes nuances, disséminés dans un mastic préparé et coulé sur une pierre de lias. Les draperies, le contour des ornements, en un mot, tout ce qui est trait dans cette figure est formé avec des filets de cuivre incrustés; les places de la tête, des pieds, et des mains, sont unies, et la pierre du couvercle est restée à nu dans ces parties; mais il est évident que les pieds, les mains, et la tête, avaient été modelés en metal. L'usage de représenter le défunt en mosaïque s'est prolongé jusqu' au XIIe siècle." One does not fail to remark that the custom of leaving the face of a mortuary slab to be represented on a detached plate of metal held in France and Flanders till very late. Most of the incised slabs of the fourteenth and fifteenth centuries exhibit this, as we shall see in the Abbey of Villers, near Genappe, and St. Bavon at Ghent.

To resume:—Chilperic was murdered, and, in the end, Brunehault governed Austrasia in the name of her son Childebert, whose children divided the kingdoms of Burgundy and Austrasia between them. Fredegonda, the peasant's daughter, ruled in Neustria until her death, in 597.* Chlotaire II., of Soissons,—who, be it remembered, represented that Belgic branch of the Franks which more than once became the main stem,—son of Chilperic I., died sole king of the Franks, in 628. Pepin of Landen—who, as he came from the neighbourhood of Liège, may be styled a Belgian—being at the head of the Austrasian lords, opposed Brunehault. Chlotaire II. captured her, his mother's life-long enemy, and, after torture, caused her to be torn to pieces at the heels of a wild horse. His sons were Dagobert and Charibert; the latter became king of Aquitaine, and in his family that province remained until 735. Dagobert was the most powerful and worthy of the Merovingians. It is not worth while to enumerate his feeble successors.

It may well gratify the national pride of the modern Belgians when they reflect that their territory not only contains Tournay, which may be called the head quarters of the Frankish nationality, but Landen, the seat of that Pepin, who, when the blind rage, hate, and lust of several generations had wrought their worst on the sons of Meroveus—the son, no doubt, originally, of a sacred race, to a belief in the sanctity of which many a member owed his life when in the hands of inferiors—applied a bridle to the failing state of Frankenric. Pepin of Heristal, the still more potent controller, founder of the Carlovingian family, conqueror of Friesland, and civilizer, came from the banks of the Meuse. From the last

---

* The imprecation of St. Prætextatus, Archbishop of Rouen, has been fulfilled by all succeeding ages with regard to Fredegonda. She caused him to be stabbed while praying in the very choir of his cathedral. After receiving the wound, he contrived to totter to the altar, stretched out his "two hands full of blood" to the vase of the Eucharist, took a piece of the bread, and returned thanks to God that he thus obtained the *viaticum*. Before death took place Fredegonda visited the archbishop, with the pretence of condolence and affection. At last his patience was exhausted by her hypocrisy, and he addressed her thus: "I feel that God is calling me from this world; but thou shalt be for ever accursed, and God will in the end visit my blood upon thy head."

The reader who is not prepared for those surprises of which Merovingian history is so full reads with astonishment that this valedictory prelate was the very man who married Meroveus his godson, son of Chilperic, to no less a person than Brunehault, the widow of Sigebert, then twenty-eight years of age; an act of rebellion against the man who had mercifully spared her life, and of treason on the part of Meroveus. It was this which strengthened the hate of Fredegonda against Brunehault, and procured the murder of Prætextatus. The history of this affair and its consequences reads like a dream, so wild and intensely dramatic is it. The most brilliant of Thierry's Merovingian narratives treats of it.

descended Charles Martel, whose son, Pepin le *Bref*, shut up the last feeble son of Clovis in the monastery of St. Bertin,* then dedicated to St. Martin, at St. Omer. This was in 752. The king was Childeric III.; he died in about a year afterwards. Thus the race of Childeric, which had begun to flourish at Tournay, died out in the silent cloisters of St. Bertin, not many leagues from where it first arose.

To Pepin le *Bref* succeeded Carloman (752—770), who left the realm to Charlemagne his brother. From this monarch a new arrangement took effect, which, to a certain extent, separated the Walloon, Flemish, and Dutch provinces from each other. He divided his kingdom, and put the sections into the charge of dukes, or military leaders, and under these were the counts of provinces. The conduct of both orders was superintended by the *missi dominici*, or travelling vice-regal judges, who came unexpectedly—it is said—upon a ruler, and called him to account for his charge.† Under this arrangement a new course of history began, which was marked by the introduction of commercial power, an element comparatively new, so far as Flanders was concerned,

---

* As this is the first time we have occasion to name this famous and once magnificent monastery, it may be well if something is said about it here. Founded in 648 by St Omer, Bishop of Therouanne, upon land given by Adroald, a noble of the place, a great but repentant criminal, the first establishment had soon to be enlarged : Bertin, who succeeded St. Omer in ruling the place, got into a boat with two companions, and was driven by chance and the tide to the Island of Sithiu, where they built a new establishment, with the same invocation as the former. The dedication was successively changed to SS. Peter and Paul and St. Bertin; until the tenth century it was known by the most ancient name, Sithiu. Four Counts of Flanders were buried here— Baldwin *Bras-de-Fer*, who took the habit here and died 879; Arnold the Simple, 1071; Baldwin *à-la-Hache*, 1119; and William *Clito*, 1128. Asser, the friend of Alfred of England, belonged to this house; here Dunstan, Anselm, and Thomas-à-Becket found refuge. The place flourished for nearly twelve hundred years, and was rifled by its eighty-third abbot, when the French Revolution swept over it, 15th August, 1790. Plundered and stripped of all its wealth, the bare walls of the hospitable house stood with little injury, until the authorities of the town, desiring to find work for some grumbling *ouvriers* in 1833, set them to pulling down the magnificent ruins, and would doubtless not have left one stone standing on another, had not a sudden call for labourers in another part of French Flanders relieved the barbarians of the opportunity to complete the wreck. All that remains now is the western tower, and a part of the nave, of middle fifteenth century work.

† The poem of Theodulph, Archbishop of Orleans, one of these Justices in Eyre, gives a very curious picture of society in Charlemagne's time: it has a certain amount of humour, and is rich in illustrations of costume. It is quoted at length in M. Guizot's *Hist. de la Civilisation*.

but of the greatest influence on Europe and civilization. The growth of this power was hardly practicable under a distant and potent king; it promised best if it could exist under rulers sufficiently strong to resist external influences, and not powerful enough to dispense with local aid. Such were the Counts of Flanders, who acknowledged a single head during the life of Charlemagne, and owned a master ever afterwards.* The traders of the Flemish cities, on the other hand, were already not without power; and above all, the Church had secured large portions of the country, which, to a great extent, were exempt from the worst evils of the age. So wide was the rule of the last that the Abbey of Nivelles alone reckoned fifteen thousand families as its vassals. The great contests which were now carried on were destined to be undecided through many centuries, and are not even yet settled. These had for questions the respective authorities and boundaries of the Frankish and Germanic races. The division of the empire of Dagobert, whereby his son Sigebert got Austrasia, did but prefigure what was to happen between the kings of France of the Carlovingian and Capetian races, with the Counts of Flanders at their backs (whenever it suited the interests of the latter to be so) on the one hand, and the German rulers—who had the Dukes of Lorraine and Brabant to help them—on the other. The brief sketch of the careers of the Flemish Counts which follows will show how dexterously they availed themselves of their position to aggrandise the province, whether at the cost of the emperor or the king, as allies or enemies of one or the other. Long before the time of Dagobert, cruel wars, of which the passionate hatreds of Brunehault and Fredegonda were but the expression, marked the antagonism

---

* Charlemagne was represented in the province of Brabant by a duke, who, after the usual fashion of his time, carried on war with the Frisons, or people of what is now called Holland. Charles Martel himself had been defeated by this race, when it was under the leadership of the redoubtable Radbod, who recovered even the city of Utrecht, where the Frankish monarch had planted Christianity. St. Boniface was the agent of this conversion, and, according to the legend, succeeded in converting Radbod, or rather in persuading him to undergo the ceremony of baptism. At the moment the Frison entered the water, he enquired of the missionary what was the fate of his old companions in arms who had died unconverted? The unwary priest replied that they were undoubtedly in hell. "Oh!" exclaimed the convert, "I would rather go to hell with them than to paradise with foreigners like yourself, who desert their friends." He came out of the water with these words on his lips, and refused to be for ever divided from his old companions.

of the races which divided Gaul between them. The rise of the Carlovingians was but a revival of the old question in stronger hands, and with less savage circumstances.

Flanders once formed, as in effect it was under the Carlovingians, we propose to give our chief attention to that province. The great wars, in which Flanders was so deeply concerned, had been carried on in the so-called Gallic provinces, (*Flandre Gallicante*) south of the Meuse, or in France proper; while, in the lower lands, the state of things was better than of yore or elsewhere. There, the indomitable spirit which kept back the Romans and the sea, still flourished, and many towns were in a thriving condition. Bruges, Ghent, Antwerp, and Courtray, all carried on large manufactures, and had considerable foreign trade. Soon after the time of Charlemagne the cities of the Low Countries banded themselves together to resist the violence of their neighbours, and for mutual aid in case of fire or inundation. The close proximity of several of these places suggested this arrangement, and something of a republican form of government obtained among them, by means of the guilds or trade associations, which survived for ages, despite internal quarrels and external foes. These turned back from their careers of aggression, *i.e.*, of plunder, many Emperors of Germany, Kings of France, Counts of Brabant or Flanders. Liège, on the other hand, got its modicum of freedom by means of the bishops, who, for the sake of personal independence, joined the commons in moderating the power of the counts who surrounded them. These destroyed many nests of nobly-born thieves which were established on rocky peaks overlooking the Meuse, or barred the roads from France and Germany, where they traversed the Ardennes. In some cases they hung the counts and even the countesses over the doors of their own castles, or burned them out like rats in a barn; ultimately these ghostly leaders held the chief authority, and became princes of the empire.

To resume:—Soon after the death of Charlemagne, the counts of provinces, none of whose honours were hereditary, contrived, one by one, to render them so, and made personal property of their official estates. When the grandsons of this emperor divided his realm between them, their boundary in the Low Countries was the Scheldt. FLANDERS went to France, or Charles the Bald, and, with more or less of liberty, remained for many centuries subject to that kingdom. BRABANT went to Lothaire (843,) and at his death to his second son and namesake, and was long a portion of Lorraine. By the Emperor Louis this province was united to Germany in 880. In 959 Brabant became the independent province of Godfrey I., under the title of the Dukedom of Lower Lorraine. LORRAINE, or Lotharingen (which took its name from the above-named Lothaire), i.e., the country between the Rhine and the Meuse, was divided between Charles the Bald and Louis of Germany, 870. The latter relinquished his portion to the Emperor Louis I., whose son, Louis II., inherited it from him; it passed to Charles the Fat in 882; he gave it to Arnulph of Bavaria, who made Zwentibold, his natural son, Duke of Lorraine in 895. Against this person, who seems to have been an unmerciful master, the people revolted; they killed him, and in 900 swore allegiance to Louis III. of Germany. When this emperor died they did the same in favour of Charles the Simple, of France (911); thus they showed their freedom. Rudolph of Burgundy, when king of France (he succeeded Robert, Count of Paris, who followed Charles the Simple), made his brother Giselbert Duke of Lorraine, and acknowledged the province to be a fief of the empire in 923. Louis (*d'Outremer*) IV. of France, re-asserted the right of his kingdom to Lorraine, and was backed by Giselbert. The Emperor Otho I. defeated them at Andernach in 938, and thus secured the province.

In 953, Bruno, Archbishop of Cologne, became duke, and the duchy was divided into Upper and Lower Lorraine, (that is to say that a strict division of the debateable land was made between the Flemish or French, and the Lotharingian or German races.) The above-named Godfrey I. obtained the latter section; the former passed through the hands of an uninterrupted line of dukes until 1474, when Charles the Bold, of Burgundy (nominal vassal of France) invaded it, while under the rule of Yolanthé and René II. (1473—1508.) Charles III., and his brothers Nicholas and Francis, governed together from 1624 to 1670; the first reigned alone until 1675, during which period he fought against the French under Turenne, and took prisoner the Marshal de Créqui. His nephew, Charles IV., succeeded him, commanded the Imperial army against the French, and was one of the great captains of that age. Other dukes followed until the death of Stanislaus Leczinsky, in 1709, when the French got it and now hold it.

LOWER LORRAINE, or Brabant, parted from the sister province in 959 to Godfrey I. Dukes succeeded each other until Godfrey of Bouillon (whose father, Eustace II.,* married Ida, sister of Godfrey IV.), having done good service to the empire, was made Duke of Lower Lorraine, 1089. He had previous investiture of Antwerp from the Emperor Henry IV., and now bore the name of Godfrey VI. of Brabant; he was elected King of Jerusalem in 1099, and died in 1100. Duke Anthony was killed at the Battle of Agincourt, 1415: his son, John IV., married Jaqueline, heiress of Holland and Hainault, who had for second husband the Duke of Gloucester.† After the death of John, Brabant was inherited by his uncle, Philip the Good of Burgundy, 1429. The son of Philip, Charles the Bold, held the duchy till his death in 1477, while fighting against the Swiss. Charles's daughter Mary married Maximilian of Austria, and the province (1477) was transferred to Austria as part of the Netherlands. A part of Brabant (now called North Brabant) passed to Holland on the German representative side of the great question in 1648; a part to France 1668—1678. In 1814, the latter, or South Brabant, joined the kingdom of the Netherlands; and by revolt in 1830 is now a portion of that of Belgium, which may be said to be dependent on France.

NAMUR was a part of Lorraine until 932. Its most famous chiefs were the Marquis Peter de Courtnay, who was elected Emperor of Constantinople, 1216; Baldwin De Courtnay, likewise so elected, 1237. John III. sold the marquisate to Philip the Good of Burgundy in 1421. At the breaking-up of the Burgundian duchy it went to Austria as part of the Netherlands (1477). It was transferred with the rest to Spain by Charles V. (1507), became part of the kingdom of the Netherlands in 1814, and of that of Belgium in 1830.

LIÈGE took the course we have referred to, and became the

---

* This Eustace II. had first married Goda, sister of Edward the Confessor of England. It was on his return to his own dominions that the affray at Dover took place which had such serious effect on the history of England, and brought Earl Godwin into trouble. His son Eustace, brother of Godfrey, rebelled against Rufus, and went to the Crusades with Godfrey. His mother, Maud of Lorraine, was descended from Charlemagne.

† Humphrey, fourth son of Henry IV. of England, the good Duke of Gloucester, murdered at Bury St. Edmund's, 1447.

diocese of the Prince Bishops, who were elective. John, brother of William IV. of Holland, was chosen, and became so noted for his cruelties that people named him "The Pitiless," and expelled him in 1406. In 1789 a bishop was expelled by the French. In 1791 the Austrians replaced him; in 1814 the province joined the kingdom of the Netherlands, in 1830 that of Belgium.

FLANDERS.—The most ancient earls of this province bore the peculiar title of Foresters,* which is of unknown origin; it is suggestive of the early condition of the country, and may derive from it. Lyderic le Buc† is said to have been the first holder of the title by the appointment of Dagobert in 621. The successors of Lyderic rendered themselves less dependent on the Frankish crown as time went by, and at length the Foresters of Flanders appear among the holders of great state offices; at a later period they bore the sword before the kings of France at their coronations. Baldwin I. (Bras-de-fer), who received the title of count from Charles the Bald, was a person of remarkable audacity, strength, and stature. Judith, daughter of Charles, and widow successively of Ethelwulf and Ethelbald, kings of the West Saxons, caused herself to be carried off by Baldwin in 862,‡ and in the end, but much to the disgust of

---

* The Flemish historians trace the descent of these personages from the Lyderic hereinafter named, to Baldwin Bras-de-fer in the following order:— 1. Lyderic le Buc, who had, says the record, "innumerable virtues," and fifteen legitimate children, (and one illegitimate) cut off the head of the eldest of his sons, married Richilde, daughter of Chlotaire II. of France, and a Merovingian princess. 2. Antoine, second son of the above. 3. Bouchard, third son of the above, forester and Lord of Harlebec. 4. Estorede, son of the last, forester, Prince of Louvain and Lord of Harlebec, died 792. 5. Lyderic II., son of the last, was made Count of Harlebec, and died in 836. 6. Ingelran, son of Lyderic II., was a great builder of castles and towns; died 852, buried at Harlebec. 7. Odoacre, son of Ingelran, built the castle of Audennerde, and the walls of Ghent, rebuilt many towns, and lies at Harlebec. 8. Baldwin Bras-de-fer.

† "Lyderic, premier de ce nom, dict le Buc, fils unique de Salnart, Prince de Dijon, et de Madame Eringarde, fille de Gerard, Seigneur de Roussillon, ayant vaincu et tué Phinart le tiran Seigneur de Buc, fut establi le premier Forestier de la contrée de Flandres l'an 621, par le Roy de France Dagobert, et porta les premiers armes ci descrites, qui estoyent gironnes d'or et d'azur, de dix pieces, au millieu une escusson de gules, trépassa l'an 692."

‡ She was married when twelve years old to Ethelwulf, the West Saxon, who saw her at the court of Charles when returning from his famous Roman pilgrimage in which Alfred, afterwards King of England, accompanied him. When Ethelwulf died (858) his son Ethelbald, passionately in love with Judith, and reckless of the curses of the monks, married her in the following

the Frankish king, *Bras-de-fer* received the title in question. He was buried at St. Bertin, 879. Baldwin II. married Alfrith, daughter of Alfred of England, 891, and obtained great victories over the Normans. He built the walls of Bruges and Ypres, and was the first of the long line of Flemish princes to be interred in the church of St. Pierre at Ghent, 919. Arnulf the Old fought with Otho of Germany to settle the boundaries of Flanders on the side of Brabant. Otho took Ghent by surprise and returned it on conditions. Arnulf died in 964, and was buried in St. Pierre. Baldwin III. reigned in the later years of his father's life, and succeeded him. He restored many towns that had been ruined by the Normans; reigned three years alone, and died in 970. He was buried at St. Bertin. It was Arnulf who killed William Longuesspée, Duke of Normandy, at a conference held on an island in the Somme (Dec. 16, 943). Arnulf II. carried off the relics of St. Valeri from Leuconaus—*i.e.*, St. Valeri-sur-Somme—to Sithieu (St. Omer). In revenge for this liberty, the saint himself appeared in a vision to Hugues Capet, Duke of Paris, and enjoined him to recover his bones from the Fleming, and place them as of old. In the event of his doing this the liberal spirit promised that the posterity of Hugues should be kings of France until the seventh generation had passed away. "Hugues readily obeyed the orders of St. Valeri," says an ancient chronicler, "and by the will of God and his own impetuous courage, so terrified Arnulf that he gave up the relics in 911." It is needless to say that St. Valeri

---

year. He repented of this act and repudiated her. He died in 860. Judith, who had returned to her father after causing great scandal, and affording means for abundant disputes, caused herself to be carried off in 862, being then but twenty-two years of age. Charles was irritated to the last degree by the flight of his daughter, and threatened vengeance on Baldwin. He was probably not sorry, however, to receive an urgent appeal for pardon to the fugitives from Pope Nicholas I., who on the 23d December wrote to that effect, and strengthened his entreaties by pointing out that the Flemish Forester might, by too severe measures, be driven to join the terrible Normans, who were then devastating Christendom, and France in particular; moreover, when Judith was married to so renowned a champion as Baldwin *Bras-de-fer*, she was safe out of mischief, and might secure a powerful friend to the father, who had quite enough to do with his quarrelsome sons, Louis the Stammerer, and Charles, afterwards of Aquitaine. Poor King Charles accordingly agreed to what was done, and made Baldwin Count of Flanders. It was this Judith who taught Alfred his letters; her son married his daughter. Baldwin died 879, and was buried in the famous monastery of St. Bertin, near St. Omer, where so many Flemish chieftains lie.

did his part of the bargain.* Arnulf II., sometimes styled "The Young," died of "hot fever" at Ghent, 989, and was buried in the church of St. Pierre.

Baldwin with the Comely Beard, fourth of the name, son of Arnulf, succeeded. He obtained Valenciennes and the islands of Zealand from the Emperor in 1006. Having captured this city from the Count of Hainault, the Emperor's vassal, and by the aid of the townspeople defeated the Emperor and the King of France, "his own suzerain," the former finally consented to receive Cambray in exchange for Valenciennes. This Count died in 1036, and was buried in St. Pierre, Ghent.+ Baldwin V. of Lille rebelled against his father, being moved thereto by his young wife, Adela of France, daughter of King Robert. He succeeded him in the county, and was styled *Le Debonnair*; he was one of the most enterprising and most successful Counts of Flanders. His four children were in many ways famous. He married his son Baldwin (VI.) to Richilde, sole heiress of Reignier, Count of Mons and Hainault, and in her right claimed the inheritance of those fiefs. His second son was Robert the Frison, afterwards Count of Flanders. His eldest daughter was the famous Matilda of Flanders, wife of William the Conqueror of England. Judith, the other daughter of Baldwin, married Tostig, brother of Harold II. of England, and son of Earl Godwin, who was slain at the battle of Stanford Bridge (Sept. 25, 1066), a few days before that of Hastings. Baldwin died a year after that event (1067), and was buried "in the middle of the choir" of the church of St. Pierre at Lille, an honourable place reserved for founders, such as he had been with regard to that edifice. His wife Adela was buried in the convent at Messines, 1071. Take what Ordericus Vitalis says of the honour which befel Baldwin V. "In the year of our Lord 1059, the thirteenth indiction, Henry, King of France, after a glorious and prosperous reign, demanded of John, a physician of Chartres, who from some accident was called 'The Deaf,' a potion which should restore his health and prolong his life; but, being very thirsty,

---

* *Acta Sanctorum, ord. St. Benedict.* V. 556. St. Valeri must not be confounded with St. Valerie of Limoges, the saint who brought her head to St. Martial at that place, and whose life is represented in the glass of the cathedral there, and very commonly in enamels.

+ *Chron. du Monastère D'Oudenbourg.*

under the influence of his inclination more than of his physician's advice, he made his chamberlain bring him water privately, while the medicine was passing through his intestines, and before they were cleared by it. Thus drinking without the knowledge of his leech, he died, alas! on the morrow, to the great grief of his people. He left the sceptre of France to his son Philip, who was still of tender years, appointing Baldwin, Duke of Flanders, his guardian, and regent of the kingdom. The duke was a fitting person to undertake this trust, having married Adela, daughter of Robert, King of France." This office Baldwin performed with great probity, and did much for France during the rest of his life. Unhappily that did not endure so long as the minority of his charge. Adela was the widow of Richard III., Duke of Normandy.

Of the sons of Baldwin we will speak presently: meanwhile let us say something of his daughter Matilda, wife of the Conqueror. It is not generally known that this lady was a widow, or divorced, at the time of her marriage to William. According to the chronicle of Tours, as quoted by Mr. R. Stapleton in an elaborate article published in the third volume of the *Archæological Journal*, Matilda was the divorced wife of Gerbod, Avoué (defender) of St. Bertin, St. Omer (St. Peter of Sithieu), and had for children Gerbod, Earl of Chester,* Frederic,† and that Gundrada who was the wife of William de Warrenne, Earl of Surrey.‡ In the charter to the priory of Lewes, the Conqueror styles Gundrada his daughter, a style which has puzzled many: she was, doubtless, the daughter of his wife. The Saxon chroniclers tell a pretty piece of scandal about Matilda in reference to an English noble, Brihtric Mawr, or

---

* See Vitalis, 4. 7, for the fate of this noble.

† In the speech which Vitalis reports as the reply of Matilda to William's remonstrances with regard to her giving aid to Robert Courthose while in rebellion against him, she is made to style Robert her first-born son. This chronicler was not likely to put such a phrase into her mouth if the fact were otherwise, and the existence of Matilda older than those she had by the Conqueror was known to him. He could hardly be ignorant of their existence, and had peculiar opportunities of learning the truth about her speech because " Samson, a Breton," Matilda's agent to Robert took refuge from the threats of William in St. Evroult, Vitalis's own convent, and would be able to talk the subject over with those who could relate it to that writer. *Avoué* was the title assumed by the first Christian king of Jerusalem.

‡ Not many years ago the bones of William and Gundrada were found in leaden coffins as they had been buried, in the chapter-house of the priory of Lewes. These relics were removed to the church of Southover, near Lewes. Gundrada died in child-birth, May 27, 1085.

the Handsome, who had been to her father's court in the capacity of ambassador from Edward the Confessor. Matilda took a fancy to the youth, who, to her lasting indignation, declined to marry her. Dugdale says that after the Conquest, Matilda asked for her own all the lands of Brihtric, and as Domesday Book attests, she had them. They were mostly in Devonshire, and included Clovelly, that sweet little nook on the coast. Poor Brihtric died in prison. There can be little doubt of the truth of this statement. Conceive the ironical smile which must have crossed the face of William when his consort of fourteen years asked for the means of vengeance on the Saxon who had rejected her advances! She furnished the ship in which William crossed to Hastings, and styled it the *Mora*; at its prow was the gilt figure of a child, pointing with its right hand and blowing an ivory trumpet.

Baldwin VI. of Mons reigned for three years only, but with "such perfect policy," says his panegyrist, "that it was not needful for any one to close his house-door at night in order to keep out thieves." His marriage with Richilde brought more trouble than profit to this model Count. Robert the Frison was, according to those authorities with whom Sismondi seems to agree, the eldest son of Baldwin of Lille; for some reason not now perfectly understood, he was made to give place to his brother Baldwin of Mons, husband of Richilde, who, in right of his wife, governed Namur and Hainault some time before his father's death. It may be that the politic father of these princes desired to aggrandize his family by the union of the heritage of his second son's wife to the county of Flanders; if so, the scheme failed exactly where it was considered safest, and the aggrandizement of Flanders came by the hands of Robert rather than of Baldwin. The story illustrates the filibustering manners of the age, almost as fortunately as does the history of the conquest of England by a man who had not the faintest shadow of a claim to this island. Robert appears to have been a wild youth who was sent forth into the world by his father with ships, money, and men, to see what sort of a fortune he could make for himself. Of all qualities, that which distinguished Robert was indomitable perseverance. Fortune, during his youth, invariably went against him; he chose for his first expedition the Spanish coasts, then in Mohammedan hands, and tried to carve out a principality in Gallicia. At first he got a great deal of booty, but, exposing himself to a counter attack, all his friends were slain, and he got away with the greatest difficulty. A second time the wild youth of Flanders joined the prince in a naval expedition, which, only a few days after sailing, was shipwrecked. Robert, rendered miserable by these repeated failures, went to Jerusalem as a pilgrim, hoping to expiate the secret sin which dogged his steps and brought ruin on all his acts. On the road he met with that indomitable adventurer Robert Guiscard,* Count of Apulia, and was easily persuaded to venture an attack on the provinces of Greece, then in the shaking hands of the emperors of the East. This scheme failed, and Robert completed his pilgrimage in a less warlike guise than that assumed by his son when, a few years later, he was styled "The Sword and Lance of Christendom." Robert returned to Flanders with a reputation which was much improved by this visit. The crusading fever was then simmering, and needed only the fierce words of Peter the Hermit, and the wild passion of Godfrey of Bouillon, to become a raging madness. Many a noble pilgrim had been to the East before Robert. Foulque-Nerra, Count of Anjou, an extraordinary criminal, ghost-haunted and stained with blood, had himself whipped through the streets of Jerusalem. Frottmonde, of Brittany, fratricide, walked to the Holy Land with chains on his body, and wrapped in a winding-sheet, as the king of France and the Bishops condemned him to do;† twice he did this, and returned to be considered a saint. Foulque-Nerra went thrice, and died at Metz, to be reckoned peculiar in sanctity. These, with Beranger, Count of Barcelona, and Frederic, Count of Verdun, were all great sinners and penitents before Robert, and all obtained much increase of credit on account of their pilgrimages. These journeys were by no means holiday excursions, they were in truth terrible penances. Beranger died of suffering; Frederic gave up his country, and returned to be a monk.‡ §

---

* Roger, brother of Robert Guiscard, married Adela, daughter of Robert the Frison, 1093.
† *Acta Sanctorum*, IV., 2.
‡ Ultimately prior of St. Vedast, at Arras.
§ It was of one of these pilgrims that the grim *mot* was made by a friend who related to another that he had met the penanced man on the way to Jerusalem, and lying in a litter that was carried by Saracens. The teller added that he seemed to be going to heaven, and borne by devils. Considering what was the opinion of the Saracens held by Europeans of that age, this is a strikingly apt expression.

Robert, whose offence was probably the least serious, was most fortunate of these noble pilgrims. His old friend Florent I, of Holland, died (1062), and left three children in charge of their mother, Gertruda of Saxony. Upon this woman he made war to such effect that although never defeated she was worried into marriage with him, as a good way of settling the matter. By this union he became Count of Holland and Friesland. When Baldwin V. died, Robert seems to have acquiesced in the ascent of his brother Baldwin VI. to the rule of Flanders. The latter is said to have been the first who attacked Robert and invaded Holland; a fight ensued (July 16th, 1070), when Baldwin was killed, leaving Richilde a widow with three children. He was buried at Hannon, a monastery of his own foundation.

Upon this, Robert the Frison claimed the tutelage of his brother's children, and being supported by the Emperor, Henry IV., he invaded Flanders. Richilde applied to Philip of France, her son's suzerain, and that prince marched to her aid in the cause of her son Arnulf III., and called upon his vassal, William (the Conqueror) of Normandy, for assistance. William was then in England, but his lieutenant in Normandy was no less a person than William Fitz-Osborn. Earl William joined the king with only ten men-at-arms, and rode with him gaily to Flanders as if he were only going to a tournament. Meanwhile Robert the Frison had united his forces with those of the Emperor, and on Septuagesima Sunday, the tenth of the calends of March, attacked his enemy by surprise early in the morning, and Philip, king of France, and his army flying, Arnulf and Earl William were slain.* This

---

* *Vitalis*, IV., 9. This earl was a noble of the greatest dignity in the days of the Conquest. He was supposed to have the warmest possible feelings for Richilde of Hainault; his going to her succour with no more than ten men-at-arms was probably due to the haste in which he set out rather than to lack of inclination or of power. Representing William, he was bound to go, and Matilda, who then ruled in Normandy, was not likely to interpose any objections to the succour of Richilde. William Fitz-Osborn was Steward of Normandy, cousin of the Duke, and a leader of such influence in his own country that when the lords there hesitated to aid their duke in his descent on England, he settled the matter with a few reproaches for their coldness, and was empowered to be their spokesman with William. Greatly exceeding his authority, he committed the nobles to the enterprize. Thus does Vitalis curse him, and triumph over the ruin of his family.—" Truly, the world's glory droops and withers like flowers of the grass, and is spent and scattered like smoke. Where now is William Fitz-Osborn (earl of Hereford), the king's lieutenant, high-steward of Normandy, and the valiant commander of the royal troops? He was,

was at Ravenchoven, near Cassel, Feb. 22, 1071. Robert appears to have entangled his enemies among canals and ditches in a strange country, and then came upon his enemy with all his might.

---

without exception, the first and greatest of the oppressors of the people of England, and amassed an enormous fortune by his exactions, causing the ruin and death of thousands by his severities." He was lord of the Isle of Wight, and Earl of Hereford. His son Roger succeeded to the latter title, and, having rebelled against William, was defeated and imprisoned at Winchester. He was of an indomitable spirit; when the king sent him some splendid robes by way of Easter gifts,—"surcoat, silken tunic, and mantle of the furs of precious ermines brought from abroad," probably hoping the rebel would, by kind treatment, be induced to sue for pardon, so that the scandal of the imprisonment of so great a noble, who was also son of a faithful servant, might cease,—the earl had a fire made, and burnt the gifts, to the great wrath of William, who swore "by the light of God," that he should never be released while he (William) lived. On his death-bed at Rouen, 1087, William referred to this, and ordered the prison doors of the earl to be thrown open. (See the words in the account by Vit. VII., 14, of William's death). This appears to have been done. The unfortunate earl had suffered for thirteen years. Vitalis speaks of his sons, Reginald and Roger, "excellent young men," as beseeching the clemency of Henry I., "which seems to them sufficiently tardy," as well it might. The curious reader will do well to refer to Vitalis for the account of the vision of the priest of St. Aubin de Bonneval, near Orbec (Book VIII., 16), a sight so terrible that some memory of it *lingers even now* in the minds of the peasants. It affords a curious illustration of the rapacity of William Fitz-Osborn by the appearance, among those who are accursed, of William de Glos, his steward. Here is an outline of the tale:—" Walkelin, the priest, was returning at night from the house of a sick man, when he heard the heavy tramp of horses and the rattle of arms, and thought within himself that it was the troops of Robert de Belesme going to the siege of the castle of Courci, before which Robert Courthose was then lying. Near 'four medlar-trees' he was stopped in order to allow the passage of a host of persons, some of whom he recognized as among the lately dead. Some were loaded with spoil, or bore heavy weights; all lamenting and urging one another on. Then came a crowd of women, riding on saddles that were stuck full of red-hot nails; some of these he also knew as not long dead; he saw the palfreys and litters of others *who were yet alive;* then came a host of clergy, who implored him to pray for them. Then an immense army in which no colour was visible, but only blackness and fiery flames; all were mounted on great war-horses, and fully armed as if for immediate battle, and they carried black banners. Then he saw Landri of Orbec, who died the year before, who uttered horrible cries and entreated the priest to bear a message to his wife; but those who rode with the troop interrupted him, and said he was guilty of deceit, a liar, corrupter of justice for bribes, and unfit to be heard. This troop passed on in a long train. The priest tried to catch a black war-horse that went without a master, but upon this four knights came shrieking, and, ghosts as they were, would have slain him had not another interfered. He also begged to send a message to his wife. Walkelin, rather ungratefully, said he knew him not nor his wife, but the knight declared himself as William de Glos, plunderer and usurer, one who had unjustly foreclosed a mortgage on a mill, in punishment for which he showed the priest how he bore a bar of hot iron from the mill in his mouth which was heavier than the tower of Rouen He charged him to desire his

There must have been something of mercy in the mind of the victor when he caused a monument to be placed over the grave of Arnulf in St. Bertin, which represented him with "a sword in his hand, and skirmishing" (*escarmouchant*.) It is worthy of note that in this war the old distinction between the Flemish towns of the hill-country and those of the low-lands displayed itself. Arras, Douay, Tournay, St. Omer, Boulogne, Aire, St. Pol, and Bethune, ranged themselves on the side of the French (or that of Richilde and Arnulf), whereas those which belonged to the more peculiarly Flemish low-lands,—*i.e.*, Ghent, Bruges, Ferns, Bergues, Capel, Courtray, Harlebee, Oudenbourg, Ypres, and Lille,—joined Robert in resisting the attempt of Philip to impose a Count upon them.

Philip made another attack upon Robert, but was most ignominiously induced to fly, with the loss of all his baggage, from St. Omer, of which town he had taken possession. It appears that Robert succeeded in making him believe that he was surrounded by traitors. A new and more formidable enemy attacked Robert in the person of Godfrey-le-Bossu V., Duke of Lower Lorraine, who had married the famous Countess Matilda of Tuscany, as his father had married Beatrice, her mother. This vigorous antagonist attacked the north side of Flanders, and devastated Holland and Friesland for three years, but was finally reconciled to the Frison by the Bishop of Liège. The terms upon which Robert secured the county of Flanders were not hard ; the second son of Baldwin VI. and Richilde received Hainault—his mother's heritage—on condition of marrying Robert's daughter which, however, he declined to do, on seeing how ill-favoured the lady was, and forfeited the town

---

heirs to restore the mill to the heirs of the mortgager, and, after much persuasion, got a promise that he would bear this message. Afterwards the priest retracted the promise, upon which the knight dashed him to the earth and dragged him along with hands that were burning like fire. Crying upon the Virgin, he was rescued by another spirit, who turned out to be his own brother, but whom he did not know. This man was enclosed in flaming armour, *that emitted a horrible stench*, and pressed him down unendurably; he was then, however, better off than before an enormous shield fell from its place about his neck. This happened when Walkelin said his first mass ; the brother trusted to get rid of his sword in another year ; when the priest asked about what appeared to be a mass of clotted gore hanging about the spur of his brother, he learned that it was really hot iron, and heavier to bear than Mont St. Michel might be." This grim narrative was written nearly two hundred years before the Divine Comedy of Dante. William, son of the William Fitz-Osborn above-named, was present at the death of William Rufus, and, hastening to Winchester, intercepted, but in vain, the attack of Henry I. on the treasury there.

of Douay in consequence. Robert, in 1085, made arrangements with St. Canute II., King of Denmark, husband of his daughter Adelais, for the invasion of England; in fact he suggested this scheme, and was about to adopt the invading tactics of the Conqueror. William was so alarmed at this that he drew together fresh troops from Normandy to oppose it. One may think it fortunate that the murder of St. Canute at Odensee put a stop to this business: the atrocities of the Normans were woeful enough to England. The cause of the quarrel between Robert and William is said to have been the refusal of the latter to pay a pension of three hundred silver marks that was due on account of assistance rendered by Count Baldwin of Lille, in the Conquest. William refused this to Robert, saying that he owed it to the Count of Flanders, a dignity he denied to him. Vitalis, however, distinctly says that Baldwin was applied to, but refused assistance to the Normans.* There is another story, which avers that when Baldwin inquired what was to be his share in case he assisted the invader, William sent a letter inscribed without to the effect that the Count would discover inside the description of what he would give for help of the kind. When Baldwin opened the letter it was found to be blank.† Robert was seated securely as Count of Flanders until his death at Wynendael, in 1093, and was succeeded by his son.

---

* The facts appear to be that the money was really due, but not paid with regularity, by William I. and II. On the return of Robert II. of Flanders from Jerusalem, he required the arrears to be paid. Henry I., who then reigned, said that he did not mind doing it if left to himself, but, if there was any fuss made about it, he would not pay anything It was agreed in 1101, that the sum should be five hundred marks, and that the Fleming should aid the king with 1,000 men in time of war. Two charters on this subject appear in *Rymer.* (See also *William of Malmesbury,* Book V.)

† St. Canute II., of Denmark, married Adelais, daughter of Robert the Frison, and was father of St. Charles I., Count of Flanders, who was murdered in the church of St. Donat, Bruges, 1127. She married, secondly, Robert Count of Apulia—(*Guiscard*).—Here is a pretty tale about a man who has been reckoned almost a saint: " She (Adelais) having collected money from all sources after his (her second husband's) death, amassed a great treasure. Baldwin the younger, King of Jerusalem, hearing this, coveted her wealth, and sent noble proxies to demand her hand in marriage. Adelais, insatiably greedy of pride, and rank, and honour, accepted the proposals of the illustrious suitor, and went to Jerusalem with a large retinue and a vast treasure. King Baldwin was pleased enough to receive her money, which he lavished on the stipendiaries who fought in the name of Christ against the Pagans ; but he repudiated the woman, who was wrinkled with age, and had rendered herself infamous by many crimes. The old woman returned to Sicily in confusion at her failure, and spent her declining years amid general contempt." Vitalis speaks of her as daughter of Boniface, Count of Liguria.

Robert the younger (II.), called of Jerusalem, went with Godfrey of Bouillon to the Holy Land (1096), and so conducted himself as to be called "The Lance and Sword of Christendom." He is often mentioned by the chroniclers of the time, and always among the foremost of the fighters. "A soldier always prompt," he was at the siege of Nice; and at the battle of Dorylæum, he shared the sufferings of that tremendous march across the desert, when the hawks died upon the wrists of the knights. He traversed those mountains "where some lords sold their armour for a little money, rather than carry it any further." One historian says it was he who set fire to Antioch, when 2,000 houses and churches were burnt; he was present at the taking of the city, and shared the hardships of those Crusaders who, being almost starved, ate the dead Saracens, an act which on account of the stringency of the circumstances was passed over without punishment. One of the chroniclers says the Crusaders did not consider it a mortal offence that those who fought for God against the Turks should use their teeth against them as well as their hands. Robert was at the siege of Jerusalem, and encamped before the gate of Herod, so that he must have heard the Turkish women sing a shrill antiphonary from the house-tops to encourage their valiant husbands against the invaders. "See!" they shouted, "how they swell and strut with barbaric pride, attacking without mercy the nations of the East, and pillaging our land! Vengeance and destruction await them; this day your enemies shall fall or perish." They sang in vain; soon the floors of the Temple were "knee-deep in blood," and only some few of the valiant defenders of the city were spared for a time in order that they might bury the dead (they were obliged to burn some of them), the accursed business was completed by the slaughter of the remnant, or by their sale into slavery. Robert was present at the election of Godfrey de Bouillon as King of Jerusalem; he left the hideous shambles on the third day, and was one of the first that were prepared to fight the Mussulmans who threatened the city from the side of Ascalon. He rode with Tancred (the only true knight among the leaders of the first crusade) in the charge that insured the victory at that place. In 1100 Robert returned from the Holy Land. He died in 1111 in a manner which was ignominious enough for one of the takers of the Temple.* Going with Louis King of France

---

* What was the end of his great friend and companion in arms, Robert

to attack Count Theobald of Meaux, the soldiers of the latter routed them, and " during the rout the earl fell from his horse in a narrow way, and, being trampled under foot by the cavalry, he was unable to re-mount, and, being raised from the ground with great difficulty, for his limbs were severely fractured, he expired a few days afterwards. Kings and princes and many people lamented his death, and as far as Arabia the fate of the warlike Crusader was deplored both by Christians and Gentiles. His corpse was carried by the Flemings with great sorrow to the city of Arras, which not long before he had fortified against Henry the Emperor, surrounding it with a stately wall of white stones. He was interred in the church of St. Vedast, the Bishop, at Arras." He married Clemence of Burgundy, daughter of William the Obstinate, and sister of Pope Calixtus II.: his eldest son Baldwin succeeded him.

Baldwin VII. was surnamed *à-la-Hache*, because he always carried that weapon in war and during peace, and displayed its image on his banner. Of him this strange story is told: " Amongst other acts of justice he caused to be hung in the great hall at Wynendael, eleven knights who had robbed and killed three Easterlings. The Count himself put them on a table, and, having had them tied by the necks to one of the beams of the hall, drew the table from underneath, leaving them hanging." This act of justice, personally done, may compare with that of Henry I., of England, when he thrust Conan of Rouen from the summit of the tower of that place. He showed the wretched man the splendour of the view, the river laden with ships and full of fish, the hunting lands; the city with its strong walls, stately houses, and innumerable people, and rejecting the most abject entreaties, dashed him backwards through the window. Hence the place was ever afterwards called " Conan's leap."

Baldwin did not forget to succour William *Clito*,* son of his father's friend, Robert Courthose,† when he failed to obtain his inheritance from Henry I., of England. He received William in his

---

Courthose, the history of Cardiff Castle relates. It is noteworthy that nearly all these chieftains of the first crusade died ignominiously.

* Clito, *i.e.*, the heir, equivalent to *Childe*, or *Atheling*.

† Contrast these words of Matthew Paris with the tumult of Jerusalem, and the songs of the Norman meretrices, who attended Robert in his time of power (1134). "The same year ended the ample time for repentance which our Lord Jesus Christ, who wishes that no one should perish, had granted to Duke Robert—namely, the period of thirty years, spent in loneliness and prison; but he had abused this gift of God, and was swollen with pride, detraction, malediction,

dominions—which were soon to belong to that fugitive prince himself, a chance, one would think, of the strangest kind—and ultimately died fighting in his cause. In this cause, "Louis, with the chief lords of France, Baldwin (*à-la-Hache*,) and Charles (*le Bon*) both Counts of Flanders, and their great men, Anmari de Montfort, Count of Evreux; Stephen, Count of Aumale; Henry, Count of Eu; Walleran, Count of Mellent," and half a score more, were of no avail against Henry's wisdom and power, yet strange to say, a noble holding was found for the son of Robert, who seems to have been a good sort of young man after the fashion of the time. Baldwin VII. was by no means a temperate man, and suffered accordingly from a wound he received before Argues in Normandy, which province he had invaded. This event happened at Roulers, near Bruges, 1119. It is said that he took the cowl before his death, as a brother of St. Bertin's, it is certain that the monks of that place claimed him as one of them, and that he was buried in their church. He named for his successor in the county of Flanders his cousin Charles of Denmark, son of St. Canute and of Adelais, daughter of Robert the Frison.

The son of Canute of Denmark and Adelais was a man of very holy life, and of undeniable distinction among the almsgivers; "He had continually in his company three notable religious men, doctors of theology, who daily, after supper, read to him and explained a chapter in the Bible. He forbade each upon pain of losing a member, to swear by the name of God, or by anything

and complaints, though he ought rather to have devoted himself to humility and prayer, for he was a suffering and afflicted old man, and ought rather to have said in tears with the psalmist that he suffered these things deservedly, because he rejected the burthen which he should have borne in the Holy Land, and despised the honours which were offered him; but in his arrogance he did not think of this. It happened one day that the king was putting on a new scarlet robe, and on this occasion he always sent a similar robe to his brother; but in trying to put it on he found it too small, and burst one of the seams. 'Carry this to my brother,' said he, 'he has a narrower head than I.' When the duke received it the seam had not been mended. 'How is this,' said he, 'that there is a fracture in the robe?' The attendants told him how it had happened, upon which the duke exclaimed, 'Alas! that I should have arrived at this pass: my brother, who has betrayed and supplanted me, and is younger than I, and nothing but a lazy clerk, has seized on my kingdom, thrown me into prison, and now treats me so contemptuously that he sends me his cast-off clothes!' Saying this he wept, and declined to eat; nor would he even touch a morsel more until he died. When the king heard of his death he did not grieve much, but commanded the body to be reverently interred in the Conventual Church of Gloucester."

which concerned God or his saints; and when any of his household was found in fault he made him dine for forty days on bread and water. He was marvellously severe against swearers, enchanters, necromancers, and others who helped themselves by similar and unclean arts. He drove out and banished from Flanders all Jews and usurers, who had previously lived without tribute, saying that he would not suffer them until they had satisfied and made amends for the murder committed by them on the Son of their Lord." This peculiarly impracticable personage, the type of a class who were the causes of nearly as much mischief as their bloodthirsty contemporaries, came by his death through excess of zeal, as we shall show in speaking of Bruges, the scene of that event.

The widow of Count Charles married Thierri of Alsace, and so became a second time Countess of Flanders. She was Marguerite of Clermont.

Several competitors for the county of Flanders appeared after the death of Charles; the most formidable of them, and that one who had probably the best right, was William *Clito*, son of Robert Courthose. Not only was William *Clito* the son of the eldest son of Matilda of Flanders, but he had the support of Louis the Fat, of France, suzerain of Flanders, who inducted him to the county. This assistance was probably less serviceable than appeared at first sight. William *Clito* had been a wanderer from the very earliest period of his life;* his father put him in the charge of that faithful friend Elias of St. Saens. On September 28th, 1106, which was the anniversary of the conquest of England by the Normans, at the Battle of Hastings, Henry defeated Robert at Tinchebrai, and conquered Normandy by the means of the English. On this day Robert was made prisoner, never to get free. Henry went to Falaise, where the young William was brought to him, "and the king, looking with an eye of compassion on the boy, who, trembling with fear, was exposed to such misfortunes in such tender years, comforted him with promises of kindness, and, for the prevention of calumny if any harm should befal the lad, gave him in charge to

---

* His mother was Sybilla of Conversano, daughter of Geoffry, Lord of Brundusium, nephew of Robert Guiscard, a lady of great beauty, with whom Robert fell in love on his return from the crusade. She died of poison. *William of Malmesbury* says otherwise. Her father gave Robert money enough to redeem Normandy from his brother; this was squandered as usual. *William of Malmesbury*, IV., 2.

Elias de St. Saens, who had married the daughter, by a concubine, of Duke Robert, and was trusted by him. Henry, moved by some fear, afterwards sent Robert de Beauchamp, Viscount of Arques, to St. Saens, where the *Clito* was being educated. Elias was absent when the messengers came, " on a Sunday morning, when the greater part of the people were in church." Much astonished, and fearing for the boy, his friends aroused William where he was sleeping in his bed—much as William, his grandsire, had more than once been roused by his mother's brother, when they hid the future Conqueror " in poor men's houses," and out of the reach of his enemies. They secreted the *Clito* from the viscount, " that he might not share his father's imprisonment." Elias removed him into foreign lands, and thereby lost his own castle of St. Saens; he appealed to many princes in his aid. Many were moved by the tale of his wrongs, and Foulque of Anjou, the younger, sometimes styled the Wily, promised him his daughter Sybilla in marriage. This was not until after the death of William,* son of Henry I., in the *Blanche Nef,* left even a nobler prospect of succession than that of Normandy open to the view of the *Clito.* Henry, in order to spoil this scheme, procured that the marriage should be prohibited, as between consanguineous persons. Sybilla married Thierri of Alsace, and became Countess of Flanders. The *Clito*, by the intervention of his great friend Adelais, wife of Louis the Fat, married her sister Jane of Maurienne. In the meantime, however, he had to wander again until Baldwin *à-la-Hache* received him. Pope Calixtus II. interfered for his benefit, and suffered himself to be imposed upon in the most open manner by Henry. William was the centre upon which the great revolt of Normandy formed; to repress this Henry perpetrated hateful cruelties, such as even in the narration of Vitalis, the King's apologist, sicken one who thinks of what caused the desperation of poor Luke de la Barre, the Trouvere, who had satirized Henry,† and

---

* This prince married Matilda, elder sister of Sybilla. Foulque went to the East, married Melisende, King Baldwin's daughter, and became king of Jerusalem, 1131. Matilda became a nun at Fontevrault, 1128, was elected abbess 1150, died 1154.

† " Making scurrilous sonnets on me, and sang them aloud to bring me into contempt; thus often making me the laughing-stock of my malicious enemies." This was Henry's complaint to Charles of Flanders, when he interposed for the sake of humanity.

led him to dash out his brains, " like one demented, fracturing his skull against the stone wall, and thus miserably expired, lamented by many who admired his worth and playful wit." The death of St. Charles of Flanders having brought Louis to avenge it on the assassins, this king appointed William *Clito* to the vacant county. The Flemings, jealous of his authority, favoured Thierri of Alsace. Another thing which moved the people was the excessive cruelty with which the traitors were punished by the *Clito*, when one hundred and eleven were thrown from the top of the tower at Bruges. The Thierri above mentioned was son of Thierri, Duke of Lorraine, and Gertrude, third daughter of Robert the Frison. He invaded the province, receiving much aid from the people, and probably some assistance from Henry of England.* William *Clito* defeated and drove his rival into the town of Alost; but in repelling a sally of the garrison of this place the prince seized the lance of a foot soldier, who drew back the weapon so that the duke's hand was wounded; St. Anthony's fire supervened to the inflammation of the wound, and he died on the 9th August, 1128.† He was buried by the side of Robert the Frison, at St. Bertin's, and near the grave of his friend Baldwin *à-la-Hache*. Thus ended the life of this unfortunate young man. The chronicler tells us that while on his death-bed he sent a petition for forgiveness from Henry I., on account of the evil he had done him. If it was so, William did indeed die like a Christian, and heaped coals of fire on the head of his persecutor. He took the habit of a monk of St. Bertin, as his epitaph testified.

Having now brought the dates of our personal relics to the time when many of the buildings here illustrated were erected, we propose to discontinue the historical and chronological manner of arranging them. Sequential arrangement is convenient to author and reader, when no better or more striking method presents itself; but when existing remains connect us with the past, it is preferable in a compilation of this sort to place those remains before the eye of the reader, and dispose about them what legendary or historical

---

* Roger de Hoveden says, " at the persuasion of King Henry."
† " Duke Robert (Courthose), who was then at Devizes, felt in a dream just at that time that his right arm was struck by a lance, so that he seemed to lose the use of it. When he awoke in the morning he said to those who were about him, ' Alas! my son is dead.' The intelligence had not been orally conveyed by messengers to that place when the duke said his."

fragments are to be shown. The men named in the latter portions of our text must have seen many of the edifices which are herein displayed, much as we may see them. For example, while Baldwin of Lille was bargaining with William of Normandy for a share of the spoil of England, or joining with St. Canute in the same holy enterprise, the builders of Tournay were busily closing the roof over the nave of their cathedral. William *Clito*, of Flanders and Normandy, probably walked under the aisles whose presentment our nineteenth-century reader may examine here. The people of the city of Childeric were great friends of his; in 1119 we find them attending a levy *en masse* in his cause. The seven towers of their cathedral were landmarks to many a mile of the Scheldt valley soon after his death. When Thierri of Alsace died, in 1168, St. Bernard had founded the Abbey of Villers (1147); shortly afterwards (1183) the first stone of the belfry at Ghent was laid by the city's chaplain, Siger. In the same place the Church of St. Nicholas was rebuilt, after burning, in the days of Charles the Good, 1119—1127.

It must never be forgotten that while the princes of Flanders and the adjacent counties were maintaining a sort of rough justice at home, or busying themselves in foreign wars, marrying, and feasting, and dying after their fashion—the great communities of the Low Countries were becoming powerful and wealthy. The original date of the freedom of the cities of Ghent, Bruges, Courtray, Ypres, Lille, Tournay, and others, is not known; probably liberty was inherent to some of them, and possessed when the first inhabitants of the Flemish sands drew together for mutual aid and founded the towns. Tournay was a city, it is believed, before Cæsar entered Belgium; the Romans settled there, the priests aided in establishing the power of the faithful Franks, and succeeded to that authority when the quarrels of the second race of kings left the people defenceless before the Normans. They led the inhabitants to Noyon, and this city was empty for nearly a generation. They returned and built the existing vast cathedral, and reigned there with varying but never ceasing dignity, so that in the time of Henry VIII. of England, the see was thought a prize for Wolsey himself. The other towns were little republics, governed by their own officers, and exercising no small influence on the external affairs of France and England.

When Guy de Dampierre (1280—1305) called together his states for advice with regard to the imprisonment he had suffered at the hands of the French king, they replied, "My lord, we are merchants, and without the arrival of the English in Flanders and the passage of the Flemings into England, we cannot traffic to any advantage; let peace, therefore, be between your nation and theirs, and then, supported by their assistance, we may despise the injuries already inflicted on us by the King of France, as well as any others to which he may endeavour to subject us." The English so fully appreciated the alliance thus suggested, that they sent fifteen thousand pounds of silver to aid in fortifying the Flemish castles. The crusades, by weakening the force of the nobles, were favourable to the liberty of the cities. Some towns actually expelled their lords and lived free within the walls; this was the case with Mechlin and Louvain in 1303. In 1100 the people of many towns appointed their own magistrates, and with the right to erect those belfries which still form effective features in the great cities, received also the right of self-defence. Ghent and Tournay were the first[*] to erect their belfries of stone. These, like the great towers of the Italian cities, symbolized freedom and power; their shadows crept at morning and at evening over enormous numbers of brave and laborious men, over houses where citizens lived in the style of princes, and enjoyed more of peace and humanity than was to be had elsewhere in Europe. It is impossible to look up at these great towers without forcibly feeling their significancy as symbols of manliness and right, and beacons of the people against their oppressors. Possessed of such power as these monuments indicate, the great hives of men grew wealthy and mighty, set examples such as Europe has followed, and by which England in particular has profited. Had not the inhabitants of those hives been divided amongst themselves, not all the power of all the Spains would have desolated the country nor tried its fertility in so tremendous a manner as is implied by the fact that in 1580 Philip II. obtained, on "loan," no fewer than twenty-four tons of gold from the Netherlands.[†] To serve the ends of the Spanish crown and the passions

---

[*] M. Schayes, *Histoire de l'Architecture en Belgique* :—"Both of these towers remain, but injured by time and the restorer; still they are noble objects."

[†] In 1550, five years after the discovery of Potosi, the whole American revenue of the Spanish crown was only 400,000 ducats annually, while the Netherlands often paid two millions and a half of ducats in the same period.

of one portion of the people, the long-established freedom of Flanders was laid so prostrate that Charles V. could take Alva—at the mention of whose name one feels almost forced " to fall a-cursing "—to the summit of the belfry at Ghent; and in reply to his proposal to destroy the great city which spread out beneath them (such was the wretch's counsel) to say, " How many skins of Spanish leather will it take to make such a *glove* as this?"* If freedom rose again, like the phœnix, it was over ashes, and even now, although the cities are free, much of their old prosperity is gone, with nearly all their power. A significant fact, indicative of much that was to follow, deserves place here. In 1132 the Flemings, who had ever since the beginning of the ninth century bought the wool of the eastern English counties, came over to this island and introduced the art of spinning it at a place called Worstead (in Norfolk, and thirteen miles from Norwich) a name not unknown to English readers.

For the sake of convenience and for after reference by the reader, it will be well to give here a list of the Counts of Flanders who succeeded Thierri of Alsace, together with the dates of their deaths. Thierri died in 1168, having been a prominent leader in the second crusade. His son Philip, by Sybilla of Anjou, succeeded him. Philip took the cross in the church of St. Pierre at Ghent, and went twice to the succour of the Holy Land and of his cousin, the King of Jerusalem. In the course of his first voyage this prince changed the arms hitherto borne by the Counts of Flanders, and above described, for a shield, *or*, with a lion rampant, *sable*. He was buried at Clairvaux in Champagne, the great house of the Cistercians, augmented by St. Bernard, at whose fiery adjuration the father of Philip had taken the cross. Philip died before Ptolemais†, July 11, 1191, having some time previously declined the

---

* A vile pun on the name of Ghent, or *Gand*—a glove.

† Geo. Vinsauf says that "he died immaturely," and that it was by means of "a very choice petraria of large size belonging to him, but after his death to King Richard of England (I.), that much of the 'Accursed Tower' was cast down after that terrible machine, 'The Petraria of God,' had done its work."—See Geo. Vinsauf's account of this siege, which is one of the most striking narratives of such events known to us, and full of examples of the use of military engines of such enormous size and power. The loss of one of them, a "Cat," designed by Philip Augustus, caused that monarch "to be enraged beyond measure, and began to curse all under his command, and rated them shamefully for not taking vengeance on the Turks who did the mischief."

offer of the kingdom of Jerusalem from the hands of the aged Baldwin. Baldwin VIII. succeeded Philip of Alsace, having married Marguerite, daughter of Count Thierri. He reigned only until 1194, in very troublesome times, and under the opposition of many competitors. He died at Mons, and was buried at St. Waltrude's in that city.

Baldwin IX. succeeded his father as Count of Flanders and Hainault, which latter province had been added to the former by Baldwin VIII; in him the right line of Flanders was restored, having been broken by Robert the Frison. In treating of Bruges, we shall have much to say about this prince, whose romantic career and unknown fate have given rise to many legends. He joined the fourth crusade in 1201, was elected Emperor of the East in 1204, and about a year afterwards vanished from human sight in a manner which is even more mysterious than that which signalized the disappearance of Sebastian of Portugal after the battle of Alcazarquivir. Baldwin of Constantinople was succeeded by his daughter Jeanne, who married Fernand of Portugal. The latter refused to join Philip Augustus in the invasion of England, and so drew upon himself the anger of that monarch. Fernand was allied with the Emperor, and John of England; their party concerted an attack on France which promised much. Philip sent a fleet to the Flemish coast, which being assailed by that of England at Damme, the port of Bruges, was destroyed. Philip captured Ypres, Courtray, and Ghent, and, marching southwards again, met the forces which were assembled under the Emperor, and amounted, it is said, to 150,000 men in all, at the bridge of Bouvines, between Lille and Tournay, and after a terrible combat defeated them, taking Fernand and William, Earl of Salisbury (Longsword) prisoners, 1214. After twelve years' imprisonment, Fernand was released; he died in 1232. Jeanne was married a second time, to Thomas of Savoy; she died in 1244. Margaret, second daughter of Baldwin of Constantinople, followed her sister,

---

There is a curious account of "Philip sitting under the mantle of a 'cerelcia,' and employing himself by throwing darts from a sling at any chance Turk who appeared on the walls of the city." Roger de Hoveden says that "Philip Augustus seized the property of the Count of Flanders, kept it for himself, and that it was in the hope of securing the county that he returned to France." See "Annals of Roger de Hoveden, 1191." Philip's rampant lion was originally borne on the shield of a gigantic "pagan" whom he slew on Mount Sinai.

and ruled with her husbands—(1), Bouchard D'Avesnes, and (2), William de Bourbon, Lord of Dampierre, and died in 1280. She was succeeded by her son, one of the most unfortunate of princes, William de Dampierre, who going with St. Louis to Tunis, was taken prisoner. He ruled not more than three years, and died, leaving the county to Guy de Dampierre, a still more unfortunate prince; he died a prisoner in Compiégne in 1305. He was a great friend of Edward I. of England, who, however, left him at the mercy of Philip IV. of France, who treated the people of Bruges like slaves until they rose against him, and drove Jaques de Chatillon, his governor, headlong into France. Philip returned with all his chivalry, and was utterly routed at Courtray with terrible loss. Returning again, he defeated the Flemings at Mons-en-Puelle, near Lille. Nevertheless, he concluded peace and acknowledged Robert, son of Count Guy, as Lord of Flanders. This was a very valiant prince; he commanded the army sent to assist Charles of Anjou against Manfred of Naples. He died at Ypres, 1322, and was buried in the church of St. Martin in that city.

Louis I. succeeded his father Robert; it was under the rule of this prince that Flanders was convulsed by the contest in which Jaques von Artevelde took so distinguished a part. He was slain at the battle of Cressy, and was succeeded by his son Louis II., *de Mâle*, whose daughter Marguerite, marrying Philip of Burgundy, took Flanders into that house (1384).

The princes of the Burgundian house followed in this order:—Philip the Bold, husband of Marguerite, died 1404; John the Fearless, his son, was assassinated at the bridge of Montereau, 1419; Philip the Good, died 1467; Charles the Bold was slain in 1476. Mary, daughter of Charles, married Maximilian of Austria, who (1494) rendered the province, with the whole of the Netherlands, to his son Philip, at whose death in 1507 Flanders fell to Charles V., who incorporated the province with Spain, and (1555) resigned to Philip II. Flanders declared against Spanish rule, and joined the "Pacification of Ghent," 1576. After many struggles, Flanders, with the southern provinces of the Netherlands, submitted to the Duke of Parma (the northern states got free under the name of the Seven Provinces). Albert of Austria married Isabella of Spain, daughter of Philip II., and they were named joint sovereigns; on the death of the latter the Netherlands reverted to Spain. Philip III. appointed various governors. At the peace of Utrecht the country was given to Austria, 1714; revolts, 1787; is suppressed, 1790; overrun by General Dumouriez, 1792; annexed to the French Republic and styled the department of "L'Escaut"; becomes part of the kingdom of the Netherlands under the King of Holland, 1814; of the kingdom of Belgium, 1830.

INTERIOR OF THE CATHEDRAL, TOURNAY

THE CATHEDRAL OF NOTRE DAME AT TOURNAY.

TOURNAY, which is presumed to have been the *Turris Nerviorum* of Cæsar, capital of the Nervians of the Sambre, is one of the most ancient towns on the northern side of the Alps. It is mentioned in the Itinerary of Antoninus, and in the third century became the centre of the missionary labours of St. Piat.* There need be little doubt that on the spot where the cathedral now stands a church was founded by this holy man, and that from his time to this prayer has rarely ceased there, except while the city was desolate for a generation (880—911), because the people in fear of the Normans fled to Noyon, and left their own town empty—a condition not uncommon to the Gaulish cities at that period. About 450, Chlodion, king of the Franks, is said to have settled at Tournay. Clovis was born here about 465; Childeric died here in 482. Sigebert besieged the place in 575; it was much injured by an earthquake in 650; and sacked by the Normans in 880. This led to that desertion of the inhabitants which is above noted; when they returned it is probable that the oldest remaining portions of the cathedral were erected. These, the side porches of the naves, are still decorated by curious sculptures in the Romanesque manner. In 1053 Tournay was devastated by the Emperor Henry III.; fire destroyed the upper part of the cathedral in 1054; after this the seven towers were built.† The nave was dedicated in 1066; it has now a semi-circular arched roof, but, according to M. Schayes, this was placed in the eighteenth century (1777): before that time the roof was flat and of wood, and doubtless of the character exhibited by those still existing at Peterborough and Norwich cathedrals. The vaulting of the aisles is Romanesque. The transept was

---

* St. Piat suffered torments in Tournay, and martyrdom at Seclin (299), in the neighbourhood. He was transfixed by huge nails; such was the method of martyrdom then in vogue. His relics were found in the latter place, where they remain in a church dedicated to him. His day is October 1st.

† Schayes' *Histoire de l'Architecture en Belgique*.

erected about 1146;* at least, such was doubtless the case with regard to its magnificent apsidal ends. The choir, which is larger than the nave, was dedicated in 1338, when the western porch was placed where the nave until then terminated in a gable; some portions of the old west front remain in the sealed doorways of the aisles. The existing choir replaced that which pertained to the Romanesque portion of the edifice, and had a semi-circular apse, like the ends of the transept; the church was therefore triapsal. Over the crossing there was originally a gigantic square tower, which formed a group with six minor towers, that were placed at the angles of the transept and choir; the towers which stood to the east of the great central one were removed with the ancient choir. The five remaining towers, and the reduced central one, form a magnificent assemblage, the obtusely-pointed roofs of which are visible far and wide over the country. When the seven towers stood all together, and the central one had its original altitude, the group was unrivalled beyond all comparison in Europe. The famous Apostles' Church at Cologne did not approach it. Even the remains are imposing to modern eyes—so vast is the height of the minor towers, so bulky is the central one.

This cathedral, in its interior, presents to the student a most effective combination of three styles. We have severe and sombre Romanesque in the nave, magnificent chastity of expression and what may be styled pure architecture in the transept; when we enter the choir, however, it is to be transported to another world and stage of society. From where all was grave, dignified, self-centred, and self-restrained, impressive without heaviness, and vast without monotony, we are suddenly removed to an expansive structure that is blazing with light, and has its windows filled with stained glass, divided from each other by the most slender piers, and having mullions like rods. A triforium of the most elegant kind takes the place of the dim and vast gallery of the nave; enormous clerestories supply that of the dim arcades which surmount the gallery of the latter and the aisles beneath it, and give an awful solemnity to the western half of the building. The latter is Egyptian in its grandeur, impressive in every feature, almost void of ornament, and seemingly indestructible by time; the former

---

* Ferguson's *History of Architecture*, p. 720.

startles the spectator by its lightness, and the audacity of the builder of those fairy piers, which have bent into two curves, one inwards and one outwards, and are hardly able to bear the roof. Whereas broad and stilted semi-circular arches rest on massive piers to form an arcade, which, dividing the nave from the aisles, is of the gravest character, we have, in the choir, keenly-pointed and richly-moulded lancets borne upon square piers of extreme tenuity, at whose angles very slender shafts are placed, while reed-like triple vaulting shafts descend from the roof to the floor. The aisles of the nave are but dimly lighted by windows placed high in the wall; those of the choir, on the contrary, are illuminated by vast glazed spaces, which seem hardly divided by the narrow buttresses—one cannot speak of walls in such a place, for there are none. Five trigonal chapels radiate from the east end, which being lighted in the same manner, and open to the choir aisle, or *chevet*, give an extraordinary aspect to this part of the cathedral. Nearly the whole surface of this section is stained glass, which although for the most part quite modern, and by no means wholly satisfactory, has been designed with unusual skill for modern works.* Notwithstanding this display of architectural daring at the east end of the cathedral, that which strikes the visitor before all parts of the interior is the immense gallery above, of the same extent as the aisles of the nave. This is a feature common in Romanesque buildings, and probably derived from the vast passages of like character, which, in Byzantine churches, were appropriated to women.† There is something of the same kind in Norwich Cathe-

---

* The subjects of these paintings are taken from the lives of Childeric and Sigebert; they represent the donation of privileges to the church, incidents connected with SS. Piat and Eleutherius, history of the diocese, &c. The most ancient portions are by Theodore Stuerbout, of Haarlem (Dirck van Haarlem, or of Louvain, died 1470), an artist of the school of Bruges, probably a pupil of Memline, and painter of the " Martyrdom of St. Erasmus," in the church of St. Pierre at Louvain, of which we shall speak presently—a picture long attributed to Memline himself, and still so described in Murray's Handbook, 1863, last edition, notwithstanding that M. Nieuwenhuy, in his Catalogue of Pictures of the King of Holland, published about 1830, shows that the work is by Stuerbout, and that the receipt of the painter for the price of his picture has been found at Louvain. The ancient portion of the glass at Tournay is but small.

† The triforium of Westminster Abbey, which is said to have been appropriated to the use of the sister-convent of Barking, is nearly as large as the aisles beneath it, but screened from view from below by double shafts and tracery of the most beautiful kind.

dral, but of less imposing character. The Romanesque naves of Norwich (1121), Ely (1174), and Peterborough (1155), although longer than that of Tournay, suffer in comparison with it, exhibiting only three arcades to each bay; the Belgian edifice has four, as the photograph shows. Each of the English works is two bays longer than Tournay, while the bays* at Ely are considerably wider from centre to centre of the piers, and those at Norwich of very nearly the same width. The noble view of the interior of Tournay Cathedral, which is obtainable from the western doors, derives no small part of its charm from the skilful manner in which the effect of light and shadow has been produced by the use of stained glass in the choir, which, although raw and crude, is effective as a whole, as it could not help being; so that, looking along the dimly-lighted nave, the eye takes in the eastern expanse, which is filled with mysteriously-hued and softened light, that—spreading behind the group of Michael defeating Satan, which is of dark bronze and raised above the screen—aids the aspect of the whole in a singularly effective manner. On a close approach to this screen, which is the work of Floris of Antwerp, 1566, and not without a low sort of merit of its own, the incongruity of its style with that of the building is painfully evident. The group of Michael and Satan is the work of Lecreux of Tournay. The ancient cross above the screen was destroyed about fifty years ago.

The lover of Art will turn from these, from this daring beauty of the choir, and even from the grandeur of the nave itself, to the severe dignity and gracefulness of the transept of this cathedral. There is nothing in England of the sort;† its apses are semi-circular in plan and semi-domical, with massive square ribs converging to the centre of the roof. Like the nave, these apses have four arcades, but in them the lowest tier is much loftier than that next above it. The piers are cylindrical, *i.e.*, pure columns of great height; their capitals are bold, while the arches which rise from the last are stilted, lofty, neither moulded nor chamfered, but set square with the face of the wall and of prodigious thickness, so as

---

* A bay is composed of arches placed one above the other, *e.g.*, from the floor to the roof of a church; an arcade is formed by arches placed side by side, as from one end of a building to the other.

† There are many examples of rounded transept ends in continental cathedrals; *e.g.*, St. Martin at Cologne, Noyon, Pisa, and St. Maurice at Gençay (Vienne).

to look as if they bore the massive superstructure with perfect ease: the effect of this is strongly impressive. The arcade which corresponds to the gallery of the nave, has cylindrical columns, short and very severe in their character, but finely proportioned. Above this, the third range is square headed, not an arcade. Between the windows of the clerestory which surmount the last, rise the mighty ribs of the semi-dome. There are seven windows in the topmost tier and but five in the gallery and lowest arcade. Although these windows are filled with indifferent modern picture-glass, the style of which is that of the seventeenth century, and quite at variance with the architecture, it is impossible to conceive anything finer, grander, or more nobly beautiful than these apses. Lovely in proportion, divested of ornament, magnificent in size and effect of light and shade, they represent architecture pure and simple.

It is interesting to observe how the three styles of this cathedral are united at the crossing from which we look upon the solemn nave and noble apses. The roof of the transept is slightly pointed —a characteristic observed by M. Schayes in the tower above; the chancel arch is acutely so, showing the progression of the styles. This union of the old flat roof, with the vault of the transept, must have been uncouth.* It is hard to believe that the roof of such a nave as this was ever originally flat. The paintings in *camaïeu* which disfigure the east wall of the transept above the altars placed there, are more unfortunate than the screen, or even the transparencies of the transept windows. These are false, imitating relief, and, in representing sculpture, are egregious shams. It is needless to describe what the photograph before us represents; suffice it that the carvings of the nave capitals have been restored, but in a good fashion. The ancient choir was ninety-eight feet long; the existing

---

* On the subject of the arrangement of the timber roofs of Norman (Romanesque) buildings, the reader will do well to consult the excellent *Mémoire* by M. Bouet on the church of St. Stephen at Caen, and Mr. J. H. Parker's learned and ingenious paper on the "Abbey Churches of Caen," published in the proceedings of the Institute of British Architects, 1862-63, where it is shewn to be beyond reasonable doubt that such spaces as the nave of Tournay cathedral were roofed in timber, supported on great transverse arches or ribs of stone, as now existing at Bernay Abbey and at the Abbey of Cerisy, near Bayeux. These, like Tournay Cathedral, are works of the eleventh century; thus the ugly flat ceiling, without arches to break its monotony, was no real characteristic of Romanesque architecture. The ends of the roof timbers rested on the transverse stone ribs. When a fire injured these roofs the ribs would go.

choir was begun by Bishop Walter de Marvis about 1219; the works were carried on until 1325, and consecrated in 1338. The aisles of the choir, ambulatories, or *carolles*,* as they are called here, are extremely broad and have a magnificent effect. The pillars of the *chevet*, or radiating arcade, immediately adjoining the altar, were originally so extremely slender that about 1435 it was found necessary to strengthen them, a process which was effected by some sacrifice of their original grace. The triforium is lighted by quatrefoils formed behind the heads of its tracery, as the photograph shows. The piers of the chancel are eighty-six feet in height; its clerestory is composed of nineteen windows.

On the wall of one of the chapels of the ambulatory is a painting with a gold ground, representing the "Triumph of Death," so frequent a subject in the period when it was executed, i.e., the thirteenth century. Parallel to the north nave aisle is a very large chapel or parish church, said to have been built by Henry VIII. of England during Wolsey's occupation of the see of Tournay (1513—1518); its style is rather "earlier" than we are accustomed to associate with buildings of that period. Among the pictures that may be worth notice is a "Purgatory" by Rubens, and an "Adoration of the Magi," by Lucas Van Leyden(?). There is a great rose window in the west end, filled with modern stained glass—not a fortunate addition. The subjects of the paintings are the "Virgin and Child," surrounded concentrically by figures of angels, prophets, the seasons, and zodiacal signs. Beneath this is the organ-loft, apparently of the same date as the screen. On the wall of the transept, high up, appear the remains of the original painting of the cathedral; figures of saints are depicted in panels one above the other, a characteristic Romanesque manner of decoration. In a side chapel of the nave is some early sixteenth-century glass, good of its kind. By the side of the altar stands the splendid shrine of St. Eleutherius, elected bishop of the city in 486, a member of a family converted by St. Piat a century and a half before his birth. By his exertions, the faith which had begun to die out in the neighbourhood was revived. In opposing some heretics he was wounded in the

---

* A term applied to the aisles of French churches that have screened chapels on one side. (Account of building the Church of St. Pierre D'Aire-sur-la-Lys.) See "Glossary of Architecture."—*Carole*.

head with a sword, and died July 1, 532.* The *châsse* is an extremely fine example of the goldsmith's work of the thirteenth century (1247), and is of silver gilt, decorated on the sides with seated figures of the apostles under tabernacle work. There are four figures on each side; at the ends appear Christ and St. Eleutherius. The gable above the last contains wingless angels bearing the symbols of martyrdom; the saint himself holds a model of the cathedral, such as is always given to founders; beneath his feet is the two-headed monstrous symbol of heresy and persecution. The shrine of St. Piat, which is visible in the photograph on the south side of the high altar, appearing close against the jamb of the door in the screen, is a much earlier work than that of St. Eleutherius; it is of wood (1280), and bears subjects from the life of Christ in bas-reliefs and medallions, and is painted and gilt. In the treasury of the cathedral is a fine collection of ancient robes; among them is a chasuble embroidered in silver, said to have been given to the cathedral by Thomas à Becket,† who stayed here in 1165; there is also a mantle embroidered with subjects from the Passion, and with the Last Supper, which was worn by Charles V. when he held the chapter of the Golden Fleece at Tournay in 1531. There is a fine crucifix in ivory by "Fiamingo" the famous Flemish sculptor, and other works of the sixteenth and seventeenth centuries.

The sculptures on the outside of the north and south doorways of this cathedral are extremely curious; above the door they are comprised in a blank semicircular arch, which is enclosed in another arch formed by three curves to the shape of a trefoil; the central curve of the latter being higher than the other two is formed by two curves, which, meeting in a point, produce the true ogive; the jambs beneath these are also richly carved. The general subjects are described by M. de Renaud ‡ as representing, under many satirical and grotesque forms, the Norman destroyers of Tournay. Among

---

* The day of St. Eleutherius is February 20; his emblem is a heated oven.

† Of this chasuble there is a sketch in M. De Caumont's *Abécédaire D'Archéologie, Romaine secondaire*, p. 308. Another chasuble with the mitre of this archbishop has been long preserved in the cathedral of Sens. A mitre from the same place, once belonging to à Becket, was in the possession of the late Cardinal Wiseman, and exhibited in the Loan Collection at South Kensington, 1862, No. 3,000. This mitre is also represented in M. De Caumont's admirable work, together with the chasuble of Sens.

‡ *Monographie de la Cathédrale de Tournai.*

the sculptures on the jambs of the north doorway we observe the devil bearing off a man who is dressed in embroidered vestments and has a bag hanging round his neck, and wears a helmet. The man is astride of the devil's neck, and holds to his horns; his legs appear in front of the strange supporter and are clasped by that personage with one hand, while with the other the latter gives his own tail a twitch. Above this is an angel, and below it the convolved serpent so common in Romanesque work and of obvious signification. The cockatrice appears as a sort of base, bearing up the detached shaft that is set in the first rebatting of the jamb on one side of the door. There is a second shaft placed in the inner rebatment; on the space between these shafts, *i.e.*, the jamb proper, are figures of a warrior and a grotesque animal, one above the other. The flat of the doorway, which is enclosed by the jambs and the architrave, bears sculptures, which are now decayed and undecipherable. At the sides, but above this last work, appear some subjects; among them is a reconciliation—a king joins the hands of two persons; the uppermost carving shows a town gate set in lofty walls, and standing half open; a man enters bearing a load on his shoulders, probably intended to suggest the return of the people to Tournay, a notion further strengthened by the representation of a very lofty tower having two stages of Romanesque windows and a blind base, which may be meant for one of the towers of the cathedral itself. The next panel shows a man cutting off the head of a soldier with a large sword; this may represent David and Goliath, but looks like an execution. The outer mouldings of the architrave have grotesques and symbolical figures carved upon them; among these, one group shows a stag pulled down by a lion—a goat, a bull, and a nondescript creature (man hunted by his sins.) The cap of one of the side shafts is splendidly carved into a grotesque, seated, beaked and winged monster (the spirit of evil), which is quite Assyrian in character. Another cap shows a man wearing large hanging sleeves; a hawk is on his wrist, two dogs are at his feet. There are many more sculptures of this sort. The exterior band of mouldings comprises palmettes,—those characteristic ornaments of the *style Romaine secondaire*, masks, griffins. To designate as barbarous the style of these carvings, as inconsiderate writers have done, is simply to ignore the intention and decorative skill of their producers; nothing can exceed the spirit and precision of their workmanship, which is only surpassed in excellence by the grotesque force of their conception. It is we who are barbarous and childish, in condemning that which we do not understand. The sculptures of the south doorway resemble the above in character; they are much less various, appear to have been restored, and comprise figures of armed men, who guard the entrance of the church; one of these threatens with his sword. The figures on the jambs of these doors are evidently allegorical; beneath that of a knight the word *superbia* is written; another shows a woman bearing a cross, and is inscribed *pietas*.*

The exterior of the cathedral may be briefly described. We have given an account of its most interesting portions—to wit, the sculpture on the north and south doorways, in the last paragraph, because they are matters of detail fitly associated with others of that order. The building is cruciform, but—the transepts being very short, the choir very wide, and the north side of the nave extended by the erection of the attached parish church before spoken of,—the plan is not very distinct on the exterior. The roof of the nave is much less lofty than that of the choir. At each external angle of the transept stands a lofty tower; that on the south-east, which is named *La Tour de Marie Pontoise*, is a noble specimen of pure Romanesque design; the others are of somewhat later date, and transitional character. These towers are about 250 feet in height, built in stages, slightly diminishing upwards and capped by an obtuse pyramid of evidently later date than the structures beneath them. These roofs have a dormer in each of their faces. The central space or roof of the crossing proper is now covered by an octangular pyramid, which is raised upon a low tower; originally this central tower was of much greater altitude. In front of each of its diagonal faces is placed a smaller four-sided pyramid, of about one-fourth of the height of the greater one. The grouping of these five pyramids with the four lofty transeptal towers gives great variety and striking effect to the cathedral, an effect, however, immeasurably inferior to

---

* We are not able to accept that interpretation of these sculptures which gives all of them a particular reference to the history of the city; like all works of their class, they have a general application to Christian life and religion. "*A toutes les epoques*," says M. De Caumont, with perfect truth, "la fantaisie a été un des éléments de l'art, et l'on ne doit pas s'étonner qu'il y ait eu dans l'ornementation, au moyen age, des figures de convention, comme il y en avait dans l'architecture Grecque et dans l'architecture Romaine."

E

that presented by the ancient arrangement when seven towers crowned the roofs of this imposing edifice. Owing to the proximity of houses to the cathedral, the tower which is most open to view is that on the north west, close adjoining to the foot of which is the richly-sculptured doorway before described. The tower is divided into stages by shallow strings, which do not exhibit those ranges of corbels beneath them which form corbel-tables in so many later works of this order. The topmost stage is pierced by coupled lights, that next below has a blind window of like character; beneath this the tower is solid, and pierced only here and there by small windows, which approach very closely to the pure Romanesque form, having, however, elements of transitional character. The *Tour de Marie Pontoise* is of severer aspect than this one.

The apsidal ends of the transept, north side, are in two stages; the upper one is pierced by seven semi-circular headed windows. At the angles these appear coupled shafts; there is a buttresset between each light; the roof above this stage bears one dormer, an evident insertion; the lower stage is pierced with two tiers of lights. The towers are connected by a gallery above the vaulting of the transept.

The exterior of the chancel exhibits the same extreme ambition, as one may style it, for slender forms and apparently impossible feats in stone working, which distinguishes the interior. Between the buttresses, which sustain double flying buttresses, are the chapels of the choir aisle, the acutely pointed gables of which come as far outwards as the buttresses themselves. In fact, the gables of the chapels rest on the buttresses, so that the bases of the gables occupy the whole spaces between them; where the wall should be is glass, and the width of the buttresses alone divides the windows from each other. The aisle windows are each divided by mullions into three lights, the central one being highest; three circlets, each enclosing a quatrefoil, fill the heads of the lights. The windows of the clerestory are equally wide, and much loftier than those of the aisle; they are also divided by mullions into three lights, the centre one being narrowest; one large circlet, inclosing a trefoil, fills each head. The windows of the east end are divided into two lights only, as the photograph shows; their traceries differ from those at the sides of the choir. There is no parapet to the choir. From transept end to transept end, all round the chancel of this church, is a mass of houses which hides the design. This is common in Belgium. Thus at Antwerp, the cathedral is hardly visible, except at the west front. The cathedral at Louvain is wholly surrounded; small houses are thrust close against the wall of the east end, but not, as at Tournay, so as to hide the entire structure. At Louvain the beautiful edifice rises above its incrustations. The cathedral at Mechlin is only less completely hidden at the east end than that of Tournay; it is, nevertheless, open on the north side. St. Gudule at Brussels stands free, but only so of late times, we believe. The case of St. Nicholas at Ghent is displayed in the photograph.*

The west front of the cathedral of Tournay has had some additions made to its original Romanesque design, which are by no means improvements. Among these, none is less fortunate than that great rose window before named, which may, although this is rather improbable, have taken the place of an eleventh-century work of similar form, but which never had an original so discordant to the structure of which it forms part as the present design of pointed character. Immediately under the roof appears a small arcade, supported by shafts, each of which rises from a step higher than that external to it, *i.e.*, nearer to the outer walls of the church. The porch is a much-injured work of the fourteenth century, decorated with statues.

Among the interesting relics of ancient Tournay are the immense remains of its walls, which are still standing on the south side of the city. Some of the walls on the north side of the Scheldt are probably as old as Henry VIII.'s time. Guarding the passage of the river there are two bastions connected by a wall, which is pierced by acutely pointed arches; these are parts of the fortifications of Philip *le Bel* (1290). The arches are closed by enormous gratings of iron, styled *herses*, like those which still exist in the walls of

---

* It is just to the photographer who produced the illustrations for this book to state that the crowded condition of the Belgian towns rendered it impossible to reproduce satisfactorily many of their most famous buildings. The Belfry at Ghent is an example of this. The deficiency of decorative carving which characterises the Belgian churches, and distinguishes them strongly from those of France, renders this less a matter of regret than would otherwise have been the case. The gigantic towers of the Low Countries, so closely are their bases crowded up, offer insurmountable difficulties to the photographer. The towers at Bruges and Brussels, here represented, were fortunate exceptions, obtainable by placing the camera at the summits of very lofty houses.

Troyes, in Champagne, and were raised or lowered by means of windlasses on the wall above. The wall between the bastions has a rampart on the inner side. Except the cathedral, no building in Tournay is so interesting as the belfry, which stands between the Grande Place and the cathedral, upon a base supplied by a Roman watch-tower. Philip Augustus, in 1187, granted the right of erecting such an edifice to the city ;* doubtless the present work is mainly of this period, or a very little later. It has less ancient additions, and now consists of a very lofty square tower, with turrets at its angles, surmounted by a spire and divided into two stages. The lower stages of the turrets are octangular, the upper ones are circular; they are roofed with octangular pinnacles, on the summits of which are statues of warriors. Each face of the stages of the tower itself is pierced with lancets; the uppermost stage bears a parapet of pierced work. Attached to the centre of the north face of the tower is a semicircular stair-turret, which is divided into two stages, and, at about half the height of the second stage of the tower, capped by a conical roof, which, being independent of the main structure, is pierced with little dormers, and ends in a finial. At this height probably the ancient tower ended; greater altitude might have been given to enable the watchers to see over the walls of the city when they were extended by Philip *le Bel*. The edifice is very picturesque; it was burnt in 1491, but, with the addition of the spire, restored in its original form very soon afterwards. On the summit is a clock (*c.* 1424), and three bells, one of which is named *Bancloque*, and inscribed :—

> "*Bancloque suis de commune nommé*
> *Car pour effroy de guerre suis sonnée.*"

"Roman Tournay," says Mr. Weale, in his excellent "Belgium, Aix-la-Chapelle, and Cologne," which is immeasurably the best guide-book for tourists, and especially rich in archæological information, "was situated wholly on the left side of the Scheldt; its walls were defended by semicircular towers built at intervals. A considerable portion of the wall and two of these towers still exist at

---

* Notwithstanding the assertion of M. Schayes, this fact is no proof that a belfry had not existed here before this date, when the king named seized the city from Philip of Alsace, Count of Flanders. The tower is the oldest in Belgium.

the backs of the houses of M. Dumortier, *Rue des Fosses*, 19, and of M. B. Dumortier, on the *Grande Place*."

The library of the place contains 30,000 volumes, comprising many manuscripts, among which is a psalter belonging to Henry VIII., a book of hours, once the property of Alexander Farnese, a copy of the *Roman de Rou*, etc. Wolsey, who was made bishop of the town by Henry VIII., and held the see for five years, must have often used this library. Erasmus was here in 1498.

Tournay contains several interesting churches ; among the most remarkable is that of St. Quentin, a transitional Romanesque church, and eminently characteristic of the style. It was an older foundation, of the ninth century, destroyed by the Normans, at the same time that the cathedral suffered. This church was reconstructed in the middle of the eleventh century. It has an aisleless nave, very short transept, and choir ; the last has a semicircular apse and an aisle passing completely round it, as in the church at Congues, quoted by Mr. Ferguson in his "History of Architecture," when treating of the development of the *chevet*. This resemblance was increased when the radiating chapels of the east end were added to St. Quentin's (*c.* 1445). The roof of the body of the church is comparatively low, the arches are very broad and obtusely pointed ; the roof of the transept is lower than that of the nave, which last is now flat, whatever shape it might originally have had ; that of the chancel and transept is ribbed ; the ribs of the crossing rest on banded vaulting shafts (a very rare feature in Belgium, where bands are hardly ever seen), which apparently descend to the floor, but are hidden by woodwork; those of the chancel rest on the caps of the piers, or on corbels, as do those of the transept. There are chapels on the west side of the transept, filling up the angles between it and the nave. Each face of the wall of the crossing, above the arches of the transept, nave and chancel, has an arcade placed before what appears to be a wall passage. The lighting is by clerestory throughout, and, on the north side of the nave, by three windows; those on the south side are filled up. The transept ends are respectively lighted by two round-headed windows, and above these each has a great bull's-eye. A noteworthy sort of triforium appears on the east side of the transept ; it is composed of five shafts, having very ancient caps, upon which rest stone lintels ; this somewhat resembles what presents itself in a similar position in the cathedral.

This church was originally founded by St. Eloy (Eligius), king Dagobert's friend, bishop of Tournay and Noyon, sees which had been united since the time of St. Médard in 512 (they were separated in 1146),* and by no means pleasant seats. Eloy became bishop here on the death of St. Acarius in 639. So serious a business was it considered, that the new bishop desired two years for preparation before he would enter upon his duties, which extended from the Somme to the Rhine. The people of Ghent and Courtray were remarkable for their virulent paganism, and did not scruple to treat bishops in the fashion which was experienced by St. Rumold at the hands of those of Mechlin more than a century later than the time of Eligius. At Tournay itself, the faith was not in a good condition, but the exertions of Eloy were so far successful that he not only founded this church but built the great abbey of St. Martin, some of the Romanesque piers of the crypt of which now remain among its gardens, which were converted into a public park about thirty years ago. Eloy did more than any one else for the dissemination of Christianity in Flanders. After a long service, he died in peace, December 1, 659, at Noyon. Queen and Saint Bathildis,† wife of Clovis II., came from Paris, and bathed the corpse in a flood of tears, and would have moved it to Chelles, but the people of Noyon would not permit it to go. Bathildis, who, with the exception of a pair of bracelets, had stripped herself of all her jewels for the sake of the poor, had a cross made of these and placed it at the head of Eloy's monument, and covered it with a canopy of cloth of gold. St. Eloy appears in ancient art as a bishop, holding a hammer, forging, shoeing a horse,‡ working as a goldsmith. Botticelli painted him erect on an anvil with Satan standing near, a picture now in the Florence Academy. These emblematic allusions are to the apprenticeship and craft of the saint as a blacksmith, in which capacity he was famous before he became a bishop.

---

* After the separation, the bishops of Tournay ranked with the twelve peers of France at a king's coronation.

† Bathildis was originally a slave brought out of Britain: it may be that on this account she forbade Christians to be made slaves. She was Regent of France during the minority of her son; her day is January 30.

‡ It is said that a horse was brought to him to be shod that was possessed by a devil, who compelled the beast to kick out fearfully. The saint, not to be defeated, simply cut off the leg of the horse, placed it on his anvil, fixed the shoe properly, and then, making the sign of the cross, not only put the leg in its proper place, but expelled the devil.

He wrought many shrines, among them that of St. Martin at Tours. The "Chair of Dagobert," attributed to St. Eloy—from which, as from a throne, Napoleon distributed honours to the army of invasion at Boulogne—turns out to be an antique curule chair, with a back of the eleventh century.

Besides St. Quentin's church, Tournay contains others of interest. Especially worthy of note is that of St. Jacques, which was partly rebuilt by the Bishop Walter de Marvis, who constructed the choir of the cathedral (1219—1251); it has fifteenth-century additions, and is especially noteworthy for the double triforium placed round the nave and above the arch which separates it from the choir. The churches of St. Magdalen and St Piat are worthy of examination. On account of its neighbourhood to the tomb of Childeric the church of St. Brice,* which dates from the twelfth century, has attracted more attention than that of St. Quentin; it stands on the right side of the river, in ancient days an open space, and has interesting features, but has suffered dreadfully in the hands of those who adapted it for what they considered modern uses. It was near the north door of this church that on the 27th of May, 1655, some workmen, while digging up the foundations of an old house, came at seven feet from the surface upon an ancient burial-place, which contained two skulls and some other bones of men, the teeth and jaw-bone of a horse, and a horse-shoe in a good state of preservation. In digging round the spot they found, at about six feet from these remains, and closer to them also, a great number of golden bees; a clasp of gold with the head of Childeric in relief, and, inclosed in a bag of rotten leather, more than a hundred gold medals and two hundred medals of silver; part of a sword, and a javelin, and the iron of an axe; a little bull's head of enamelled gold; a crystal ball; a gold case, with a stylus for writing; fragments of the same metal from the sword and its scabbard; enamelled gold from the bridle and harness of the horse; two gold rods with red enamel upon them, apparently formed to hold together a pair of tablets; a gold ring of considerable size; four clasps for the girdle and baldric; and lastly, and most important, as enabling us to identify the remains as those of the father of Clovis, a large gold ring bearing a seal, upon which was engraved a figure of a man, surrounded by the

---

* St. Brice, Bishop of Tours, died 444.

words CHILDERICI REGIS, in Roman letters. One of the skulls is supposed to have belonged to the marshal of the king of the Franks; the crystal ball was probably an amulet.

There were the bones of him whom Basina followed from her home! There were the mighty limbs of Childeric! While they lay still, what things had been done above his head? The very tumulus which distinguished his grave was levelled, and that ground the Salians marked as sacred to the memory of their king re-consecrated to a saint of whom Childeric thought little enough when the holy man died some forty years before the time came for digging the hole and heaping the mound on the side of the river, which ran through fields near that capital which his people had clutched, mint, wool-factories and all, from the Romans.* St. Brice's very ground itself was trenched upon in course of time, and a house built close to the walls of his church, right over the resting-place of the king. One house had followed another in decay, and all sorts of domesticities had gone on without waking the son of Pharamond. At last some one thought of doing a little justice to the saint, and clearing the rotten old houses from the neighbourhood of his church. A few strokes of the shovel and the pick, and there lay Childeric in the light of day again.

The royal houses that had risen and fallen during his interment were quite as numerous as those habitations of the Tournay citizens, who, above his head, lived, worked, ate, drank, danced, and died in their generations. Merovingian, Carlovingian, Capetian, Valois, Orleans, Angoulême, all had passed; Bourbon itself—which through all the rest boldly assumed to have some of his blood in it, had come to a strange pitch; and that wonderful man, Louis XIV., who, after a fashion, was very soon to capture Childeric's own city—was alive, with many wigs and women of outlandish styles. Chlotaire, Sigebert, Chilperic, Fredegonda, Brunehault, Pepin, Charlemagne—counts of Flanders, counts of Hainault; kings of England—Edward III., Henry VIII.; emperors—Henry III., Charles V., and the Prince of Parma—with centuries of blessed peace and silence between some of them—every one of them came and conquered and went while

---

* Tournay was reported to the Empress Placidia as great in wool manufacture.

Childeric lay in the darkness, and, if he heard at all, could only hear the priests chanting in St. Brice's church. One would think it strange to Childeric to hear only this during five hundred years, and probably the chanting would be more annoying to him than the dead silence of the eight hundred years which preceded the erection of the church so near his place of rest. As if to complete the strange chances of the monarch, the very clasp with his head upon it serves to decorate the scarf which the Dean of St. Brice's wears on festival days when he goes in procession with the singers and the people of the church. Did Childeric and his marshal think of such a thing as that? Could the faithful man who shared his tomb from the death-day to that of digging up venture to hint that their bones would be put in a museum, he would gladly have added to their unpleasant information the fact that Napoleon, a greater than he, would assume his armorial bees,* and vaunt them above the lilies of France.

Whether the people of Tournay derive it from Childeric, Clovis, or the ancient Salian race in general, it is certain that for courage

* The reader will remember that these precious objects of antiquity are not the only examples of their kind which have been taken from the graves of kings. Most important of these are the treasures removed, in 979, by the Emperor Otho III., from the grave-chamber of Charlemagne at Aix-la-Chapelle, then as now at Vienna. See Dr. Bock's account of them. In the treasury at Aix is the cross of King Lothaire, with its inscription, "*O Christ, aid King Lothaire!*" The jewels at Monza, popularly supposed to have been taken from a tomb, were given to the Cathedral by Queen Theodolinda. Nothing of the sort equals the discovery of the eight crowns of gold, worth about £2,000, which happened in clearing out an ancient cemetery at Guerraza, near Toledo, in 1858. They were votive crowns, offered before a shrine of the Virgin, by Recesvinthus, the Visigothic King of Spain (650—672), and, probably, his queen and nobles. From the lower edge of the largest crown the name RECESVINTHUS REX OFFERT—formed in Roman letters, is supended by chains of gold; it is eight and a half inches in diameter, and has, hanging from the centre, a splendidly jewelled cross. Five of the larger crowns have similar crosses suspended from them, and all have gold chains, by which they were hung before an altar. The king's crown contains some sapphires, thirty rubies, and thirty-five pearls. Each letter of the name is separate, having a separate chain, and from them again, hang pendents of gold and pearls; these support twenty-four pink rubies, and form a fringe all round the crown. The cross is set with gems, and has three pendents. From the inscription on one of the other crowns, it appears that these ornaments came from the Church of Santa Maria de Abaxo, at the foot of the hill on which Toledo stands; they were probably concealed and forgotten when the Moors captured Toledo in 711. They are now in the Hôtel Cluny, Paris. The beauty of their workmanship is marvellous. Some other crowns have been found since the above in the same neighbourhood; these are now at Madrid.

the inhabitants of few cities have a greater reputation than theirs. Letalde and Englebert, brothers, of Tournay, who went with Godfrey de Bouillon to the first crusade, were before all others in Jerusalem on that blood-stained July 15th, 1099. They scaled the walls, and were the first to enter the place by means of a ladder, while Bernard de St. Valery was struggling to go astride on a beam that had been let down on the battlements from a wooden tower. Although Bernard de St. Valery was a Norman, and Duke Robert's own cousin, it was not right of Raoul de Caen, the chronicler, to give the Flemings' meed to him. The people of Tournay may well be familiar with sieges and captures, seeing that their city's first appearance in history refers to its capture by Cæsar. About 350 the Vandals came upon it; 575 brought Sigebert against Chilperic; in 880 came the Normans, who so desolated the place that none lived there for nearly thirty years; 1054 brought Henry III., nearly as bad a foe as the Normans were; in 1340, being then a French town, it held out valiantly, under Sir Gondemar du Fay, against the English, under Edward III.,* the Flemings

---

* For an account of this siege see Froissart, chapters 53 to 63. Edward encamped before St. Martin's Gate, before walls that are still standing. Van Artevelde and his 60,000 Flemings sat down before that of St. Fontaine, *i.e.* the *Pont des Trous*, where the Gothic bridge and bastions before-named still are, and drew a bridge of boats across the Scheldt. The Brabanters, with their duke, were at Ponteries-on-the-Scheldt, "as you return from the fields by the gate Valentinois." The Count of Hainault sat down between the last and the King of England. The Duke of Gueldres and the Germans were on the Hainault side; there were one hundred and twenty thousand men in all, "so that the city was very completely surrounded." The Flemings did the greater part of the fighting. Froissart tells us one assault of theirs lasted a whole day. This was made before the *Pont des Trous*. The Kings of Navarre, Scotland, England, and Bohemia, were present at the siege. Philip of France stayed at Arras, because Robert, king of Sicily, "who was a great astrologer," had declared that he would be beaten whenever he faced Edward in person. Then came the Dukes of Lorraine, Brittany, Burgundy, and Bourbon, on the French side, to raise the siege, together with the Counts of Flanders (Louis Mâle), Savoy, Geneva, Alençon, Armagnac, Blois, and a host of others. Froissart's narrative is full of his delightful and masterly episodes, which give such life to his pages. No reader will forget to rejoice with those poor peasants whom the German knights from Bouchain succoured so fortunately when they set out " to seek adventures, and to see how things were going on." We remember how these good fellows met the " Knight from Burgundy, Sir John de Frelais, under the orders of the Lord of Beaujeu," and his marauders, driving before them two hundred head of cattle, and certain peasants, prisoners, and how with a loud shout they set upon them full gallop; and how the Burgundy knight fought well, but was taken prisoner, and many of his rascals were killed by the peasants, "who had armed themselves with

who followed Jaques Van Artevelde, and their allies. The siege lasted eleven weeks, and many deeds of arms were done on both sides. It was raised at last in consequence of the entreaties of the "good Lady Jeanne de Valois, mother of the Count of Hainault," who "frequently, on her knees, entreated the King of France her brother, the Duke of Brabant, and others," so that Edward's allies left him, and the city was delivered. In gratitude to Tournay for its valiant defence, Philip—who could not forget that only three days' provisions were left in the town—granted back to the citizens their franchises, which they had lost for some time. He also chose from among them a special body-guard, entitled *Familiers de l'Hotel*. In 1513, Henry VIII. took Tournay, and gave the see to Wolsey; but returned it, together with Therouanne, for 600,000 crowns.* Charles V. took it in 1521, and it was abandoned by France at the treaty of Madrid in 1525. In 1581, the Prince of Parma (Alexander Farnese) besieged it, when it was most valiantly

stakes;" the re-captured booty was given to the right owners, "who were thankful to the Germans ever after." We remember, too, how Sir Vauflart de la Croix persuaded about one hundred and twenty knights and squires (Hainaulters), to set out one day "for love of each other, and to do some deed of arms," and how, with the best intentions, they went for wool and came home shorn, for Sir Vauflart got lost in a fog, met a party of Liégeois—whose bishop had made them promise " to go out and see if they could find any chance to profit by,"—was beaten by them; had to hide in a quagmire, be taken prisoner, given up to the King of France, who sent him to Lisle, where, "as he had done much harm to the inhabitants, they would not accept any ransom, but put him to death." We remember how this before-named Lord of Beaujeu amused himself with a lance that had a sharp hook, with which, "when he made his stroke," he entangled those who attacked the walls of Mortagne, and drew them into the river; and all about the "handsome engine," which was destroyed by another in three wonderful shots.

The neighbourhood of Tournay has been strangely fertile in chroniclers and memoir writers. Besides minor men of this sort, there is the prince of all in the good Canon of Chimay and "Lille," rector of Lessines, native of Valenciennes, John Froissart himself, who is supposed to lie buried—for, although he rescued so many from oblivion, no one knows for certain where he is interred—in the chapel of St. Anne, in the church of St. Monegunda, at Chimay. Enguerrand de Monstrelet lived, and was probably born, at Cambray, where he was buried in the church of the Cordeliers. Philip de Commines takes his name from the place of his birth.

* The secret reports of Sebastian Giustinian, Venetian ambassador at the court of Henry VIII., to the signory, give a strong idea of the importance of this relinquishment.—(See "Four Years at the Court of Henry VIII." Smith, Elder, and Co. 1854.) Monstrelet, chapter 236, relates the capture of the city, and it appears that Henry frightened the citizens by a terrific display of wooden cannon.

defended by Christine, Princess d'Epinoy, of the noble family of Lalaing—whose statue now stands in the *Grande Place*. Her husband, the governor, was absent; she was wounded, and lost three-fourths of the garrison ere the place fell to the Spaniards. Tournay was taken by Marlborough in 1709; returned to Austria in 1714; besieged by the French in 1745. It capitulated when the Duke of Cumberland was defeated at Fontenoy, while advancing to its relief; four years afterwards it was restored to Austria; it was captured by the army of the French republic in 1792; relinquished in 1793; retaken in 1794 by the same, and retained until 1814. To say how often its fortifications have been built, demolished, rebuilt, and again destroyed, might give an idea of the military importance of the place, but need not be stated here. May the existing ones never be used!

RUINS OF THE ABBEY, VILLERS LA VILLE.

THE ABBEY OF VILLERS.

ABOUT twenty-five miles from Brussels stands the great and ancient Cistercian abbey of Villers. Like all places belonging to that order, it is at a distance from towns, close to water, and well sheltered from cold winds. The charming situations of the English monasteries of Tintern and Valle Crucis are examples of such choice by the founder of the house in Brabant, which is placed under the shelter of a hill that has been quarried to furnish materials; on the south and west, however, the land stretches smooth in sward from the abbey doors and, even now, when the space in front of the church is strewn with wreckage, there is level green as far as the edge of the wood, that encroaches again on ground which, seven centuries ago, was cleared by order of St. Bernard himself.* From that time (1146), when it arose under the

---

* The wolves were not the only disturbers of the forest about Villers; there was a sort of leathery goblin called Kludde, a brother, no doubt, of Robin Goodfellow, and friend of our English Puck. This Kludde, like the others, had his good qualities, but was often mischievous. For example, he would bother a peasant when returning home at night, and seeking his way through the wood by signs and the positions of trees, Kludde, for love of evil only, would take the form of a tree and stand in a place where none had been before, to the great bewilderment of the good man. At other times, he would appear as a shrub, and, starting up before the feet of men, cause them to stumble over him, and then, while they lay cursing on the ground, stretch himself enormously and become gradually a great tree, to the horror of the peasant. He would sometimes, in the form of a huge black dog, jump on the backs of people, throw them down, and vanish with a howl. Taking the shape of a dirty, half-starved horse, he would now and then get into a field where was a full-fed one, turn the last out, and remain, till morning brought the farmer's man to clean that which could not be cleaned, and refused to work. He appears by various names in different parts of the country, and we shall hear of him again. One of his freaks was to come down the chimney of a cottage, after all the folks were gone to bed, light up the fire, and sit by it till morning. It is averred by many that, although but little of the winter store of wood is sometimes left by Kludde, that little will outlast the season if the house-wife does not curse the intruder as she sees him sitting in her husband's chair, burning the winter fuel as fast as possible. Many a woman of the forest, failing in the trial, has lost her temper and her timber too.

direction of Laurent, first abbot, to the date of its destruction in 1796, the house flourished, with few changes, except such as were symptoms of decease in the later days. As we find, when in 1789 while the establishment was ruled by Bruno Cloquette, seventy-fourth, and, as it happened, last abbot, revolution broke out in Brabant, and the Austrian army retreating from the province pillaged Villers,* Abbot Bruno did his best to repair the damages, but did not foresee that a wider fury was to sweep the land with the French Revolution, and that the long reign of his order was to come to an end. In the years 1792 and 1794, the army of " La Republique" surrounded the place, and joined the people of the neighbourhood in plundering it. The order for the dissolution of monasteries followed, and on the 23rd Frimaire an V. (13th December, 1796), the community learnt its last hour was come. The monks received two days' notice, to quit their ancient and find a new asylum.† Abbot Bruno succeeded, it is said, in saving three loads of treasures—for the use of the monks, let us hope: he died in 1828. The last brother of Villers, Placide Adant, died no longer ago than 1852 : a woman who lives in the neighbouring mill remembers to have seen the monks walking in their gardens, wearing their black scapularies and white robes, and heard them chanting in the choir.

There is this about the Abbey of Villers which strikes the imagination of an Englishman with much force. He stands almost face to face with an ancient and powerful house gone to ruin within the memory of those alive. The vault of the nave, although it is half destroyed already, and the long arcades of the aisles, although they seem to totter, have echoed but lately with the chant of St. Bernard, ordained when his friend Laurent and twelve monks, with five lay-brethren, laboriously set about their work here. A visit

---

* *L'Abbaye de Villers*, par Jules Tarlier, Bruxelles, 1857.

† The devastation which took place at Villers hardly approached in violence that which wrecked the sister Cistercian house at Orval, in 1793, when the Republican army plundered the place for eight days, and at last heaped timber with shells and gunpowder in the church, and blew it up. At Lobbes, and at Alne, near Charleroi, much the same was done ; at Altenberg the monks were turned out, and the abbey became a manufactory of Prussian blue. Dilegem was destroyed, so were Cambron, near Lille, Jardinet, La Cambre, and many more. The great parent of all these, St. Bernard's own abbey at Clairvaux, actually escaped the Republican fury to be utterly destroyed in the first year of the Restoration, because more room was wanted for a prison yard.

to this place is as if we were set back in time to within one man's life of the dissolution of monasteries in England, while some which are now utterly wrecked retained their noblest features. We question if the work of destruction could have been more complete in England than it was in Belgium. The reader sees how the nave of Villers appears, and that the figure leaning against a column is waist-high in herbage, while three bays only of the nave retain the vault above them ; the roof of the choir and transept has fallen down, and the triforium and clerestory of the southern side bend inwards to their fall.* Wild birds sing on the summit of the arch, farm-beasts soil the sole remaining monumental slab, the inscription of which tells us how a knight and lady were interred beneath, in 1348, the year when Rienzi was journeying to Rome, and Alfonso of Castile making a truce with Yusef ben Ismael, Moorish lord of Granada, just three years before the battle of Crecy, while Louis I. was Count of Flanders, and John of Gaunt but three years old, and John III. ruling in Brabant. Neither the beauty of the engraving, nor the hands pressed together in prayer, saved the memorial when the crown of the vault came down upon it, and some huge stone smote the knight in the face and the lady on her breast, starring the enormous flag as if it were a sheet of glass. Although, as in all Cistercian houses, the western towers of Villers did not exceed the height of the roof, yet vast masses of masonry lie at their feet upon the sward without, just as fallen rocks lie before a cliff.

The founder of this house needs little notice from us ; men know him well, although few have learnt how before his birth his mother dreamt she would be delivered of a great white dog, whose barking would fill the world ; she complained to a monk, and was comforted with the assurance, " You will bear a son who shall keep God's house, and bark against the enemies of the faith ; " and so Bernard did, sure enough, for if making a noise was serviceable, to say

---

* The destruction of the building followed so complete a pillage that not a single relic of all the *mobilia* of the vast establishment exists here. In the parish church at La Ville is some oak carving, removed from the abbey ; elsewhere are a few fragments of antiquities. The superb tombs of the dukes of Brabant and many others, their very bones, indeed, have been destroyed. In the choir in the church a huge hole was dug, in order to search for treasures. Fire appears to have been freely employed.

nothing about his share in the second crusade, he was a noted persecutor, as Abelard found to his cost on being condemned as a heretic. Like a dog, Bernard sometimes barked very loudly at chimeras, fantastic delusions, and whims of heated brains, such as had better have been let disperse themselves: the times were full of such. He attacked Arnould of Brescia, Peter de Bruys, etc. (1150), and did not content himself with barking, says his satirical apologist; he was more successful in exterminating heterodoxy than in the ruin of infidels, yet he attacked the latter with arms of the flesh, with prophecy, and when he was accused by his adversaries of procuring the deaths of many thousands in the crusade, he replied that their sins had caused the failure of that enterprise,—no unreasonable answer.

It was while he was preaching the second crusade that St. Bernard visited Belgium. He was a man of such extraordinary influence as to have terrified King Louis VII. in a letter reproaching him with having burnt thirteen hundred persons, in a church at Vitri, where they took refuge, when the place was assaulted by the king's troops. In behalf of the Church he wrote,—"*I will fight for her to the death, not with swords and shields, but with the arms of a servant of the Lord,—my tears and my prayers.*" These words, not more, let us hope, than the revulsion of passion in a human heart, brought horror, shame, and repentance to the soul of Louis. Fear of death before he could offer the compensation of sacrifices for the Lord's sake, *i.e.*, a repetition on the unhappy Moslems of Syria of those atrocities for which he suffered, led him to accept with joy the hint of St. Bernard, that no act would be so efficacious as that of taking the cross, as Robert the Frison, Robert of Jerusalem, and Robert of Normandy had done before him. The Pope, seeing that great benefits must accrue to the Church by the diversion of men's minds from those detestable questions which Arnould of Brescia and others had raised, gladly and with all his might helped the enterprize suggested by Bernard. The famous meeting was held at Vézelai, and men shouted madly in answer to Bernard's harangue," *Id Deus vult! Id Deus vult!* "* Thierry of Alsace, Count of Flanders, was one of the first to take the cross, together

---

* The pulpit from which Bernard preached remained at Vézelai until 1789, a year curiously fatal to the remains of his influences.

with Louis of France, and Conrad of Germany. No wonder they did so, for they actually believed, or pretended to believe, that the Abbot of Clairvaux gave sight to the blind, hearing to the deaf, and performed miracles not less potent. He preached all along the Rhine, and multitudes followed him. All ended in dreadful discomfiture, ruin and wreck on every side.

While this crusading torrent was beginning to form, Bernard had promised to found a monastery in Brabant, which should transport to the Low Countries those virtues and their attendant blessings which were centred upon Clairvaux in the lonely valley of Champagne. His martial labours over, he remembered that a crusade of another sort might be profitable, although the more violent one failed miserably. He sent the men before-named to a place now styled Gemioncourt, which proved unsuitable, and the whole plan was about to be abandoned, when the monks demanded to return to Clairvaux, and Abbot Laurent resigned in favour of Gyrald. Upon this Bernard himself came to the rescue, visited the place, and recommended that the house should be removed farther into the great forest,* which then extended as far as Nivelles, and to the borders of the Thyle, a river which, lower down, passes Louvain. This was done; before leaving Abbot Gyrald and his monks in their huts, Bernard helped to erect a little oratory of stone, and, at the moment of parting, struck his staff into the sward in front of that structure and gave it his blessing, so that, rapidly taking root, it sprang into a magnificent oak that outlasted even the stone

---

* In the days of Abbot Gyrald, the forest round Villers was supposed to be infested with evil spirits, and those metamorphosed men who are recognized by the name of Werwolves, one of which in the form of a wolf would sometimes jump out of a thicket on an unlucky passenger. On one occasion, long after Villers was built, a young girl was attacked by a creature of this sort, as she was sitting at evening watching cattle, not far from the borders of the forest. An archer was attracted to the place by the screams of the girl as she clung to a sapling, and the evil thing tugged to make her loosen her hold. The archer shot the creature in the side, and it ran howling into the wood. A few days after this, the man was riding through the village of La Ville, no great way from the abbey, when some one asked him to go and see a man who had been shot in the side, by robbers of the wood, as he said. No sooner did the archer see the arrow, than he knew it was his own, and that the wounded man must be a Werwolf. Collecting himself, and knowing that the wretch might accuse him of being one of the robbers he had spoken of, the archer turned everybody out of the room, and roundly taxed the dying man with endeavouring to carry off the girl in order that he might eat her. The fellow confessed, and died instantly.

edifice by a hundred years, for Bernard's oratory stood on the high bank above the abbey transept until the end of the sixteenth century, while it was not until 1697 that a stroke of lightning converted into relics that which was a tree when Louis came back from the crusade, and his wife, Eleanor of Guienne, innocently, as her friends said, was flirting with the handsome Turk. Bernard, in defending himself against the charge of too often quitting the cloisters,—to which, as a Cistercian, he should have been peculiarly devoted,—replied that he could not always remain "the disciple of oaks and beeches." Here was a disciple, so to say, of his own, which shadowed his house long after men had ceased to quarrel about him and his deeds. He died soon after his friend Suger, Abbot of St. Denis, and Chancellor of France, 1153.

The invocations of so ardent a preacher as St. Bernard were not less powerful in filling his monastery at Villers than those strange measures which were practised in Merovingian times to augment the number of inmates of great religious houses, when nobles gave their serfs to seclusion—a sort of vicarious retirement it might have been, —and slaves were purchased from the Norman markets, to be, by pious founders, relegated to the cloisters. Queen Bathildis, herself a purchased English slave, as we have seen, spent large treasures in the redemption of her countrymen for the monasteries, so did her friend St. Eloy.* The fact is that the convents of this early age, and for some time later, were noble industrial establishments, wherein the life prescribed to the Bernardines of Citeaux or Villers would have been as impracticable as they were needless. We see this in thinking that in summer as in winter, long before the eastern sun could strike the loftiest lancet of the choir before us, the Cistercian was astir; from three o'clock in the morning until nine he prayed unceasingly, after which came complines and vespers at two and at six o'clock. So rigorous was the silence held in these houses that, even in the cloisters, men might speak but for a single hour *per diem*. An order devoted to labour could not pray continually, as did some of the more ascetic associations. Yet a stringent rule was observed at Villers during the early centuries of its existence; in later days, however, we find these practices much

---

* *Acta Sanctorum, St. Bathildis.*

relaxed, and time given to the education of pupils,* who were received into the house. The loss of their estates in the political changes of the eighteenth century probably led to this peculiar direction of the energies of the monks. The noble library, the apartments containing which still astonish the visitor by their great extent, offered facilities for study.

St. Bernard's influence wrought not only powerfully but rapidly; in 1160, we learn that Godfrey IX. of Brabant confirmed the gift to Villers by Engelbert de Schroter of his allodium and all its dependencies. So soon as 1231, Villers produced an offshoot in the form of the Abbey of Grand-Pré, near Namur, and, in 1238, the house established the Abbey of St. Bernard-upon-the-Scheldt. Henry II. of Brabant testified to his belief in the sanctity of the monks of Villers when he said in reply to one of his gay companions, who urged him to examine the relics of the saints which were preserved in the church, that it was enough for him to have seen the bones of the monks who were interred in the *colline*, to the east of the abbey.

This duke was buried here, 1248, as was his successor, John III., 1355.† In 1272, Villers contained a hundred monks and three hundred lay-brethren: this was in the days of Abbot Arnould II. In 1314 (Jaques II., twenty-fourth abbot), the monks of Villers not being willing to pay the heavy land-tax levied upon them by the guardians of John III., quitted the abbey, carried away all their mobilia, and found refuge in other houses of their order. Under John III., twenty-fifth abbot, famine drove them out. Poor John VI., thirty-sixth abbot, managed so carelessly that the monks were compelled to beg bread in the streets of Genappe, instead of distributing doles at their own gates: no wonder that in 1414, the

---

* The Cistercians were of the second order of the Benedictine rule; their manual labour was serious enough; "in summer, after chapter, which followed prime, they worked till tierce, and after nones they worked till vespers. In winter, from after-mass till nones, and even till vespers during Lent. In harvest, when they went to work in the farms, they said tierce, and the conventual mass immediately after prime, that nothing might hinder their work for the rest of the morning, and often they said divine service in the places where they were at work, and at such hours as those at home celebrated it in the church." Such was the practice in England.

† This was the duke whom we met before Tournay, attacking that place with Edward III., of England: his desertion caused the siege to be raised, 1340.

council of the Bernardines interfered to re-establish the severity of the ancient discipline, which had already been relaxed. At intervals during the fore-named periods and in those which succeeded them, the Abbey suffered and rose again. Thus Abbot Robert II. built a great deal, and repaired the ravages of the religious wars of the sixteenth century; he was the forty-eighth abbot, and was succeeded by Henry II., abbot, in whose time the troops of General Lamboy and those of the Duke of Lorraine, the Imperialist general, devastated the neighbourhood, burnt the abbey farms, and kept the monks in misery for three years. Under Robert III., abbot, the house contributed about 250,000 florins towards building a royal palace at Brussels. The revenues were sadly reduced, and in 1776 there were not more than fifty-four monks and eleven lay-brethren of Villers; its time was nearly come, its work was done.

So vast was the establishment in its palmy days, that even now the ruins extend over a parallelogram which is 285 yards by 195 yards, and enclosed by a wall nearly ten feet high; in this wall there were formerly three entrance gates, those of Namur, Brussels, and Villers la Ville. We enter now, not by one of these grand portals, but by a little doorway in the wall which brings us at once to the ruins of the Guest House, the Library, Abbot's House and Prior's House, with the great Court of Honour on one hand, under part of which is a range of cellars, yawning here and there for the unwary passenger, now covered by grass and shaded by great trees: beneath the rooms of the Procurator is a prison. The immense extent of these premises astonishes one, room succeeds room, and doorway, doorway; all is ruin and desolation, roofless, floorless, and the scrawls of visitors* deface the naked walls; the Guest House and Abbot's House are of red brick, rebuilt in 1729. Beyond the Court of Honour, and on the same side of the range in question, is the Court of the Novices, with the Library on the east, and once divided from the Court of Honour by a range of buildings comprising dormitories, which was at right angles to the

---

* Such evidences of want of respect for antiquities are much more common, we are bound to say, on the Continent than in England: the range of chambers at Villers is an expanse of scrawls; the church itself has not entirely escaped.

Abbot's House. These structures were all built in the second quarter of the eighteenth century. It is true that these edifices have no architectural interest; their extent, however, and the knowledge that they replaced ancient structures, impress one. The wrecks look raw, unfit to be a ruin, and shock us like the corpse of a young man, dead before his time; the sight of them is not the less painful because they fail to evoke that veneration which does so much for antiquity.

The Thyle traverses nearly diagonally the great Court of Honour. If we go in the same direction it will bring us to the older parts of the Abbey; first of these is the refectory, built in 1190, and of Romanesque or transition character, a parallelogram of about 110 feet in length, by 50 feet in width; beneath its north-east corner runs the Thyle. Five columns divide the interior into two aisles, which are vaulted, that on the northern half being semi-circularly arched, that on the south pointed. There are six windows on either side, each of which is divided by a shaft into two pointed lights; in the heads are bull's-eyes; discharging arches inclose all. There are two windows at each end of the refectory; four round-headed windows are placed above these; on the north a third tier, which fills the gable, is composed of three, the central one of the group being highest and placed immediately above the great buttress which divides the end of the structure into two parts. The arrangement of windows in the south gable is nearly the same as that in the north. As the chimes were placed in the summit of the refectory, the windows there, *i.e.*, the three at each end, were probably never closed. Clocks were forbidden to Cistercians, but sun-dials allowed. The north end of the refectory has a door which admitted the monks from the cloisters that abutted it; on the east of this apartment is the dark and vaulted kitchen, the aspect of which leads the visitor to imagine that the cookery of Villers was primitive; it is about thirty-eight feet by twenty-eight feet; its groining rests on each side on five unequally placed engaged cylindrical columns; the chimney is on the west side, near the door of the refectory. The Thyle passes across the room and may be seen by looking through a breach which is made in the enormous walls that separate the refectory from the kitchen by an interval of seven feet. On the opposite side of the refectory is the calefactory, or place where the monks were allowed to warm themselves after the kalends of November. Here the censers were lighted, and, if the weather was very cold, chapters were held. It was built about 1200, has three pointed and one round-headed window, and is divided by six columns standing in pairs. On the south wall of the refectory are the remains of a very ancient painting of the Virgin enthroned, with Jesus on her knee: on a corresponding wall Da Vinci painted his "Last Supper" for the convent of San Domenico, Milan.

In this neighbourhood we have also the vaulted rooms which were once appropriated to the buttery, and the scullery (*Lavoir de cuisine*). The last has a closet opening upon the river beneath it; in the south end angle of the scullery is an apartment from which access is obtainable to the great range of cellars under that building, which once divided the Court of Honour from the court of the novices, and comprised probably the dormitories and work-rooms of the monastery. The mere basement of this range remains. About half the west side of the refectory is occupied externally by the calefactory before named, the other half is appropriated to a small court, on the opposite side of which, and parallel to the refectory, stands the infirmary (*c.*1190), and the dispensary (1784), which last has attached to its south side the herbary, or physic-garden as we should style it in England, open to the sun, and in fact, part of the vineyards of the convent, which faced that side. The infirmary and dispensary occupied only the upper floors of the structures which abutted on the small court, and the calefactory; under the dispensary the road from Genappe to Gembloux passes, and divides the vineyard from the great court of the Abbey, which is on the west side of the infirmary, a space which extends beyond the west front of the church, and gives a fine view of the grave architecture of the ancient buildings, and is about eight times as large as the Court of Honour. The dispensary is probably the most recent part of the Abbey, built by Abbot Bruno Cloquette in 1784; it stands supported on pseudo-classical columns, between which the road runs, is of brick with stone facings, and by the motto, "*Fideliter et suaviter*," which is inscribed upon its front, attests the vanity of the builder's hopes. One half of the lower floor of the infirmary is occupied by the chapter-house, like it of Romanesque character (*c.* 1197), and lighted by round-headed windows; the other half of this lower stage comprises three rooms, probably *scriptoria*, or places for special study; a wretched eighteenth century façade, erected at an enormous cost, hides the ancient work of the last mentioned structures. Between the scriptoria and the chapter-house is the great entrance to the Abbey, which, to be in keeping with the regulations of the Cistercian order, has no pretensions, being a mere doorway to a passage leading direct to the south side of the cloisters, *i.e.*, that abutted by the refectory, calefactory, and kitchen.

The west arch of the cloister is formed by the chapter-house and infirmary above it; the south by the offices of the *cuisine*; the east by the dormitories; and the north by the church, as in the parent house at Clairvaux: the cloister was, in fact, the common passage of the house, giving access to and connecting its principal offices, exactly as did its prototype, the *atrium* of a classic villa. Few ruins in England have so picturesque a character as the cloisters of Villers, as they are surrounded by the wrecks of conventual buildings, draped with creepers, and with trees growing in the enclosure or garth, which last was probably used for the interment of great personages,—for those of ordinary character, doubtless, the *garenne* or cemetery, on the slope of the hill to the west of the church, sufficed. The cloister is 164 feet long by 131 feet wide; its north and west sides were built about 1230, that on the south sixty years later, that of the east or dormitory side in the sixteenth century. The arcades on the north and west are entirely destroyed; five arches only of the south walk remain, but the west side is still perfect; they are in the best manner of the *style ogival secondaire* of M. De Caumont, or *Decorated* of the English archæologists. In the north-east angle was, as usual, the entrance to the church; near this was interred the Blessed Gerbert, a beatified crusader of the Aspremont family, Count of Montaigu, who took the cowl at Villers, and died in 1263;* close to it is a magnificent rose window, which once gave light to the south end of the church transept, which was darkened, and this rose removed from it, when the staircase to the dormitory was built close against it. A doorway at the west end of this cloister gives access to the crypt, which

---

* Weale. The Gerbert in question edified the monks by the severity of his devotion; for ages after his death every cowled head was bent when passing this grave.—*Tarlier*.

extends beneath the vestibule and part of the nave of the church; here the abbots of Villers were interred.

We will not enter the church as the monks did, by the door in the corner of the cloister, but as strangers, between the western towers, by one of its three Romanesque doorways, and pass the vestibule, which is not larger than sufficed to cut off the external world. From the extreme west end of the nave the photograph was taken, which will serve to give a better idea of the present condition and original beauty of the building than many pages of words could evoke. Its plan is cruciform, with a short transept, its extent is nearly 300 feet long by 130 feet at the transept; the nave is 81 feet in width. The nave and aisles, which are nearest to us, were built between 1197 (under Abbot Charles) and 1220, and are noble examples of the first pointed style. The reader will observe the beauty and severity of the columns, which are cylindrical, gently changing to octangular at the upper parts of their capitals, and having beautifully moulded octangular abaci: the bases of these pillars are very finely formed, so are the rings from which the capitals spring. Nothing that can be strictly styled decorative carving appears in any part of the interior of this church; the leaflets on the caps of the triforium shafts have more architectural than decorative character. All is pure architecture of the finest sort, unaided by ornament. The nave, including the vestibule, consists of eleven bays; the figure leans against the pier of the sixth of these, counted from the east. That part of the vaulting which remains serves to show how exquisitely fine was the outline of the whole.* The vaulting shafts, which are triple, rest on the caps of the columns, and are traversed by a string which forms a band.

---

* We are sorry to say that the course of destruction in these beautiful ruins is rapid, and threatens to be considerably extended by the curious manner in which the keystone of the rib which traverses the vaulting of the north aisle of the nave from the first pier has been thrust upwards; an inch more of this and it seems certain that the vault must fall, upon which, there being insufficient resistance to the thrust of the vault of the nave upon the wall, the whole angle of the crossing on that side, and those portions of the structure which are connected with it, must descend from their place of pride and beauty. The centre one of the three holes in the roof is said to have been produced by two foolhardy Englishmen, who, with equal regard for the mischief they might effect and for their own necks, climbed to the top of the church. They came to a place where the rain had washed away the cement and, their passage breaking the vault, sent a shower of shrubs and stones to the floor beneath. Fortunately, they did not follow the rubbish; but lived, let us

Between the triforium and the great arcade, the caps of these vaulting shafts are connected by a second string close above the triforium, and from them spring the ribs of the roof. As in all Cistercian churches, there was no wall passage behind the triforium; this arcade is therefore blank. The clerestory was composed of a single pointed light only in each bay, and that of comparatively small size; thus, although these lights were never filled with stained glass, the use of which the rules of the order forbade, the nave must have been but dimly lighted. The west window was, doubtless, small for its place; there were no windows in the south aisle, the cloisters standing there; those in the north aisle, whatever they might have done originally, could, at a later date, give little light to the nave, because in the fifteenth century seven chapels were erected in place of so many lights, and greatly obscured the interior. The severity of the architectural ordinances of the Cistercians appears in the absence of mullions to the clerestory windows. Here, in course of time, as we see at Tintern, this rigour was mitigated, and exquisite tracery introduced. It is probable that the church at Villers was not painted in the first case, and that the plaster which still appears on the walls and pillars is a later addition; this original bareness would add greatly to the severe character of the structure, and the solemnity of its effect on the spectator, and, to the learned eye, give a charm wherever it recognized the subtle purity, dignity, and delicacy of architecture, standing unaided by its sister arts. Of old, neither the sculptor nor the painter helped the architect at Villers.*

The idea of making the simplest means conduce to the gravest and noblest impression ruled the erectors of the transept and

---

hope, to regret having aided in defacing so noble a ruin as the Abbey of Villers. Probably these persons were only slightly hastening the too sure utter destruction of the place. The vibration which passes through the whole edifice when a train and its engine rush along the railroad from Louvain to Charleroi, at a distance of about thirty yards from the east end of the church, is like a shudder preceding dissolution.

* It is evident that colouring of some sort has been placed on the walls; everywhere are its traces, and obviously of different dates; brilliant patches of red may be observed in several places, and beneath a barbarous smearing of coarse yellow wash, which was undoubtedly put on in the eighteenth century, because it is lined out to represent a sort of Flemish bond, with double lines of white and red, so as to hint at the chamfered edges of stone work then in vogue.

chancel of this church. They set to work on these eastern parts soon after the nave was built. The style here is that of a transition of later character than appears in the nave; it is even more beautiful. The whole work seems to have been finished about 1273, under Abbot Arnould de Ghistelles, a date when structures of elaborate and highly decorated aspect were completed in Belgium, *e.g.*, the chancel at Tournay; and in England, *e.g.*, parts of St. Mary's Abbey at York, the Chapter House at Wells, and the choir and transept of Westminster Abbey. The reader will notice that the character of the nave of Villers is more archaic than many structures of the same date in this country, and will remember that the choir and north transept of Lincoln Cathedral were built between 1190 and 1200. There are six bays in the transept at Villers; it has double aisles. The roof, except that of the crossing, is wholly gone; the photograph shows the remaining portion of the vault here stretched like a tent over it, and having the circular opening at its apex which communicated with the sanctus turret, which once stood above. The pillars of the angles of the crossing are clustered about octagonal piers, and banded; they rise to the level of the spring of the vault of the nave; from their caps spring the ribs of the roof, except the diagonal ones, which rise from short baseless shafts of their own, placed on the caps of the crossing-pillars. The most striking feature of the east end is that which suggests the general idea of the architect when he concentrated a great amount of light about the altar. Seven tall lancets stand in the lower tier of the chancel, their sills being scarcely higher than a man's head; above these is the very remarkable arrangement peculiar to this church and that of the Abbey of Floreffe,* *i.e.*, the manner in which the round-headed windows of the second tier have been filled with slabs of the slaty stone of the country, which have been pierced in each window, with two large circles or bull's-eyes, one above the other. In the chancel, it is noteworthy that, alternately in the upper and lower ranges of the circles, a sort of quatrefoil has been rudely formed by four cusps being allowed to remain when the circles were cut out of the slabs. The alternate openings in this extraordinary plate tracery, if such it may be styled, are not cusped, nor do those cusps appear in the similarly

---

* Schayes.

lighted transept ends. It is remarkable that such work as this should have been constructed at the date in question, which was at least seventy years later than that of the roses of Lincoln and Peterborough cathedrals, and ten years after the tracery in the triforium arcade at Westminster was executed. Above these bull's-eyes rise seven lancets, taller than those of the lower range. The whole of this portion of the church is exquisitely beautiful. The ends of the transept are flat; that on the north, which has not been affected by the erection of buildings close upon it, exhibits three lancets in the lower range, and in the second, three round-headed arches, all of one size, as in the chancel, divided *externally* by square built-up shafts with square caps. These arches are filled by slabs, pierced as in the chancel, but with three bull's-eyes instead of two, placed vertically, making nine in all. Externally, a discharging arch without mouldings of any kind, is carried over these openings, and the head of this strange window is pierced by two round openings; these alone have an external moulding, a plain roll. While speaking of this part of the building, it may be well to say that a singular sort of external wall passage appears beneath bull's-eyes. All round the east end and transept is a sort of gallery, or rather ledge, formed between the buttress by thin slabs of stone, and carried through the buttresses themselves; this was probably intended for use in cleaning the windows. A similar pathway exists in the east end only, below the upper range of lancets. The archaic look of this part of the work is sustained by the semi-circular flying buttresses, which, without even a chamfer, rest on plain piers of stone. The profoundly ascetic appearance of the exterior may be surmised. As usual with Cistercian houses, the staircase remains in the south end of the transept, by means of which the monks came from the adjoining dormitories at three o'clock in the morning to matins, and retired after vespers.

The other buildings remaining at Villers comprise the brewery, which is said to have been a refectory devoted to the lay-brethren before it found its recent use; erected in 1197, 140 feet in length by 40 feet in width, it is divided in the middle by five cylindrical columns, with naked vases or capitals, and supporting a round (Romanesque) roof. It has a sort of vestibule, containing six columns disposed in a rectangle, and bearing a pointed vault. On each side of the brewery are the workshops and residences of the craftsmen who served the Abbey. This range of buildings formed the north side of the great square of the Abbey; on the front of the brewery is placed the sun-dial. On the escarped rock which is on the north side of the church, stands the Chapel of St. Bernard, a seventeenth-century structure, which replaced the ancient one before mentioned; near it, lower down, was the *Léproserie*, or *Maison des Pestiférés*. Above the Abbot's garden rises the rock whence most of the stone for the buildings was taken; it was cut into terraces, laid out as gardens, and named the amphitheatre. There was a reservoir for feeding the fountains, a tannery, a stable, and a grange. The ancient mill of the Abbey is now a little inn; it is a structure of the twelfth century.*

---

* The first edition of "*Brabantia Sacra*" by Sanderus, contains a view of the west front of Villers, as it appeared early in the seventeenth century; that in the "*Trésor Sacré de Brabant*" shows the additions of the last century. For the early history of the Abbey see *Hist. Monast. Villar, apud Martene et Durand.—Thesaur. Anecdot.*, as quoted by Schayes. See also Mr. Ferguson's "History of Architecture," p. 723.

CHURCH OF ST. NICHOLAS AND BEFFROI, GHENT.

CHURCH OF ST. NICHOLAS AND BELFRY AT GHENT.

T is far from our intention to write a history of Ghent, that theme would demand a volume three times as large as this; suffice it that we describe the buildings photographically illustrated here, and give a general account of some of the most interesting structures in the city. The church of St. Nicholas, in the *Marché aux Grains*, is the most ancient in the city; it is cruciform in plan, with a short transept, apsidal choir or *chevet*, retro-choir and radiating chapels : there are chapels also in the south aisle and ambulatory. Originally founded in 912, St. Nicholas was burnt in 1120, a fate which, considering how closely the churches of Belgium are surrounded, is less common than one would expect. The reader will notice in the photograph that a row of little houses is stuck against the north side of the church, and that their chimneys go like buttresses above its roof; should one of these burn, it is hard to see what can save the church, those great bald windows are no protection against fire.

Rebuilt soon after the conflagration, St. Nicholas' Church presented a beautiful example of the transition from the Romanesque style to that of the First Pointed, or what we call the Early English style. Of this re-construction there remain the lower part of the tower over the crossing, the west front which is before us, the walls of the nave, and its clerestory; the last formerly exhibited a range of narrow Romanesque windows, which, although now filled up within, show their heads above the lean-to roof. The transeptal turrets appear to be of rather later date than those of the west front; the bases of the latter are ornamented with a Romanesque arcade, which, if compared with the like decorations of their upper stages, happily illustrates the progress of transition from the pure Romanesque to the early pointed manner. The highest arcade shows trefoil lancet-heads. The west window is an extremely beautiful lancet of great altitude; the doorway beneath it is of course modern, but probably, in its mass, reproduces the ancient archivolt. The upper stages of the central tower, having decayed early in the fifteenth century, were replaced, as we now see them, by Thierry De Staenhoukefelde in 1406.* The apse was rebuilt by Jean Colin and Liéven Boene in 1427, when the second pointed style was adopted, and the windows and piers altered to suit the fashion. There was formerly a very lofty wooden spire on the tower, an ornament lost, it would appear, in the course of the last century. At that time many spires were suffered to decay, among them the beautiful one which gave its architectural character to the Belfry at Bruges.

The interior of the church of St. Nicholas is almost as effective as the exterior, which from the south side is peculiarly striking in the disposition of its masses and great altitude. Entering, we are moved by the loftiness and simple gravity of the place; the height of the choir is aided in impressiveness by the massy but gigantic cylindrical pillars of the crossing, which bear up the tower. There is neither clerestory nor triforium to the nave; the former, however, appears at the east end. The vaulting of the nave, which is very fine, seems supported by short shafts that descend to corbels, the carving of which, although late, is good. Thus the wall space is unbroken by arcades above the great one of the aisle. Owing to the narrowness and height of the nave, the interior seems unusually tall, an effect not reduced by the shallowness of the aisles, which form a complete path round the church. The interior suffered much during the wars of the sixteenth century, when it was used as a stable. The pictures here are not of importance; yet, however commonplace, they are delightful if compared with the vile stained glass of the choir clerestory. With its whitewashed walls and deficiency of carving, the interior looks bald, being without clerestory or triforium in the nave. It is hard to say what sort of art-feeling induced the decorators of the seventeenth century to deform the beautiful pillars of the nave by sticking against them those ugly figures of the apostles which, as in scores of Belgian churches, are perched on brackets in a painful manner, and with cumbrous emblems and rococo draperies, attitudinize in the face of the chaste and perfect art of earlier times. The ugly seventeenth-century rood-

---

* Schayes.

screen was, fortunately, pulled down fifty years since; nevertheless the pulpit (1670), remains: it is not a worse example of bad taste and ignorance of art than most of its class, of which we shall speak when treating of that wonderful specimen which disgraces the interior of the church of St. Romuald at Mechlin.

Among the treasures of this church are the relics of St. Anne, preserved in the third chapel of the north aisle: they are said to have been brought from Jerusalem by Godfrey de Bouillon in 1101, (this must be a mistake): in honour of these a confraternity was established. Among the members whose names appear on the chapel walls are those of Margaret Duchess of Burgundy, sister of Edward IV. (1473), and Queen Mary of England, 1552, the last inscribed just before she became queen. Mr. Weale tells us that in the sacristy is some oil from the tomb of St. Nicholas of Myra and Bari, a star of the church whose legend follows here.

St. Nicholas, of Myra, born in Lycia, died 342, was a wonderful personage; even in infancy he kept the fasts, which were in his days appointed for Wednesdays and Fridays, by refusing to suck the breast of his nurse. "Happy are they," says simple Alban Butler, "who from their infancy and innocent age are inured to the exercises of devotion, penance, and perfect obedience." Such is the trash with which the fond folly of later days has overlaid the life of a good and devout man. "He performed an incredible number of stupendous miracles," and is famous in the Greek, French, Roman, English, Spanish, and German calendars, and great patron of the empire of Russia. His day is the sixth of December. He looks after children, young women, sailors, and travellers,* and protects houses against thieves. With regard to the first, no doubt his extraordinary abstinence above mentioned suffices; as to the second, he is said to have privately endowed for matrimony three marriageable maidens, whose virtue was exposed to danger through the poverty of their father. He did this by secretly throwing through the window money enough to portion them; twice he did this unseen, but on the third occasion, when the last daughter

---

* Roger de Hoveden tells us St. Thomas of Canterbury appeared three times in a vision to people on board a London ship going with Richard I. to Palestine, and averred that St. Nicholas, St. Edmund the Martyr, and himself, were appointed by the Lord to be special guardians of the English fleet.—*Annals*, 1199.

was imperilled, he was detected by their father—(see the picture by Fra Angelico, in the Vatican). By prayer St. Nicholas stilled a storm; and when one of the sailors of a ship in which he travelled was drowned, the saint restored him to life. While he was sojourning in secret at Myra, there fell a vacancy in the bishopric of that place; a vision declared to one of the priests that the first man who entered the church on a certain morning should be chosen. Nicholas appeared, and was, much against his will, made bishop. He was travelling soon after this, and came to a tavern kept by a man so wicked that he fed his guests, unknown to them of course, on the flesh of young children. The saint readily discerned the crime, and going to the pickle-tub where the carcases of the poor little things were laid in brine, invoked them by the cross, revived them, and returned them entire to their parents. Alive and dead, St. Nicholas performed abundant miracles.* Buried at Myra, he wrecked the fleet of Haroun Alraschid when it was sent to attack the place, and often foiled others who would have removed his bones. During many centuries his tomb attracted endless pilgrims and was unviolated, but at last, in 1084, three merchants of Bari, near Ragusa, succeeded in the feat. The neighbouring country had been desolated by the Turks; the Barians, however, found that the relics were safe at Myra, but on offering abundant gold to the four remaining monks of the shrine to be permitted to take away the bones of St. Nicholas, they were informed that no human being would dare to do so, so often had the saint ruined the best-laid plans, and punished their devisers. The monks ironically pointed out the place of deposit of the bones, and the Barians were really alarmed by the tales they heard concerning former attempts at violation; but, divinely inspired—by Nicholas himself, no doubt—they persevered, and setting guards to watch against interruption, broke up the pavement of the church until they came to a white marble sarcophagus: this being opened was found to be filled with oil that emitted a most delicious fragrance, that intoxicated the searchers, and gave them strength to proceed. Matthew, one of the sailors, dipped into the sarcophagus, and came forth all dripping

---

* The emblems of St. Nicholas are three golden balls upon a book, or lying before him; he is painted in episcopal vestments, standing before the children in a pickling tub, and otherwise.

with the sacred fluid; he found the relics, which, in fear and trembling lest the Myrians should discover the theft, were wrapped in white cloths and carried to the ships. These set sail immediately, not, however, without a quarrel among the captors, ere it was settled which vessel should carry the spoil. That to which Matthew belonged was appointed, on his taking an oath not to separate from the others. The Myrians came to the church only to tear their hair and beards at the success of the audacious robbers, who had deprived them not only of the saint's protection but of the profitable visits of pilgrims. Near the shores of Mackery the robbers were detained by contrary breezes, so that they began to doubt if the body of the saint, so potent with winds, was really theirs, or if he did not intend to stop their further journey. A dream settled this matter, and so terrified those mariners who had concealed some of the precious fragments for private benefit, that they gave them up to the common stock. After this all went well, the stiff-necked saint consenting to be borne away by men who were compelled to exhibit that honour which should be amongst thieves. The odour of the holy oil was round about them everywhere, and a bird, supposed to contain the soul of the saint, attended their voyage. It is strange that St. Nicholas delayed to punish one Christopher, a knight, who—as it appeared by his confession to Abbot Berenger, of Venosa, in whose convent he took refuge when sick—had concealed one of the ribs in his sleeve; this he presented to the house at Venosa, and was incontinently cured. Purloining the bones of St. Nicholas was not to cease on their deposition in the magnificent church which was built on a spot miraculously indicated in the city. Stephen, chanter of the church at Angers erected in honour of the saint by Fulque-Nerra, Count of Anjou, of whom we spoke before, in his zeal for the honour of that edifice, and by permission of his Abbot, Natalis, disguised himself, went to Bari, got familiar with the sacristans of the church there, and actually stole the arm-bone of St. Nicholas, which was kept outside the shrine in order to bestow benedictions on the people. Pursued by the men of Bari, the chanter was reduced to such extremities as to sell the silver casing of the relic for food. They caught him at last by means of Erembert, a Norman, and took back the bone. After all, the saint seems to have made no account of a tooth which somebody stole in the translation, for William Pantulph, a Norman knight of note, contrived to buy such a thing, and to endow therewith his church at Noron, 1092. The oil preserved in St. Nicholas' Church at Ghent is, by some, believed to be a portion of the contents of the sarcophagus of Myra. The awkwardness of this story is apparent when we recollect that the monks of the Church of St. Nicholas at Myra, which still stands, aver that the relics were never stolen, because they possess them to this day. The narrative of Vitalis, condensed above, is almost cotemporary.

On one of the pillars of St. Nicholas' Church is an inscription in memory of Amelberge Slagen, who had thirty-one children—twenty-one boys and ten girls. At the head of the former their father, Olivier Minjau, appeared to welcome Charles V. on his entry into Ghent, 1526. In August of this year all died of sweating sickness, father, wife, sons, and daughters, and were buried in the cemetery of St. Nicholas here.*

---

* John Lyon, Dean of the Guild of Boatmen, and valiant captain of the White Hoods of Ghent, was buried in St. Nicholas' Church with as much state as if he had been Count of Flanders. He seems to have been poisoned at a feast in Bruges (which city he had captured two days before), it was said by order of Louis Maele, in revenge for the Gantois having burnt his palace at Andreghien, near Eecloo, which was in effect a disguised fortress, capable of annoying Ghent sadly. (See Froissart's account of these matters, vol. ii. c. 39, 40, 41.) What a monster of slaughter Count Louis really was, may be understood by Froissart's assertion that he beheaded at once five hundred men of the lower crafts at Bruges, in revenge for their having joined John Lyon, and, shortly afterwards, seven hundred weavers and fullers of Ypres, and sent three hundred of the principal inhabitants of the latter town to prison at Bruges, and two hundred of those of Courtray; this was besides two thousand five hundred men slain in battle. The Canon of Chimay has no commiseration for these fellows who were slain in fighting for the liberty they had bought and paid for, but when a couple of the Count's knights perished in the streets of Ypres, he says—"it was a great pity." There still exists a vulgar prejudice to the effect that the Flemings were ignoble fellows, and their leaders ruffians. Most of the latter were of noble families, as the Van Arteveldes, Rasse de Harzelle, &c.; and their conduct was better than that of the Count's party.

THE BELFRY OF GHENT.

N *terra firma* the distance is short between the tower of St. Nicholas and the Belfry; for an aërial promenade, however, it is considerable. So, one would fancy, must it have appeared to those citizens who, during the celebration of the birth of Charles V. (February 25th, 1500), traversed the space in question by means of a gallery of ropes that was stretched high in the air, between the edifices, and which remaining many days was illuminated at night.

The Belfry is seen in the photograph behind the church of St. Nicholas, and greatly diminished in apparent altitude by the distance. It was the most famous edifice in Belgium, and the centre or mouthpiece of democracy in the Low Countries. In reply to its clamorous call the men of Ghent assembled to fight for their city, or to invade others. On its summit originally hung a bell which, after one of the twelve peers of France, was named Roland,* and bore the following inscription in Flemish:—

*Mynen naem ist Roelant, als ick clippe dan ist brant
Als icke luyde, dan ist storm in Vlaenderlandt.*"

or,—

"I am Roland; sound I low, there is fire at hand,
But, sound I loudly, it means foes in Flanderland."

The original Roland was cast in 1314, but, notwithstanding the

---

* Bells were most frequently named in England after the apostles; in France the Paladins were equally favoured. Ancient church bells generally bear an invocation to a saint. St. Katherine has a peculiar interest in bells. Ingulf of Croyland, A.D. 975, tells us that his noble abbot Turketul had a very large bell cast, and named it after Guthlac, patron of Croyland; Egelric, his successor, had six bells made, and named them Bartholomew (after the apostle whose thumb Turketul received from the emperor Henry I., and gave to Croyland), Bettelm, Turketul, Tatwine, Pega, and Bega. The Roman Pontificale contains the ritual for baptizing bells; they were furnished with regular godfathers and godmothers, and named with ceremonies of the same kind as those still used for ships, but with prayer and supplications that they might serve good purposes.

assertion of Mr. Murray's "Guide," no longer exists. It weighed twelve thousand five hundred pounds, or one thousand pounds more than the great bell of St. Paul's, London. We believe Roland was broken up when, after the occupation of the city by Charles V., February, 1540, that tongue of Ghent was taken out of the tower and lowered to the earth, as the emperor desired to lower the pride and curb the independence of the Gantois. According to one version of the affair which led to this, it appears that, bent upon carrying on the war with France, Charles, or his vicegerent, Mary of Austria, demanded four hundred thousand gold florins from the city. The people, who had already paid an enormous sum beyond their due, refused to add to it, but proposed to maintain a certain number of soldiers for the war. Charles was too astute a person to consent to this; while further negotiations were going on, the question got mixed up, probably not without the Emperor's contrivance, with religious affairs, and especially the wild theories of the *Creesers*, a section of Anabaptists. The arch-duchess arrested many of the merchants of Ghent and the towns near; an insurrection broke out, Ghent was fortified against Charles, and the magistrates driven away, with many of the nobles. Charles came, breathing vengeance, but, before he arrived, the wiser citizens regained the mastery, and begged him not to punish too severely a great city, his own birthplace, on account of the turbulence of some of its inhabitants. The Emperor would not waste the opportunity afforded him, but entered Ghent like a conqueror, inflicted the most insulting chastisement, and plundered it by heavy fines.*

---

* What were the wars of earlier days, the reader may guess from Froissart's account. The Lord D' Anghien, cousin of Louis Maele, on a Sunday, in the month of June, stormed Grammont, a town attached to Ghent and the party of Philip van Artevelde. "When the inhabitants saw their town was lost beyond recovery, they sought to escape; few were so fortunate. The slaughter was very great of men, women, and children, for to none was shown mercy. There were upwards of five hundred of the inhabitants killed, and numbers of old people and women burnt in their beds, *which was much to be lamented*. The town was set on fire in more than two hundred places, which reduced churches and all to ashes; nothing remained." "For this," a writer adds, "may God remember the Lord of Anghien." It would appear that the matter was not forgotten. The ravager returned to Louis, who was besieging Ghent, and was received with applause; "*Fair son*," said the latter, "*you are a valiant man, and if it please God, will be a gallant knight, for you have made a fair commencement*." Knowing the foolhardiness of this burner of women,

On this occasion the accursed Alva proposed, it is said, to destroy the place. Woeful Ghent, like other cities of the Low Countries, endured the cruellest and most iniquitous treatment from Charles and his son Philip, so that it seems a just retribution that here, in 1579, the famous "Pacification of Ghent" was signed, which, by uniting all the counties, except Luxembourg, against the Spaniards,

---

the people of Grammont, who had fled to Ghent, laid an ambuscade, caught him, and put him out of the world with their pikes, together with others, his companions. Upon this the Count was much distressed that his fair son should be cut off in his youth; nevertheless, he had to pay a thousand francs for the body, and quit the siege of Ghent. Well for Louis Maele if he had died at that time. How the good towns held together, how, in the stress of the second siege, twelve thousand persons left Ghent under the guidance of Frank Atreman, and wandered *en masse*, but harmless, let the reader learn from Froissart, the apologist of the nobles, who could not, however, refuse his sympathy to the citizens. The chronicler tells us that the people of Brussels fed the multitude for three weeks outside their own city, after which they went to Louvain, and were helped there, and, sending to Liège, were allowed to purchase six hundred wains of flour, and assured that had the bishopric been nearer to Ghent its people would have helped that place more effectually to maintain its privileges and the freedom of commerce. The twelve thousand set out to return with their food, and were met with joyfulness by the Gantois, who came in procession to meet the convoy, saying to the merchants and drivers, "*Ah! good people, you do an act of great charity, and bring comfort to the poor who have not wherewithal to eat. Let us give our thanks and praises to God, and then to you!*" So the food was fairly divided, and an escort returned with the wains. The Duchess of Brabant, in pity for the great city, intervened, but in vain, with Count Louis, and the messengers of Ghent with Van Artevelde at their head, who met those from Liège and other towns at Tournay, Easter, 1382, received after long waiting a reply from the Count to the effect that he would not grant peace, although they were willing to submit to any conditions which did not involve the lives of men; Van Artevelde and others agreed to submit to banishment for life. Louis rejected this exception, and further required that the whole town from fifteen to sixty should meet him on the road between Ghent and Bruges, in their shirts, bareheaded, and with halters round their necks. The Bailiff of Hainault, on his part, assured the Gantois that "he would not put them all to death, but only such as had angered him most." Even to these conditions Philip agreed, but required that they should be submitted to the people of Ghent, who had made the exception named. "When Van Artevelde returned to Ghent with his companions, great crowds of the common people, who only wished for peace, were much rejoiced at his arrival, and hoped to learn from him good news. They went out to meet him, saying, '*Ah! dear Philip, make us happy, tell us what you have done and how you have succeeded.*' Philip made no answer to their questions, but rode on, holding down his head; the more silent he was, the more they followed him, and were the more clamorous. Once or twice as he was advancing to his house, he said, '*Get you to your homes, and may God preserve you from harm: to-morrow morning, be at the market-place by nine of the clock, and you shall hear everything.*'" What took place on the morrow the reader will best learn from Froissart. Suffice it that these conditions were rejected, and the Gantois determined to make a last effort for

deprived that ruthless nation of the Seven United Provinces, its most valuable possessions, and involved it in those terrible debts and wars from which it has never recovered. This is the history of the destruction of Roland, which was probably not the first bell hung in the tower; that which now bears the name is a seventeenth-century work, with decorations of that date and character. So Roland is not Roland.

The old bell was nobly hung; from the topmost gallery of the tower, as it now exists, we see beyond Bruges on the one hand, near to Audenaerde on the other, and in the opposite direction can discern Antwerp. These great cities lie so close that the sound of Roland might easily be heard all over the vast panorama, and summon the inhabitants to union, or even give notice that the Gantois were preparing to oppose a scheme of their neighbours: as

---

liberty. Five thousand picked men set out " with seven carts of bread and two of wine," to whom, at starting, those who remained said, " *Good friends, you see what you leave behind, but never think of returning unless you can do so with honour, for you will not find anything here. The moment we hear of your defeat or death, we will set fire to the town, and perish in the flames, like men in despair.*" Those who were going out replied, "*You say truly: pray God for us, he will assist us all.*" The five thousand marched like men prepared for death, and encamped about a league from Bruges on Saturday, the third of May, 1382, " a fine bright day," says the good Canon of Chimay. He tells us how the Count came out of Bruges with forty thousand men, and saw the Gantois breakfast on their little bread and wine, "after which they found themselves more determined and active on their feet than if they had eaten more." He tells us how the Brugeois attacked the sacrifice of Ghent with cannon, and how the last replied, and how they wheeled to place the sun in the eyes of their opponents, and fell upon them, shouting " Ghent !" Hereupon the traitors—for such the Brugeois were to the common cause—ran like sheep, so that "neither the son waited for the father, nor the father for his child," and the five thousand smote them freely. At night the Count got into Bruges, " the first of all," with only forty men of all the forty thousand that went forth at dawn, and tried to keep the city by going into the Great Place with torches, and shouting " *Flanders for the Lion, Flanders for the Count !*" It was in vain: he had to put his torches out, change clothes with his servant, and owe his life to a poor woman " who had often received alms at his door," and now hid him under her children's bed, where " he contracted his body into as little a space as possible," and who " lied for him when the pursuers came." Bruges was a conquered town and well deserved hard measure, but " no people ever behaved themselves better towards their enemies," than did the men of Ghent. They remembered the starving folks at home, took six thousand tuns of wine out of the stores of Damme, the port of Bruges, and bought of the foreign merchants of Sluys great quantities of corn and flour, and sent them by road and river to Ghent. The news of this defeat spread over Europe, and all the towns rejoiced; Paris, Rouen, Liège, and Louvain especially. The very Pope could not refrain from improving the occasion. The Gantois sent detachments and took possession of Ypres, Courtray, Cassel, and other places dependent on Bruges. All the towns except Audenaerde received them.

before the fight of Minnewater—when, the people of Bruges having received from Louis Maele the privilege of taking the waters of the Lys to their own city, whereby Ghent would have suffered in the trade in corn, the citizens of the latter assembled and dispersed the workmen. Ancient Roland must have been sounded when Artevelde set out to Bruges, as we have described; there might have been some among the crowd of leave-takers, who remembered to have seen it hoisted into its place. It was probably not hung until a few years before 1339, when the Belfry was finished. (Schayes). The peal of bells which now occupies the tower is very sweet and full in tone. The *carillons* or chimes of Ghent are pleasant on account of their clear and ringing notes; these mixing, as they often do, with the booming of the great clock bell, produce a concert quite different from the uproarious clangour of London steeples, the performers in which seem to ring more for the sake of exercise, and of the boiled legs of mutton, or what not, which inconsiderate persons have bequeathed, than for love of music. One of the bells at Ghent has a shot-hole in its side, said to have been made when Louis XIV. besieged the city in 1679. On the summit of the Belfry may be seen a figure of a golden dragon, as large as a great bull, and made of plates of copper, gilt, on an iron frame. Few popular legends are so well supported as that which avers that this strange object was given by Count Baldwin IX., in 1204, to some of the people of Bruges who accompanied him to Constantinople, and that it was taken from the summit of St. Sophia, or a gate of the Bucaleon, in that city. Placed on the top of the spire of the Belfry at Bruges, it remained a trophy until 1382, when, as here related, the men of Ghent captured the golden dragon, and transferred it to the apex of their own *Beffroi*, then not long finished. It has an Oriental character of execution. Its present height from the ground is 280 feet. The modern Roland does not hang so high by a great deal as his predecessor[*] seems to have done.

---

[*] Let us here complete that part of the history of Ghent to which Roland introduced us. Van Artevelde, "an Englishman for courage," went to besiege Audenaerde, and among other formidable machines, took the great gun which now stands in the *Mannekens Aert*, Ghent, named "*De dulle Griete*," or "Mad Margery." "A bombard," says Froissart, "which was fifty feet in length, and shot stones of immense weight. When they fired off this bombard, it might be heard five leagues off in the day time, and ten at night. The report of it was so loud, that it seemed as if all the devils in hell had broken loose."

The first stone of the Belfry was laid by Siger, chaplain of the city, April 28th, 1183, or four years earlier than that of Tournay. A wooden tower probably preceded it; it was not completed until 1337. M. Schayes seems to believe that it was finished according to the original plan, which must have been about 355 feet in height. Mr. Ferguson says that in 1376 a wooden spire was added, carrying the whole to 237 feet altitude. It is noteworthy that the tower at present contains 355 steps, a number which may have some relation to the elevation suggested by M. Schayes. The great tower at Westminster is 325 feet high, to the top of the vane. Mr. Ferguson, in his "History of Architecture," *p.* 729, gives a reduced copy of the original design for this tower belfry, which, like most of those relating to buildings in the Low Countries, has been carefully preserved in the archives of the city. It is an extremely beautiful composition, differing much in proportion and character from the vulgar and commonplace aspect which has been imparted to the grand old edifice by the wretched additions made in 1856 by M. Roelandt who, working in cast-iron—such is the material now in use—has foolishly aimed at mocking the style proper to stone. There appears to have been originally a lofty *grille* in place of the blank where the dial is now hung, with high pinnacles at its angles, and crockets of very bold form along its edge. Above this rose a diminished stage of stone, the height of which was about one-fourth that of the square body of the Belfry, and surmounted by a pierced parapet which was carried on corbels beyond the tower, and fringed a platform from which, between four slender pinnacles, rose a great square spire; all five ended in vanes. At the angles below the parapet, were bold gargoyles, eight in all. It is noteworthy that the old drawing shows a trumpeter sounding his instrument from the upper platform, as if notes of command were issued in this manner.

Of course, this is a frightful exaggeration; the real size of the piece is nineteen feet in length, ten and a half in circumference, and three in diameter at the mouth; it is of wrought-iron, and weighs nearly 38,000lb. Evelyn calls it "a basilisco." How the king of France, in aid of his order, having taken out the oriflamme itself, came against Philip, and how the last met him at Rosebecque, to perish on Mont D'Or, is a story that has been told perfectly by Froissart. After the battle, the most noteworthy thing the French did was to take down the seven hundred gilt spurs which had been hanging in the chapel of the Counts in Notre Dame, at Courtray, ever since the battle of Golden Spurs, July 11th, 1302; when the flower of France perished before the men of the Flemish cities. The French also burnt Courtray without ruth.

MAISON DES BATELIERS, GHENT.

MAISON DES BATELIERS, GHENT,

HE Boatmen's Hall, which is situated on the *Quai aux Herbes*, no great distance on the west of St. Nicholas' Church, is a very picturesque edifice, built in 1531. It displays the arms of Charles V., and of the powerful Boatmen's Company, in carved panels above the first-floor windows; above those of the third tier, on one side, are figures of men in high relief, one with a great anchor beside him, while another holds a rope; on the other side is a pair, with an oar and rudder respectively. Over the door a ship is carved. Lower down the quay, and next door but one to the above, is the *Halle aux Blés*, looking quite as rude and solid as a house of the twelfth century, but in truth, not built until 1323; its walls are five feet thick, the windows of the third tier are divided by a plain, round shaft, supporting a rude block capital. They are square-headed, and surmounted by a round arch. The corbie-steps of its gable are amongst the earliest known examples of that picturesque element of Belgian, French, and Scottish street architecture. The canal in front, is one of the innumerable streams which penetrate Ghent. Behind us, as we look at these old houses, is the large and picturesquely situated church of St. Michael, a cruciform structure, on a twelfth-century foundation, with an apse, radiating chapels, and very wide transepts. Here are some interesting reliquaries.

THE CATHEDRAL OF ST. BAVON, GHENT.

S it now appears, this edifice is an example of late Gothic architecture, which is singularly free, as Mr. Ferguson says, from the vices of the Renaissance. At the time of its erection most of the buildings in France and England were but mockeries of art, or displayed the results of attempts to foist the ornaments of one style upon the forms of another, without consideration for the uses and true characteristics of either. The plan of St. Bavon's Church is cruciform, with chapels round the aisles and east end; the choir is apsidal, with a retro-choir going completely round it. The chapels are twenty-four in number; these, although having special invocations, are best known by numbers which begin on the right of the west door. The exterior is heavy and plain, but redeemed to some extent and dignified by the noble tower which rises above the western entrance. Begun on the 26th of May, 1461, when the first stone was laid by Philippe Courould, Abbot of St. Pierre, this tower was completed in 1534, from the designs of Jean Stassins. In 1533, on the 7th of August, the nave and transept were begun to be rebuilt on the older foundation; they were unfinished in 1550, when Charles V. gave 15,000 crowns of Italy, "each of the value of thirty sous," towards its completion.*

The platform which now terminates the tower is two hundred and sixty-eight feet from the ground; from its summit may be seen Brussels, Antwerp, Mechlin, Bruges, and Flessing; there was originally a fine wooden spire, destroyed by lightning in 1603. As it exists, this tower is divided into three stages pierced by four

---

* With regard to this magnificent donation it will be remembered that the emperor destroyed the ancient Abbey of St. Bavon in order to make room for that potent bridle for the Gantois, an enormous fort known as the *Château des Espagnols*, now levelled with the earth. Until this time the cathedral was styled the Church of St. John.

tiers of lancets, with moulded archivolts and deeply recessed, with crockets and a finial to each; the upper stage is octagonal, having four detached buttresses, or counterforts, connected to the tower by flying buttresses. The west door is very deeply recessed, not a common thing in Belgium, and has rather clumsy mouldings about it. There is no parapet to the roof of this church, except under the gables of the transept, which are flanked by two long and slender octagonal turrets. Over the west door is a sort of minstrels' gallery—so we should call it in England; this has a parapet of panelled quatrefoils. Nearly the whole of this structure is inclosed by houses or lanes so narrow that it is impossible to obtain a good view of the exterior for the camera. For this reason it will be best to turn to the interior in order to gain an idea of the celebrated church.

Although late, this interior is a very noble one; the nave is wide, so is the transept (1534—54), which is aisleless. The choir (begun in 1274) is very large, and completely occupies the space from the crossing to the apse, and is raised much higher than the nave floor; this grand feature, which appears in several English cathedrals, is induced by the existence of an enormous crypt remaining at the east end, and part of the ancient church. The columns of the nave arcade (c. 1533) are clustered; the triple vaulting-shafts descend from the roof to the bases of the piers in the nave; the crossing, on account of its breadth and height, is singularly effective; the triforium, or rather gallery of the nave and transept, is hidden by a long row of panels of arms of knights of the Golden Fleece, painted on a black ground; the triforium of the choir, which is very large and fine, consists of pointed arches inclosing coupled openings with trefoil heads; the clerestory, which contains none but modern stained glass, is very handsome; that of the choir (c. 1320) is expansive and noble. The ends of the transept are pierced by two enormous flamboyant windows, which display armorials in stained glass of the sixteenth century; in the treasury of this cathedral are drawings of the stained glass which formerly filled the clerestory. The choir-screen is one of those abominable shams of the last century which deform so many noble Gothic interiors in Belgium; of *pseudo*-classic form, it is *painted* in black and white on wood to imitate marbles, and has gigantic pictures in *camaïeu*, in mockery of sculpture. The stalls of the choir are in the worst *rococo* manner; on the wall above them appear more *camaïeu* pictures (1774). The pulpit in the nave is an exaggerated example of what is vulgarly called "the thunder and lightning style;" we refrain from describing it because that at Mechlin—the most preposterous of all—is in view; let us say that it cost no fewer than 33,000 francs (1745), and effectually mars the beauty of the surrounding architecture.

This church is remarkable for its enormous quantity of bad furniture; *e.g.*, at the north end of the transept is a font, in which Charles V. was baptized, a bowl of granite inclosed in brass and sustained by angels. Above this appears a sort of transparency representing a dove hovering over the bowl; this trick, which is quite worthy of Vauxhall Gardens, and painfully startling in a Gothic cathedral, is not uncommon in Belgium, as a similar toy in the church of St. Quentin at Tournay testifies; it is produced by making a hole in the wall behind the font to receive the transparency. The high altar is an enormous gewgaw, of which the statues of SS. Bavon, Livinus, and Amandus alone cost about 100,000 francs, or rather more than the tower of the cathedral. It is composed of huge gilt rays, marble (pancake) clouds, a broken entablature, and what not, contrasting painfully with the beautiful arcade of the aisle and *chevet*. In front of the altar are four tall copper candlesticks, bearing the arms of England in relief, brought from Whitehall after the execution of Charles I.; they were purchased (1669) for this cathedral by Bishop Trieste, whose monument stands near them at the side of the altar. It is the work of Jerome Du Quesnoy, sculptor of the famous *Mannekenpis* at Brussels. The guide-books are of course enraptured by this statue,—" It represents Bishop Trieste contemplating the cross of the Saviour," say they, which it certainly does not, for the bishop as he is placed could not see the cross, which a heavy *Amorino* holds up at his feet.* There is a certain kind of technical skill shown in the carving of this and its companion tomb, especially that of Bishop Maes, by Pauwells, which satisfies all who do not look for genuine expressiveness and fidelity. With the exception of the figure of Bishop Maes,

---

* There is a ghastly story to the effect that on the day when this tomb was erected here, Jerome Du Quesnoy was detected in a horrible sin in the very church. He was strangled and afterwards burnt in the *Marché aux Grains*, opposite St. Nicholas' Church, 1654.

nothing can be more corrupt in style than these works; they are as low in that respect as Bernini's carvings, but without that *bravura* which is at least picturesque and effective, if not sculpturesque and honestly pathetic. The brass gates of the altar are very good of their kind, the work of W. De Vos (*c.* 1700).

In the chapels of St. Bavon there is a multitude of pictures; of these few call for notice here. Among others are the *Decollation of St. John*, by G. De Crayer, in the First Chapel. In the Sixth Chapel, as we ascend to the upper part of the church, is *Christ with the Doctors*, by F. Pourbus, containing, with many others of the same period, powerful portraits of Charles V., Philip II., and the painter. In the Fourteenth Chapel is one of the masterpieces of Rubens; it represents St. Bavon received into the convent which St. Amandus of Maestricht founded here. It is a masterpiece of art in art, wonderfully vigorous and exuberantly splendid in painting, a triumph of robust execution, but might as well be styled an incident in the life of Theodosius as in that of St. Bavon. As the National Gallery contains a fine version of the subject by Rubens (No. 57), we need not examine this one, which was formerly the altar-piece of the cathedral. The Eleventh Chapel is styled the *Chapelle de l'Agneau*, on account of its containing the famous pictures by Hubert and John Van Eyck, representing the *Adoration of the Lamb*, as described in Revelation, chapter vii. verse 9; and in the minor compositions surrounding this, the glory of God, and the life, redemption, and punishment of men. The central picture, which was begun by Hubert Van Eyck, is remarkable for its characterization, vigour, and depth of colouring, and the variety of the expressions; it is one of the most perfect examples of the early Flemish school in the hands of the Van Eycks, 1420—32. Of the Memlincs at Bruges—which we regard as examples, almost exceptional, of a much later period, and of nobler quality altogether than these works at Ghent—we shall write hereafter. First: of the history of the composition before us, let it be said that the chapel containing it was appropriated to, if not erected by, Jodocus Vydts, Lord of Pamèlle, his wife, Isabella Borluut, and family, as a chantry and tomb-house for themselves; the pictures are placed on the east side above the altar. The whole now comprises twelve parts, which may be considered as divided into two lines—the upper one of seven, and the lower of five pictures. The most important element is the central picture of the lower row,* which, although begun by Hubert, was finished by John Van Eyck; it has given a title to the whole composition, and is named above. This shows the wounded Lamb standing upon an altar, his blood pouring into a chalice, while at the sides are kneeling angels, singing or rapt in adoration; some bear the emblems of the sacrifice—the spear, nails, and sponge—others hold the cross and the pillar; two angels kneel in front tossing censers. It must be confessed that one looks with considerable apathy upon this piece of pure allegory, the soul and spirit of which has gone out of it, leaving a mere symbol which is gross and low; there is a sort of Bunyanish tangibility in the idea which, however serviceable in the Englishman's curious prose, becomes exceedingly crude in a pictorial representation. It needs all the intense purity of the adoring angels' countenances, exalted and lovely as these are, to move us with this part of the work. The other elements of the painting, having a direct human interest that is unimpaired by exploded symbolization, show that the artist felt his subject and reflected himself in the faces of innumerable figures. All symbols of Christ's suffering must be inferior to the occasion; least so is the human figure on the cross, an emblem which is infinitely the most pathetic if treated apart from the posturing and mere *bravura* of Rubens, and the grossness of the coarser and late Italian schools, whose vulgarity is even lower than the earthiness of Murillo; or, if we turn to literature, the stark-naked prose of writers like Bunyan, who, being incapable of imagination, present a writhing creature in place of a suffering Saviour.

It is wonderful how very low these vulgar artists went—so low that by common consent men for a great while, and indeed probably always, have ignored the title of a picture wrought in their way, and chosen to accept such productions as works of art *per se*, with no reference to the subject which was fantastically represented.

---

* There was originally a third line representing hell, which, being painted in tempera, was damaged and destroyed long ago. There is no engraving of this portion. The most accessible engravings of the entire work as it now appears are the outline sketches published in Kugler's "Handbook of Painting; German, Flemish, and Dutch Schools;" this book contains a general sketch and several outlines of parts, which although little better than diagrams will serve as keys. The Arundel Society has in hand a copy of the whole to be reproduced in chromo lithography.

Thus, a "Crucifixion" was regarded as a display of deft handling, exuberant colour, "mastery," and what not, qualities which seemed to gain a sort of piquancy with connoisseurs if evinced in depicting the tremendous mystery of Christ's sacrifice. The contrast is certainly effective: one would think, however, that such exploits were most apt to flowers of the earth or clouds of the air. Having ignored the subject, the next thing to be attained in painting was ignorance of the art; this, of course, came in due time—indeed, with astonishing rapidity, with rapidity so astounding that, although there is no other cause for decadence visible to the human eye than that named, yet, in one generation, (thirty years), after the death of Rubens there did not exist in all Europe a painter worthy of the title and not past his prime, although it had taken at least three hundred years and ten generations to attain the footing of Rubens' master. Is not this strange?

The difference between the prose-painters and Rubens is very great, inasmuch as there may be grossness and crudity in them, but not anything dramatic—as is ever the case with him; with them there is nothing of the vileness of the theatre to give its peculiar stain of falsehood where nothing but holiest truth should be. On the other hand, John Van Eyck was evidently susceptible of that strange passion which moved German painters—such as Albert Durer—to produce grotesques of an awful kind, such as seize the souls of men and hold them over unfathomed gulfs of thought. It is hard for the English sense of art to put itself in perfect possession of Albert Durer's ideas; but even when they are partially obtained, all feel that not even the epic flight of the early Italians surpassed the attainment of the Teutonic intellect.

The rest of the picture before us calls for another standard of criticism than that which is proper to the intended highest aim of the Van Eycks. Four great masses occupy the respective corners of the composition, if such it can be styled; of these, two, which are behind the altar, are composed, on the right of the picture, of beautifully varied figures, representing the Virgins famous in the church; and, on the left, the martyrs. The masses in front are, on the right, composed of patriarchs and prophets; and, on the left, apostles and doctors of the church. The wonderful variety and intensity of expression, rapt earnestness, and pathos, of most of these figures, move every spectator; some are beautiful, some worn with study, but retain noble features; some strong, some submissive in ecstacy; some appeal with all their hearts in their faces. But whether his saints be old or young, demonstrative or absorbed, there can be no question as to the painter's loyalty to nature, and the perfect freedom of his work from vulgarity. Hubert was far less literal than his brother, and, consequently, however ordinary some of his subjects have been, his intense sympathy has sufficed to exalt them in a manner which, while simple, is marvellous. One example of John Van Eyck's style—for we cannot doubt that he wrought this portion of the picture—may serve for many, to show how strictly literal the painter was. The six apostles who kneel in the foreground are, as was right, being travellers, bare-footed. Now, the drawing of their feet, the soles of which are towards us, has been made from those of men unaccustomed to shoes, and the forms of nature are reproduced with extraordinary minuteness, yet without an inkling of aught that is coarse in treatment or style. The man who could work in the spirit which indicates itself by the faces of the angels and saints before us, as well as in this particular, deserved the glory he has won. The composition of this picture is of an artless kind; each group stands *en masse*, and like a bed of splendid flowers set in a swarded garden, the grassy paths of which pass between parterres and are studded with daisies and blooming herbs. The masses of the front have between them a Flemish fifteenth-century fountain, intended for that of Life, pouring its waters into an octangular tank, from the foot of which the surplus fluid runs away. The leading characteristic of this picture is perfect veracity, uninspired but noble, because an exponent of the grand simplicity of the artist's mind. One would say he must surely be a just man who would paint like this.

The other pictures which surround the "*Adoration of the Lamb*" are, above it, three life-sized figures; that in the centre represents God enthroned in a glory, wearing the triple crown and something like the papal habit; these are evidently employed in no low spirit by the painter. He is sceptred, and in the act of benediction: on His right hand sits the Virgin, a beautiful figure, crowned and holding a book; on His left is John the Baptist; at His feet is the crown of the Lamb. The wings of this, the upper line, contain, on the side of St. John, St. Cecilia, attended by angels—an aggregation of exquisite countenances; and, on that of the Virgin, a group of angels singing. There is very little doubt that, with the exception of the last, these panels were painted by Hubert Van Eyck, the elder brother of John, who died before the work was finished, and who had received the commission to produce it from Jodocus Vydts. Outside the composition of St. Cecilia and the angelic choir, there appear on either hand life-sized figures of Adam and Eve, the one holding the apple. The originals of these pictures are undoubtedly the work of Hubert Van Eyck, and now at Brussels; copies supply their places at Ghent. Some absurd squeamishness at the sight of the utter nudity of these figures led a modern bishop to remove them to the sacristy, whence, after lying by for many years, they have been sold for 30,000 francs to the Belgian government. All these works, with the exceptions named, are no doubt productions of Hubert Van Eyck, and display much that serves to characterize the man as of bolder and more robust intellect than his brother. In the mere execution of the elder painter's share this appears; although the shadows are hot, rather hard, and dark, and possibly a little opaque—as if painted in a chamber with a confined light. The handling is fuller, richer, and more free, what we style more masterly, yet not without the greatest delicacy and refinement of form; indeed, the figure of Adam could hardly be finer than it is,—that of Eve is less good, on account, probably, of the ever-recurring difficulty with models. Many writers appear to have misunderstood the meaning of the painter in regard to this figure, and, accordingly, do not hesitate to criticise it as if it were not proper to make the mother of mankind with something of maternity in her form. The difference between that which men seem to expect, and that which we believe the painter intended, may be seen—however exalted by the supreme art of the Greek sculptor—by comparing the Venus of Milos with any good virginal antique. It would be hard to find a finer and more sweetly inspired figure than that of the Virgin, or a grander and more purely abstracted conception of the Most High in all the ranges of Art than those which dominate this marvellous production. The manner in which this tremendous theme has been treated by the later Italian artists is simply puerile; the immortal who is merely bearded and draped voluminously seems but a very ordinary mortal when we look close. It is hardly needful to say that representations of the most awful themes may be made effective to a wonderful extent, provided they are but sufficiently vague and broadly enough generalized; that which looks everything mostly means nought, but every vague conception of a sympathetic spectator will centre upon the inchoate hint so as to grow whole and gigantic; every one sees much of himself in Art—*i.e.*, gives as much as he takes.

Of the adjuncts of the lower row—that is, the pictures which form the wings of the "Adoration" subject—there are four. Those on the right of the work represent the soldiers of Christ and the righteous judges journeying to worship the Lamb. The whole is perfectly literal, but at the same time perfectly noble, however *naïve*. Knights and judges are mounted on barbed or caparisoned horses, and bear banners, lances, coifs, or crowns—just as they did in Van Eyck's time. Some are in full fifteenth-century armour, mailed, with sword at side and vizor up; others wear ermine, velvet robes and embroidery; the travellers ride through a romantic country, neither hasting nor resting; they keep converse like Spenser's knights, but seriously, without sadness and without affectation; the horses chafe at the bit and stoop their heads, going gently on over grass and between rocky heights that are crowned by towns and churches. There is something wonderfully affecting in this—it is a true poem—the tried soldiers and the just go earnestly but not anxiously onwards; all is calm and bright with summer. This is undoubtedly the work of John Van Eyck, and should be compared in technical respects with the extraordinarily painted portraits of Jean Arnoulphin and his wife, now in our National Gallery. In the last, a later production than that just described, it appears that the painter was approaching the greater vigour and more potent solidity of his elder brother; and, at the same time attaining a power of dealing with colour, *chiaro-scuro*, and tone beyond Hubert's. We do not think John would have approached, his brother in the higher qualities of design. The opposite wing gives us companion subjects to the last, by representing the Holy Pilgrims, male and female, journeying on foot towards the same goal. There is a remarkable difference between these wings, perceptible enough by experts, but showing itself chiefly to others in the greater exuberance of invention, greater variety of actions, attitudes, and expressions, displayed in the last than in the counterpart; a host of saints are travelling, some hermits, some preachers. The student of character loses himself in the wonderful variety of the visages; scores of subtle differences of intelligence and of feeling—mental or physical—are expressed with a cunning that excites our wonder to excess. It appears a fanciful thing to write, but some of the figures seem to us as intended to represent men who do not exactly know what is the object of the all important journey, but who go on, led by a will interior to their own. Others are self-centred,—even a little proud of their act; some think; some converse; others move their lips as in talking to themselves; many hasten along, but none loiter, although several go slowly with limbs that age or weakness deprives of power.

So much for the inner sides of the centre and wings of this work; when the latter are closed upon the former, another series presents itself, divided like the interior into two lines horizontally. The whole is by John Van Eyck. The upper half represents the *Annunciation*, an extremely beautiful composition, the background of which, the Virgin's chamber, is said to have been painted from the atelier in Ghent, where the artist wrought. "The view from the window gives us the steeple of the Weavers' Church, and behind it a gate, since destroyed, bearing the name of 'Walpoorte.' On the left is St. Martin's Street and the Steen van Passeghem." * The house thus indicated stands at the corner of Koey Street, No. 26, near the Place D'Armes. The lower parts of the exterior comprise, on the external sides respectively, kneeling portraits of the donors, Jodocus Vydts, and Isabella Van Borluut. Between these, painted in *grisaille* to represent statues, are SS. John the Baptist and the Evangelist. It will be remembered that the original dedication of St. Bavon's Church was to the former.† The originals of the lower wings here described are at Berlin, those at Ghent are exquisite copies by M. Coxcie.

---

* Crowe and Cavalcaselle, Early Flemish Painters. London: Murray. 1857.

† We cannot better complete our account of the wonderful picture than by the inscription on the grave of Hubert Van Eyck; he was buried in the crypt of St. Bavon, immediately beneath his greatest work:—

"Take warning from me, ye who walk over me; I was as you are, but am now buried dead beneath you. Thus it appears that neither art nor medicine availed me; art, honour, wisdom, power, affluence are spared not when death arrives. I was called Hubert Van Eyck; I am now food for worms. Formerly known and highly honoured in painting, this all was shortly after turned to nothing. It was in the year of the Lord One thousand four hundred and twenty-six, on the eighteenth day of September, that I rendered up my soul to God, in suffering. Flee sin! turn to the best objects; for you must follow me at last." (Translation of M. C. and C.)

The crypt, which extends under the whole choir of this church, is the most ancient part of the edifice, and one of the oldest and the largest in Belgium. It was constructed by St. Transmarus, of Noyon, in 941, and re-constructed some time in the thirteenth century, and retains, for the most part, its original form. It is divided by twelve massive piers of various dates, some of them earlier, and others coeval with the chancel above. The vaulting is rather flat, and covers no fewer than fifteen chapels. Several of these are of great size, and still used. There are some good incised slabs ranging from the fourteenth to the sixteenth century. In the treasury and sacristy of St. Bavon are many valuable works of ancient art, e.g., a beautiful chandelier of iron, painted (fifteenth century), with statuettes of saints, and a pyramidal roof with dormers, &c., the silver shrine of St. Macarius (sixteenth century), embroidered vestments, illuminated books, reliquaries, and other articles.

No visitor to Ghent should omit seeing the scanty ruins of the ancient monastery of St. Bavon, destroyed by Charles V. as before stated, together with about seven hundred houses. It was founded early in the seventh century under the invocation of St. Peter, and received its present name in the thirteenth century. Here were buried several of the early Counts of Flanders, and King Alfred's daughter, as mentioned before; here Edward III. of England lived, 1338, and John of Gaunt was born, 1341; here Philip of Burgundy was married to Margaret, daughter of Louis Macle, 1369, by which Flanders passed to the Burgundian house. Destroyed by the Normans in 649, it was re-built (651) by St. Amandus, who here received St. Bavon as a brother of the house.* Burnt early in the ninth century, it was again rebuilt (c. 820.) Again destroyed by

---

Compare this with the boastful inscription over the grave of Rubens. Vaernewyck's *Hist. Belgis.* tells us that the right arm of Hubert was placed in a coffin and above the entrance of St. Bavon's Church, where it remained until the sixteenth century. John Van Eyck was buried at Bruges (1441), in the church of St. Donat, destroyed in the French Revolution. Its site is now marked by a statue of the painter.

* The history of St. Bavon is one of the most striking among those of the early Flemish saints. His first name was Hallowin, Lord of Hesbain, Liege, surnamed *Baro*. He led a wild life in youth, more probably from excess of energy than proclivity to evil. A sermon by St. Amandus brought him to a passionate sense of error, and resolution for a new life. He distributed his

the Normans, Arnold the Old, son of Baldwin the Bald, Count of Flanders, rebuilt it, 940. The earliest part now remaining, unless we except some stone fragments and cinerary urns of terra cotta (the former attributed to a temple of Mercury, and the latter undoubtedly Roman), may be part of a wall which exhibits herring-bone work, said to be of the seventh century, and by St. Amandus. Part of the cloister was erected certainly early in the eleventh century; an early pointed doorway is of about the year 1180. The most complete fragment is the baptistery, once a chapel of St. Macarius, which is octangular, with a groined roof, showing remains of paintings, Romanesque, c. 1060, with a chapel above it, the windows of which are round-headed; one of these is, however, cruciform. The floor of this chapel is of the greatest archaeological interest, on account of its superb and nearly perfect pavement of encaustic tiles, as originally laid, c. 1260. The cloister resembles Decorated English work, a brick vault with stone ribs, and good carvings. Beneath the last are preserved some beautiful incised monumental slabs, including one c. 1250, and others of later dates. There is a monument to two of the maids of honour to Mary, Queen of Scots. Under the baptistery is a fragment of a carved altar, and

---

goods to the poor, retired to a lonely place, and practised severe austerities for the time, so as to satisfy himself of repentance, before he applied to St. Amandus, and was admitted to the monastery of St. Pierre. A close communion with monks convinced him of the necessity for still more stringent penances, or at least a stricter seclusion than theirs. Retiring to a forest near Ghent he lived for a long time in a hollow tree, and afterwards built a cell, and led the life of an anchorite. It is probable that before taking the cowl in St. Pierre, the incident occurred which gives us the first idea of his character, and throws so strange a light on the contrasted states of society in the seventh century. His life in the *Acta Sanctorum* says—"One day he saw a man, whom, before his repentance, had been one of his slaves, and as such was sold. The idea of having thus sinned against a fellow-creature moved Bavo to despair, so that he fell on his knees before the man, and cried aloud. 'Be merciful, I implore; remember not that I sold thee into slavery, and tied thee with thongs; remember not this injury, and, in proof of forgiveness, do as I entreat. Strike my body with thy staff, and shave my head as they shave those of robbers, bind my hands and feet, and cast me into prison. If I thus receive thy chastisement, God may spare that which is due to me, inasmuch as I have sinned against Him and thee.' The slave refused thus to treat the noble whose soul was abashed, but, at last, the adjurations of Bavo compelled him to do as desired. He beat the penitent, bound him and bore him to the gaol, where he remained a considerable time, deploring his former life. Returning to his convent, Bavo remained but a short time ere he built himself a new cell, wherein he died October 1st, 653. His life and death impelled sixty gentlemen to lead penitential lives."

sculptures of the ninth and tenth centuries: among them—Adam and Eve, the Expulsion, and the Angel guarding the gates of Eden. An eleventh, or early twelfth, century cap shows Samson bearing the gates of Gaza, lions ramping, and some very spirited foliage. The Crypt of St. Mary (1148), shows cylindrical columns, and several stone coffins *in situ*. There is a host of other buildings in Ghent deserving record, none more so than the Hôtel de Ville, 1481—1618. Here the " Pacification of Ghent " was signed, November 8th, 1576.

HOTEL DE VILLE, YPRES.

THE HOTEL DE VILLE AT YPRES.

IN the great square before us Philip van Artevelde addressed the people, when he thought the French king would not be able to cross the Lys nor break into Flanders. "Good people," said he, "do not be alarmed if he should march against us, for he will never be able to cross the river Lys, as I have had all the passes well guarded, and ordered Peter du Bois to Commines with a large body of men; he is a loyal man, and one who loves the honour of Flanders. I have sent Peter le Nuitre to Warneston and broken down the bridges on the Lys, and there is neither pass nor ford but these two. Our friends in England are coming to help us—keep, therefore, to your oaths sworn to us in the good town of Ghent; and now let those who will maintain the rights and franchises of Flanders hold up their hands." At these words all held up their hands in sign of loyalty; so Philip descended from the scaffold, and went to Audenaerde the next day. Even while he spoke the words were falsified, as Froissart tells us, all the hopes of Flanders were wasted for a season, and, with them, the prospect of freedom for the people throughout Europe, whether in England—as by the murder of Wat Tyler in Smithfield, under whom the cruelly-treated populace arose—or in France, where the Parisians idly waited to see what would come of the Flemish efforts. It must be admitted that the Flemings had much less to complain of than either the French or the English.

The Hôtel de Ville, with which is united the Cloth Hall, at Ypres, is the largest in Flanders; the façade is not less than four hundred and thirty-seven feet in length, of which extent a good idea may be obtained by recollecting that the National Gallery is four hundred and sixty feet long. The building which faces us, standing upon an arcade, and abutting the Gothic structure so as to hide its east end, was finished about 1630. It is picturesque, though far inferior in art value to its beautiful neighbour. The latter, the plan of which is like a very long parallelogram, has been greatly impaired in its effect by filling in the square-headed colonnade at the base of the façade; this has rendered the design rather flat in appearance, deprived it at once of richness and of the expression proper to its office as a place of meeting analagous to our Exchange in London (as built anciently), and its prototype, the Bourse at Antwerp. The reader will conceive how great would be the improvement at Ypres, if the bald filling in of the colonnade were removed, and powerful shadows permitted to fall as the architect designed they should. The work as it now stands displays two ranges of windows above the colonnade, which last, it must be remembered, was originally an *arcade*, not, as now, with flat heads between square and clumsy piers, but probably composed of lancets corresponding to those of the windows. The windows are of the most beautiful design; in the lower row they are comprised within a pointed arch, and separated by a finely-formed group of clustered shaft. The heads are filled with rich tracery, and bear a quatrefoil. The upper windows are much loftier and more acutely formed than those beneath them, their traceries are richer; one with a quatrefoil in the head alternates with another exhibiting a trefoil. Battlements that are borne upon a corbel table, running very deep upon the face of the building, and sculptured with children's heads, are placed along the front; above this rises an extremely steep roof crowned by a picturesque crest. In the centre stands the splendid belfry, having four crocketted pinnacles at its angles, and an octangular spire of the most elegant proportions. At two of the angles of the building appears a charmingly-designed octangular pinnacle, crocketted and corbelled out on the wall. It would be difficult to conceive a more beautiful work than this; whether as regards its composition or execution, it is nearly perfect. There is nothing in Belgium to compare with it.

The tower served as a belfry to the town; the first stone of this part of the *Hôtel de Ville* was laid by Baldwin IX., Count of Flanders, and Emperor of Constantinople, March 1st, 1201, in the company of his wife, Mary of Champagne, and Herlibalde, Grand Bailiff of Ypres. Ypres was one of the towns which profited by the crusading fever so far as to buy freedom and privileges from the ruler who desired to carry his energies to foreign wars, freedom not always respected, and privileges which were often valueless when the wants of those who had power induced them to sell over again that which they could retake by force. The belfry was in hand until 1304. The right wing, or Old Hall, as it is styled, was finished in 1230; that nearest to us, the left wing, or Cloth Hall, was begun in 1285, and finished in the same year as the belfry. At the rear of the building is the Conciergerie, built 1342; it faces the south side of the church of St. Martin; to this we may get access by passing through the opening, which is guarded by three posts, and under the seventeenth-century additions to the Cloth Hall. Until the last was erected, the *Hôtel de Ville* and Cloth Hall stood free of buildings at this end, as it does at the opposite one. The façade before us was originally decorated with statues of the Counts and Countesses of Flanders, erected 1513, and destroyed by the French, December 13th, 1792: these have been lately replaced; the reader may see them in the photograph, placed alternately with the windows of the first floor. There was added in 1513 a double flight of steps, which rose from the fourth opening at the base on either hand to the first floor; by this the Town Hall was approached. It formed a very remarkable feature of the building, rebuilt in 1822, but not long ago destroyed. The statue which stands on a bracket and beneath a lofty tabernacle is that of "Our Lady of the Palisade," who was adopted patroness of the town, during the siege of 1383.* The reader will observe that the

---

* After the death of Philip Van Artevelde at Rosebecque, and the conquest of Flanders by the French—for such the result really was—the only important place which held out against Louis Macle and his master was Ghent. The French victory raised again all the jealousy of the English who, although they would not help their old allies, were indignant at the good fortune of their enemies. Among other modes by which this feeling found expression, was the outrageous attack of Henry Spenser, Bishop of Norwich, grandson of Edward II.'s favourite, who had been appointed general against the Clementists by Pope Urban. This bishop set out from Calais with a large force, on what he pretended was a crusade against Clementists; he committed shameful atrocities upon the people of Gravelines and Dunkirk, invaded the territories of the Duchess of Bar, for which he had not the shadow of justification, and desolated those of Count Louis—who was a rigid Urbanist. The bishop then sat down before Ypres, and besieged it strictly. He was, in fact, an ally of Ghent; Froissart says he believed that Franz Atreman, captain of Ghent, was his guide and companion. The Gantois joined the English with 20,000 men. The Count's garrison in Ypres was badly off, because they distrusted the people within as much as they feared their enemies without. The latter were so urgent that in one day there were picked up of arrows shot into the town so many as filled two tuns. The siege lasted some time, and a great deal of fighting took place at the palisades, especially on one occasion when fire

bells hang outside the campanile; the *carillons* of Ypres indifferent. The whole of the ground floor was originally open, so as to form a great hall; it is now divided, but one of the parts is 164 feet long by 100 wide. Upstairs is a museum of antiquities, with some ancient distemper pictures on the walls.

Behind the Hôtel de Ville are seen the unfinished west tower, beautiful *flèche*, and chancel roof, of the superb church of St. Martin, which was between 1559 and 1801 the cathedral of Ypres. This edifice was founded by Robert the Frison,* in 1083; the chancel, which is now the most ancient part of the church, was rebuilt in 1221, by Hugues, Provost of St. Martin. In 1240, the west part of the church was burnt, and by the successor of Hugh, who died in 1232, recommenced in 1254; finished twelve years afterwards, it was consecrated in 1270. The tower, which is of brick, was burnt in 1234, and the first stone of the existing one laid by Anastasie D'Oulne, Viscountess of Ypres, in 1434. The architect was Martin Utenhove of Mechlin. It is square, and although never finished, is 188 feet high.

The east end of the church has been well restored of late; it is of brick, with light buttresses close to the wall; lancets between each pair of buttresses form the clerestory. There is a very pretty carved moulding under the dripstone of the windows, which is composed of flowers and leaves; the lancets are very sharp. The tracery is different in each window; those of the choir are triplets, and have detached shafts in front, so as to form a rear-vault between them and the proper mullions of the windows. The effect is extremely

---

was used. It was all in vain; the approach of the king of France caused the bishop to decamp; he was literally hunted out of Flanders. Not long after, Louis Macle died,—was stabbed, they say, in course of a dispute with the Duke of Berri, raised on account of a claim of homage for the county of Boulogne, which the latter held on behalf of his wife. Froissart describes his funeral, a very curious account of a fourteenth-century burial.

* A grandson of Robert the Frison was made Viscount of Ypres, and had a strong castle there, a great enemy of William *Clito*, being bribed thereto by Henry I. It has been supposed that he had some knowledge of the murder of Count (Saint) Charles of Flanders, in St. Donat's at Bruges, (1127); he was besieged in Ypres, 1127, by king Louis; captured, and afterwards set at liberty and expelled the country by Thierry of Alsace. He became a leader of mercenaries in Normandy and England, under Stephen, and as such, was distinguished by his atrocities; he was the first to run away at the battle of Lincoln. See the *Acta Stephani*. Ord. Vitalis, etc. (See the quaint story of the escape of William *Clito* from a trap laid for him at Ypres, which he discovered by observing the tears of his mistress while she *washed his head*. Ord. Vit. xii. 45.)

good and remarkably elegant, much aided by the existence of an external wall passage at the sills of the lancets; for this the buttresses are pierced.

At the intersection of the transept with the chancel appear two polygonal chapels beneath the flying buttresses; the last are pierced with quatrefoils and very broad. The buttresses throughout terminate in crocketted pinnacles, which rise above a fine parapet or balustrade, pierced with different patterns, which the pinnacles interrupt. The south end of the transept has a very beautiful rose window, one of the finest in Belgium, a work of the fourteenth century; of this date is the porch beneath it, which contains statues of the Virgin and saints, a very elegant design. There is a blind arcade, with tracery in the gable above the rose: the gable is flanked by *tourelles* of Decorated character, apparently recent additions. The tower has a deeply recessed and lofty doorway, less rich in decoration than that of the transept; above it are two pointed windows. On the south side is a large chapel, that of the Sacrament, built 1623, in a style which pertained to an earlier date; it has large pointed windows, and, in the gable of the west end, a very elegant modern pierced rosette or air-hole. The plan of the church is cruciform, with an aisleless polygonal chancel; the south end of the transept has double aisles; that on the north has but one, the aisle on its western side being omitted. The transeptal aisles on the east are divided from the chapels before mentioned by very elegant cylindrical shafts; one of these, by the way, is strangely out of the perpendicular; the tower is open to the nave, and has hanging beneath it a votive ship.

The general effect of the interior is very good indeed, owing to the great breadth and length of the nave, to the absence of the customary seventeenth-century choir-screens, and, above all, to the beauty of the chancel, than which we remember none so fine of its style in Belgium. The six piers of the nave are cylindrical, with octangular bases and caps, carved in volutes, common at the time they were wrought, and in excellent taste. The triforium has six openings to each bay, with trefoil heads; the clerestory is large, occupying the whole wall space, and, being without tracery or stained glass, looks bald and cold; the vaulting-shafts are triple, banded by the strings which run above and below the triforium; the lower string is carved very elegantly. Alternately the central shafts of these groups rest on the head of a canopy, that has once held a statue, and on a corbel. The outer shafts of each group rest on the caps of the nave piers. The chancel has a very elegant triforium carried entirely round it; that of the nave and transept resembles this, being composed of twin lancets, divided by cylindrical shafts, and a quatrefoil between the lancets. In front of the piers of the apse are ugly Renaissance statues; there is a good deal of elegant though rather formal carving in this church; there are demi-figures on the caps of the transept.

The chapel of the Sacrament is an interesting one; it is very large, and divided from the aisle by a fine seventeenth-century *grille* of brass, mounted in coloured marbles, and having its piers decorated with statuettes of saints and rich carvings. The roof is of wood, divided by shallow, closely-approximating ribs into square panels, and obtusely pointed; the intersections of the ribs bear bosses and pendants. The original painting of this roof remains, together with much faded carving and gilding; the effect of the whole is quaint, and, although unarchitectural, picturesque, a result which is due to the harmonizing labours of time rather than to those of the designer. There is a curious sixteenth-century font of brass in this church. Four figures, probably meant for the Virtues, support, caryatid fashion, a sort of canopy which pertains to the cover; a very large Gothic swing bracket of iron serves to move the latter from the basin; its spandrel is filled with rich Gothic foliage. The bowl stands on four *terms*. There are many curious old paintings on the walls here: one in the parish chapel, i.e., the east aisle of the north limb of the transept, shows "*Ipra ab Anglis et Rebellibus obsessa, Anno* 1383,"—a story we have just told by Froissart's help. This is said to have been painted by Frank Hals (?), but is certainly a curious performance. We have a view of the town, which is on fire in one place, and of the country round about it. The English army appears in tents; among them is seated a prince of the blood royal, having *or*, three lions *passant gardant gules* emblazoned on his surcoat, and on the banner above his head; a knight kneels before him. A knight wearing the same arms, by way of repulsing a sally, thrusts a lance into the stomach of a man who issues from the burning city. Near to these is a group of knights with the English prince at their head, and attended by two standard-bearers who hold banners, one of which shows *gules* three lunettes *or*, the other *azure*, a lion rampant *argent*. Bombards are firing into the city, attacks going on, &c. On the other side of the picture, divided from the last by an open space where the tents are on fire, appears something like a repetition of the above. Here the town receives a long procession of monks and nuns, who bear a statue of *O. L. Vrouwe van de Thuyne*, "Our Lady of the Palisade," through whose means— supplemented by the advance of the French, who appear behind —plundering Bishop Spenser was made to run away from Ypres. In the treasury of this church are a ciborium and an altar-cross with enamels, very good, of the fifteenth century, and some embroideries of later dates. Whenever a funeral takes place, a loaf and a cruet containing a piece of money are placed on the altar by the chief mourner, a custom known to be more than three centuries old.* The cloister of St. Martin, once a priory of Austin Canons, now a convent of Poor Clares, adjoins the north aisle (*c.* 1380), and contains the grave of Jansen, Bishop of Ypres, originator of the sect which bears his name; he rebuilt the priory for a seminary.

In Ypres are several buildings worthy of notice, among them the old front of the *Hôtel de la Chatellenie* in the Grande Place, with a series of demi-figures placed in roundels between the first and second floors, and a good grille to the parapet, *c.* 1530. The old butchery has its lower story of stone, *c.* 1250. The Hospital of St. Mary contains some remarkable monumental brasses, and a series of incised slabs of extraordinary interest, commencing from 1333. There are more slabs, but later, in the Hospital of St. Nicholas. Many old houses remain in Ypres, and more have disappeared within recent years. No loss has been inflicted on the town for a long time so great as the removal of the beautiful Gothic organ gallery from the interior of St. Martin's—a lamentable mistake.

---

* Weale. Belgium, Aix-la-Chapelle, etc.

THE BELFRY AT BRUGES, GRANDE PLACE.

THE name of Bruges refers to an ancient bridge (*brug*) of wood, pertaining to a fortress that stood on the road between Oudenbourg and Aerdenbourg, a sort of pass in the district, which was included in the country of the Menapians, or first free men of Flanders, who barred out the sea and began to trade. Baldwin *Bras-de-Fer* brought Judith, the runaway widow of Ethelwulf, of Wessex, to his strong fort here, and made it his chief seat. At the foot of the bridge arose a town which Baldwin fortified, so that under his eye, and that of his successors, it was able to defy the Normans—those terrible ravagers of Flanders. The site of Baldwin's castle is now occupied in part by the *Hotel de Ville* at Bruges. By way of giving a sacred quality to the neighbourhood, he brought here the relics of St. Donatian, and erected a chapel over them which was long afterwards the chief temple and mother-church of the city. Baldwin *le Cheuve* carried on the establishment of his father's little town, so that it grew populous enough to incur the penalty of crowding by pestilence, which in 1006 killed twelve thousand persons. Baldwin with the Comely Beard continued and extended the walls. Philip of Alsace was the great patron of the city, and instituted the Court of the Liberty of Bruges. Jane, his sister, who took the title of Count of Flanders to her husband, Baldwin of Hainault, and her sister Margaret, who married Bouchard of Avesnes, did a great deal for the place; the latter built a mint in 1274. Guy de Dampierre, son of Margaret of Constantinople, brought Philip *le Bel* of France to his aid against the citizens. The massacre of the last, which took place in 1300, was the first event of importance witnessed by the existing belfry of Bruges.*

---

* Guy de Dampierre, Count of Flanders, had a daughter Philippine, who was betrothed to Edward (the Second), Prince Royal of England, but the French king, Philip *le Bel*, asserted that as a vassal he had no right to ally the lady without his consent, and, by a stratagem, captured Guy and kept him safe until he sent for Philippine to Paris, where she died in prison, and of poison.

The old belfry, which was of wood, and built c. 1040, was burnt August 15th, 1280, together with nearly all the records and charters of the city, pledges of freedom won by the people from their lords, sometimes by fighting and often by purchase. Count Guy, whose miserable fate has brought sympathy he did not otherwise deserve, ignored all these rights, and did as he would with the people, but in a few years found himself compelled to acknowledge at least a part of these liberties, so that in 1291 the foundations of the tower

---

as they say. The iniquity of the charge is made deeper against Philip by the addition that, in his wrath at the defeat of Golden Spurs (July 11, 1302), he ordered the death of the innocent and beautiful Philippine. It is remarkable that the effect of Philip's policy was retributive, thus:—he procured the betrothal of Edward to his own daughter, Isabella of France in 1303: they were married in 1308, and thus strengthened the claim of Edward the Third, son of Isabella, to the crown of France, with all its consequences. The battle of Golden Spurs, or of Groeningen, was fought under the walls of Courtray by the men of Ghent and Bruges, 20,000 in number, commanded by John, Count of Namur, and the Count of Juliers, when the French invaders, under Robert, Count of Artois, were defeated so utterly as to lose 1,800 knights and 27,000 soldiers. Seven hundred gilt spurs of so many knights—they wore but one each—were found on the field, and hung up on the roof of the Chapel of the Counts adjoining Notre Dame at Courtray. These were the spurs which we saw the French so anxious to remove after their victory of Rosebecque and the death of Philip van Artevelde. As soon as Count Guy was released, he applied to Edward the First and obtained aid, but Philip came with a greater force and defeated the Count, and took him prisoner. Edward returned to England, and Philip made a tour of Flanders, during which he came to Bruges, and was received with such splendour that his foolish queen, Jeanne of Navarre, jealous of the dresses of the ladies of Bruges, cried out that instead of one queen (herself) she found there were many queens in the place. Conduct of this kind exasperated the upper classes of Bruges and Ghent, so that they seem to have united with the lower crafts in resisting payment of taxes levied to defray the expenses of the French visit. The bells of Bruges and Ghent answered each other over the flat. There were riots in both cities, and the intruders were expelled—Guy de Chatillion, the French governor of Bruges, riding for his life. It was when coming to reinstate them that Philip was met and beaten at Courtray. Philip had victory in his turn at Mons-en-Puelle; but meanwhile Count Guy died, and Philip was forced to acknowledge his son Robert of Bethune as Count of Flanders, receiving his homage and 200,000 livres. The fight of Golden Spurs was one of the most important in its consequences recorded in modern history. Robert of Bethune is said to have beaten Yolanthe of Burgundy, his second wife, to death with the bridle of his horse, because she had poisoned Charlemagne, his son by her predecessor, Catherine of Anjou. Robert III. was buried in St. Martin's Church, Ypres, 1322, and succeeded by Louis I. of Nevers, or of Cressy, so styled because he was killed in that battle, 1346. He too had experience of the Brugeois and Gantois; the former locked him up in the first case, and both expelled him, and it took all the power of Philip of Valois (VI. of France), to re-establish his vassal. Such, however, was the issue of the battle of Cassel, 1328. (See Froissart, I. 28.)

before us were laid, and the freedom of Bruges reinstated. The design of the structure has been attributed, on doubtful grounds, to one Simon of Geneva. As it stands the edifice is two hundred and ninety feet in height, or about ten feet higher than the gilded railings outside the dome of St. Paul's, a tremendous altitude, which looks even greater than it is on account of the straightness of the tower, and the shortness of the façade of which it now forms part. As the wings of this façade do not appear in the original design, and were not added until 1364, the reader must exclude them from view, if he wishes to conceive the primary aspect of the belfry. However much this may improve its architectural effect, we must go still higher in the air ere the whole structure reappears as of old. Upon the summit of the third stage of the tower stood, until 1741, a very lofty *flèche* or spire, which, after having been struck by lightning in 1493, and rebuilt in 1502, was burnt in 1741, and not rebuilt. A low roof took the place of the spire, but this, in 1822, was supplanted by the pierced parapet now before us.*

From the summit of the belfry may be seen the towns of Ostend and the sea, which is fourteen miles off, Thourout, Courtray, and Ghent, which last is about twenty-seven miles distant. At the apex of the *flèche* formerly stood the Golden Dragon of Constantinople; this was removed by the Gantois in 1382, as before related, and placed where it now is, but still in sight, on the spire of the belfry of Ghent. From this summit might be seen the men of Philip van Artevelde, as they set out from Ghent to the fatal battle of Rosebecque; the white hoods they wore would clearly mark so large a body of men. Hence have been seen the marchings and counter-marchings of the armies of every nation in Europe—English, under the Edwards, Elizabeth's generals, Marlborough, and Wellington; French, under the kings of the fourteenth century; Spaniards,

---

* The chimes placed in this tower consist of four octaves, from the largest bell of 11,539 lb. to the smallest, which weighs 12 lb. There are 47 instead of 49 bells; the *b* and *c* of the lowest octave are wanting: the whole weigh 56,166 lb. The *bourdon*, originally the great bell of Notre Dame, cast in 1680, weighs 22,600 lb.; it was removed hither by the French in 1800, and rang for the first time on account of the Peace of Amiens. The whole is valued at 3,000,000 francs (Weale). Chimes are not known to have existed here before 1631; doubtless they did so at a much earlier period. At present (June, 1865,) the machinery by which the chimes are played is out of repair; performances by hand occur three times a week. The bells have the sweetest tone in all Belgium, although they are not quite so clear as those of Audenaerde.

TOUR DES HALLES, BRUGES.

with Alva and his butchering companions: Austrians; Italians; Russians even—so that the people with whom the merchants of Bruges of old traded in utmost Novogorod, have sent descendants to war within sight of the great emporium of the middle ages. This tower saw the institution of the Golden Fleece,* and Charles the Bold going to be married to Margaret of York in St. Donat's church close by (1468). Among other ominous objects, the Belfry might have observed Ignatius Loyola cross the square at its foot, wearing that black dress which never seems black enough to human sight: this was in 1525, a time when most of the houses of the Grande Place were in existence. It saw also, on April 1, 1482, the funeral procession of Mary, wife of Maximilian, daughter of Charles the Bold, when she was borne to the vault where her bones lie "scattered about," together with those of her father. Thus they still remain, as Mr. Weale tells us, beneath the choir of Notre Dame, where her splendid monument of brass, and that inferior one of his, fill a chapel. Charles's daughter left her crown to the Chapel of the Holy Blood, at Bruges, where it still hangs. The student will not forget that she died in pregnancy in consequence of miscarriage, produced by a fall while hunting near Bruges, the effect of which, through weak delicacy, she concealed so long as it was possible.

---

* The order of the Golden Fleece was instituted by Philip the Good, Duke of Burgundy, at Bruges, in 1429, on his marriage with Isabella of Portugal, and to commemorate the wealth of his possessions as derived from woollen manufactures. When Mary, Philip's granddaughter, married Maximilian, the Order became Austrian, and since 1748 it has been shared between Spain and Austria. Its knights must belong to no other order; the motto is "*Autre n'Auray;*" the ribbon is red; the collar is composed of steels and flints, emitting sparks. The institution of the Golden Fleece has an interesting connexion with John Van Eyck, the painter, and trusted servant of Duke Philip. John was sent to Portugal to paint the portrait of Isabella; the result so pleased the Duke—who had already been twice married, and not long before rejected by Isabella of Arragon—that he caused a third marriage to be celebrated by proxy, and the young bride came to Flanders with all speed. After a very bad passage, during which the Sieur de Roubaix, Philip's ambassador, was dreadfully sick, the party, Van Eyck included, reached Bruges on Christmas Day, and was received with the greatest splendour. Van Eyck got 150 livres for his portrait, and many compliments. (See the account in Moustrelet, *Chron. ii.* 77.) The same writer gives the names of the first knights of the Golden Fleece; it is probable that the first abasement of the order took place in Bruges during the revolt against Philip, when the Lord Villiers de l'Isle-Adam was killed in the streets and his Fleece torn from his neck, January, 1437.—(Monstrelet ii. 213.) Philip died in the palace at Bruges, June 12th, 1467, and was buried in St. Donat's, afterwards at Dijon, by the side of Isabella.

The Belfry, if it had eyes to open, might have seen Maximilian on his knees in the Grande Place swearing to do a great many things which—although the bones of St. Donation and a portion of the true Cross were under his hands at the time—he never did; but, on the contrary, as the Belfry knows quite well, made the magistrates of Bruges come out in their turn and, kneeling, beg his pardon, telling down also three hundred thousand gold florins by way of fine. Not many months before, it also saw Maximilian led into durance vile in the house which still stands at the corner of the Rue St. Amand, where he must have got dreadfully sick of the *carillons*. Maximilian seems to have been merciful under provocation, and quite another sort of man than Count Louis de Maele, who caused "five hundred men of the poor crafts" to be beheaded at the foot of the Belfry; this was in 1382—when the tower was not a hundred years old. If Bruges Belfry had any ears at all, it must have heard Mad Margery of Ghent pounding away at Audenaerde with Philip van Artevelde, in the last-named year, and again in 1452. Undoubtedly, it many a time heard the cry of "FLANDERS FOR THE LION!" but never did so with more satisfaction than when Louis de Maele put out his torches in the Grande Place, and went into hiding with the widow Bruynaert, at her little house near the chapel of St. Amand.

We fear the bell of Bruges did not toll when Louis Maele died at Lille, January 30th, 1383, nor during the siege which was instituted by his successor with one hundred thousand men, against Franz Atreman with fifteen hundred in Damme, the port of Bruges, the last hope of the freemen of Flanders; but it might well have rung two years later, when peace was made by Philip conceding the privileges of the towns and receiving their submission. This bell was rung for centuries daily at the working hours of morning, noon, and evening, when the weavers crossed the bridges in such multitudes that they could not be raised to admit craft, an obviously convenient regulation in cities intersected by many canals and rivers, and of itself striking enough to express the density of the population, so as to render superfluous the exaggeration by which men have averred the rushes of workmen to have been so great that women and children were commonly trampled to death. The artizans of Bruges in the fifteenth century were fifty thousand strong, or about the number of the present entire population.

Having had concern in these things, and many more than this book could tell, were it entirely devoted to the Belfry of the Brugeois, one may readily guess at the tower's opinion of stately Mr. Evelyn, our worthy friend who came here on the 9th of October, 1641, and, as he tells us, saw nothing in the Grande Place but "cheeses and butter, piled up in heaps." It is true that the master of Wootton seriously believed that the centuries between the destruction of the Roman Empire and the advent of Leo X. were benighted, and hardly worthy the attention of a civilized creature. It is true, also, that not many days before this, Evelyn had parted with Sir Kenelm Digby, " travelling towards Cologne," so that the matter-of-fact diarist may be excused some confusion of ideas and forgetfulness. Moreover, on the night preceding this sight of eatables at Bruges, he "supped with the abbot of Andoyne,* a very courteous and pleasant priest."

Of the structure of the Belfry itself, let us now speak. It is of brick, with what carvings there are of stone; rising to so vast a height as it does, we cannot be surprised that it has inclined nearly thirty-four inches towards the east, *i.e.*, on the spectator's right hand. Standing on such soil, we may well wonder that the foundation laid, even at a depth of thirty feet, was sufficient to bear the enormous weight. The name of the architect who constructed the lower portion of the Belfry is unknown; he who built the octagonal part and the four pinnacles which are connected with it by flying buttresses, was Jean van Audenaerde, 1393—96. It is more than probable that the unknown original architect did not intend to carry the tower to the enormous height it attained at the hands of his successor. The octagonal stage is by no means an improvement. Fortune has been unkind to the second architect, by allowing his work to appear as at present, and without the spire. As we find the town of Bruges to have been enlarged at about the middle of the fourteenth century, the additional stage was probably required to enable the watchers stationed on the summit of the tower to command the city and its environs; this became practicable on the addition of the upper stage. The tower originally stood alone. The *Halle aux Draps*, which occupies its sides, was not begun until

---

* Probably of Antoing, not far from Tournay, where was an ancient religious foundation, now a school.

1364; behind this is an open oblong court surrounded by similar buildings, part of which, begun in 1284, is older than the tower; that side of the quadrangle which is parallel to the façade before us dates only from the sixteenth century.* The open space within is sometimes used as a cloth market; the west wing serves for this purpose in wet weather; the north front which faces us is occupied by the garrison of Bruges, the east and south sides are appropriated to a meat market. In the quadrangle at the south side appears a picturesque staircase, giving access to the old Hall of the Cutlers; this has been spoilt by the introduction of clumsy shafts to the arcade which covers the stairs. The arcade on the base of the façade before us was originally carried entirely round the building, a constant feature in structures of this kind; on the three fronts in the side streets it has been walled up. The balcony over the central entrance was originally a place of proclamation; above it is a modern statue of the Virgin, which replaces that destroyed in the French Revolution.

---

* Schayes, *Hist. de l'Architecture en Belgique.*

THE HOSPITAL OF ST. JOHN AT BRUGES.

BY far the most interesting things in Bruges at this time are the pictures in the Hospital of St. John, painted by Memline, it appears, for various members of that institution, and left as heir-looms. The hospital is a charitable institution for the benefit of the sick of Bruges and Maldeghem, its suburb, and attended by sister hospitallers of St. John, who have done so since the middle of the twelfth century; until comparatively recent times one half the patients were attended by monks. The ancient house is picturesque with its quaint recesses of the hall, wherein the patients lie; its aged and dutiful women, and its church. The last is a work of the fourteenth century, and contains a beautiful stone tabernacle with pierced work in brass about it, a chandelier, reliquaries, embroideries, etc. The hall was built *c.* 1350, and has a pointed roof supported by columns, which divide the apartment into galleries or aisles, comprising two hundred and forty beds. The chapter, or council-room, contains pictures, and, among them, the most complete and valuable works of Memline, the great artist of Bruges, whose place of birth is unknown* as well as the date of that event. It appears that he was resident here in 1478, and probably before. The date of his death also is uncertain; "between the 1st of June, 1492, and the 10th of December, 1495," says Mr. Weale, who is one of the best authorities; Vasari avers he was a pupil of Roger de la Pasture, of Tournay, better known as Roger Van der Weyden.†

---

* Descamps says he was born at Damme; Van Mander, the writer who first called attention to his works, speaks of him as "of Bruges," which no one doubts; the Germans assume that he was of a family settled at Geneva—anywhere, in fact, but where he lived, worked, and probably died. There have been squabbles about the spelling of his name; we have had Hemling, Memling, Hemmling, Memmeling, Memmelinck. Memline seems to be right, the main difference is in the termination. Van Mander very nearly agrees in the "line."

† Roger Van der Weyden, an artist in great repute at Brussels, and pupil of

Apart from a few pictures scattered in distant galleries, Hans Memline might well be content with the honour all pay to him who enter the quaint Council-chamber of St. John's at Bruges. It is a quiet and rather dusty-looking nook in the world, and of all we have seen most apt to a reputation and a genius such as his who produced its treasures. The great windows of the chamber admit plenty of light; through them we see to the quiet hospital-yard and its old buildings, with here and there a slender tree that seems as if it would never look old, but moves gently in the breeze and rustles in the sunlight, venerable although undeveloped. Here is a broken red-brick wall with plaster peeling off, and there a piece of carving tumbled down ; under an arcade near by moves a ministering woman, black-robed and deliberate ; there an aged man totters in his walk and work. Further off one sees the high-peaked gables and tall windows of houses in the city; these do not come too close to mar the character of the place—there is plenty of room in Bruges now—but they complete a prospect which is made pathetic by the silence which is peculiar to hospitals, so soothing to the senses, and sometimes really *felt*. The Council-chamber is high and square ; a lofty Flemish fire-place comes forward over at least one-third of its width ; the walls are entirely covered by pictures ; there a row of kindly-eyed but resolute looking ladies of the hospital, in wide hoods of black and white ; there several sad-faced " tutors" of the house ; there a demonstrative Vandyck ; here a good coast-piece, *called* a Miraculous Draught of Fishes, by Teniers the younger ; and, mixed up with these, several hideously depictured sacred subjects.

At one end of the room is Memline's *Mystical Marriage of St. Catherine*, a large triptych ; at the other end hangs the *Adoration of the Magi ;* by the side of the window, so that you can sit down

---

John Van Eyck, spent the early years of his study at Bruges ; painted for the Hôtel de Ville at Brussels, where he illustrated the splendour of justice, also for Charles the Bold, and at various places besides. One of his most excellent pictures was in the church of " Our Lady-without-the Walls," at Louvain, taken thence by Mary of Hungary and sent to Spain ; the ship which contained it was in danger and the work was thrown overboard, but ultimately came to land safely. Roger died June 16th, 1464, and was buried in the nave of the Church of St. Gudule, " before the altar of St. Catherine, under a blue stone." There is one of his pictures in the National Gallery, No. 661: *The Deposition in the Tomb.*

and look at it easily, is a superbly painted triptych, displaying on one wing, *The Virgin and the Infant Saviour*, and, on the other, a portrait of the donor, *Martin Van Nieuwenhove, Burgomaster of Bruges in* 1497. With regard to the last it appears to us, so far as technical qualities go, in colour, modelling, richness of tone and brilliancy, the finest of Memlinc's works. Inferior to the portraits of *Jean Arnoulphin and his Wife*, now in the National Gallery, by John Van Eyck, in respect to solidity and ineffable finish, there is more of freedom in the Nieuwenhove portrait than in any other picture of the time; few at any time have surpassed it in this matter. On a table in the centre of the room stands the famous shrine of Saint Ursula. On the wall is a triptych representing the *Deposition of our Saviour*, with the donor, Adrian Reins, and six saints in the wings. Also a portrait of Catherine Moreal, styled the *Sibyl Zambeth;* six works in all.

Of the first of these let us write that it presents the Virgin robed as a queen, but not crowned, seated on a throne and bearing the naked Child upon her knee; behind her is the high baldaquin of cloth of gold; two angels hold the crown of heaven over her head; a wingless angel, robed in white, kneels in front and holds the Book of Wisdom; he has the Flemish type of face, handsome enough, but peculiar. She turns a leaf of the book. On the right of this group is Saint Catherine, towards whom Christ bends, and places the ring of espousal on her outstretched finger; she is half kneeling, half sitting. The action of the saint is charmingly *naïve;* bride-like and yet reverent, her figure is altogether perfectly lovely. Behind her is a little angel clad in cloth of gold and playing on a regal or portable organ, so commonly seen in Italian pictures of this character. In its exquisite grace, this figure is worthy of any painter; it is a personation of melody of the most wonderful kind, and seems palpitating with a soft delight that strangely infects the spectator. Behind stands St. John the Baptist, with a thoughtful, happy expression, leading his lamb; and, on the other side, St. John the Evangelist,* having the chalice, and the serpent issuing

---

* This mode of depicting the Evangelist is common in sacred art; a legend grew up, as such things mostly did, with the vulgar, from a pictorial allusion to the answer of Christ to the mother of John when she asked high places at the table in heaven for him and James. Our Lord said, " Ye shall indeed drink of my cup." The legend sprung from the symbol was to the effect that some

from it, in his hand; a noble face and grave attitude. In the foreground is Saint Barbara, dressed in a green robe, and with the high-pointed frontal of the fifteenth century. She holds a book and reads from it with an expression which is marvellously faithful to nature and singularly mild and sweet, having withal a look of elevation and spirituality which is infinitely higher in art than the simply faithful and pathetic beauty of John Van Eyck's women, while it is less austere than his brother's holy faces. Saint Catherine's robe is brocaded, of black and gold; she has a vest of delicate white fur, and, beneath this, a bodice of brilliant crimson. In the background are pillars, the carved capitals of which represent the vision of Zacharias, and scenes in the early life of the Baptist. In the distance is a landscape with figures; the subjects are the Baptist preaching, praying, distinguishing and baptizing Christ, &c.*

On the left wing of this triptych appears St. John at Patmos, with the Apocalyptic signs, and the vision of the crystal sphere. On the right wing is represented the decollation of the Baptist; the head of the saint is placed on a charger, held by the maid of Herodias. The figure of the last is a triumphant study of expression; she turns away from her ghastly load, the weight of which is told by her action, with a shudder of the most natural order. The executioner is full of vigour.† Behind, are other subjects from the life of John. On the outside of the wings appear striking

---

one attempted to poison the Evangelist in the Eucharistic chalice, but the potion failed of effect, and its evil power took the form of a serpent or dragon, that crawled forth while the traitor fell dead at the foot of the altar.

* As from Memline's point of view the whole of the scene before us is mystical and never had a reality other than as a symbol of intense interest in its application to human life, there was no incongruity observable by him, nor by ourselves if we will but give time and think, in the appearance of current costumes and incidents in a picture which was directed to his own as well as any former or future period of time. Hence, before these holy and lovely countenances, serene and unaffectedly graceful figures, no one feels startled by the brocades, fur, gold, horned head-dresses, nor even by the presence of John Floreins, bursar of St. John's, and donor of this picture, who appears twice, once in the exercise of his duty, in gauging barrels that have been landed on the quay at Bruges. The bursar could take his Christian faith into the exercise of his business, nor would forget everything but gold in labouring.

† Among the many extraordinary legends which gathered about the life of St. John the Baptist, none is so startling as that which avers that Herodias was in love with him, and that her husband, in order to remove the object of her affection, caused St. John to be decapitated, and that the head was brought her on a dish. When she bewailed her loss, and sought to kiss the dead lips, they blew out so

portraits of some male and female officers of the hospital, kneeling, and having their holy patrons behind them. The whole picture, although the restorer's effacing fingers have been very active upon it, looks what it is—an admirable work of the highest art. It is five feet seven and a half inches in height, and of the same breadth in the central composition; the wings are two feet seven inches and a quarter wide.

The shrine of St. Ursula contains an arm of the saint, but is more in repute with us on account of the pictures on its exterior than for anything that might have been deposited in it in 1489 by the bishop of Tournay. It is of the ordinary high-roofed, house-like form of shrines, of wood, mounted in metal, and two feet ten inches high, three feet long, and thirteen inches from side to side. On its sides are six subjects from the life of St. Ursula and her attendant virgins, whose legendary number of eleven thousand the artist has wisely reduced; the ends of the chest are decorated respectively with pictures of the Virgin and Child, and a figure of a gigantic St. Ursula, sheltering young maidens beneath her mantle. They huddle about her form with expressions scarcely to be seen equalled in Art elsewhere, so wonderfully subtle are their varieties, and so delicate are the differences between face and face, and figure and figure. On each side of the sloping roof are three medallions, containing on one side in the central medallion, which is the largest, the saint seated in heaven, and receiving the crown from the hands of the First Person of the Trinity; Christ seated by her side, the Holy Ghost hovering above in the form of a dove; while the larger medallion on the other side of the roof, contains the saint in heaven with her companions—nine of the sweetest faces and most ex-

---

strong a breath, that she was sent floating in the air, and has never since set foot on earth. At dawn, and while the cocks crow, it is said, she reposes on the branches of oak-trees. The former part of this outrageous legend gives a key not often suspected to the intention of certain painters, who have dealt with the Decollation by giving a woeful expression to Herodias. She is further said to have carried off the head, and buried it in her palace-garden, having pierced the tongue with a bodkin from her hair, lest it should again rebuke her for sin. Every one knows that Herodias became a sort of Hecate in medieval imaginations, that witches assembled round her at midnight, and invoked her aid for evil things. After Herod's disgrace, he and Herodias were banished to Lyons, where they died miserably. Salome, the *saltatrice*, as the Italians style her, slipped on ice and, falling through, had her head chipped off so that it rolled along crying out.

quisite figures that ever painter wrought. The four smaller medallions of the roof contain single figures of young angels, playing respectively on the regal, violin, lute, and dulcimer. In the larger medallion, of the saint in heaven with her companions, and at the end of the chàsse, she holds an arrow, the instrument of her martyrdom. Nothing can exceed the beauty, delicacy, brightness, variety, and above all, the tender flower-like chastity of the saints in all the pictures; nothing can be conceived more varied than their attitudes, more exquisite than the painting of their dresses, and those—armour and robes—of the persecutors. About the angels music never seems to fail; winged, they are like " birds of God."

The subjects of Memline's pictures on the shrine belong to the legend of the saint whose bones it contains. With regard to the extraordinary number of her companions, which has been assumed to be incredible, many efforts have been made to reduce it to a "practicable" amount. Eleven is the favourite number, and one needlessly ingenious critic has reduced it to *one*,—a damsel astonishingly designated *Undecimilla*, who, as he says, not only accompanied the virgin-saint of Brittany in all her journeys, and perished with her, but has shared the honour which was her due among eleven thousand sisters in imaginary martyrdom. The account given by those who are determined not to believe in the host of maids is to the effect that an early writer (Herman of Cologne), 922, mistook in an ancient MS. the abbreviations XI. M.V., *i.e., eleven martyr virgins*, for *undecimillia virgines*,—" or eleven thousand virgins." Ursula was the daughter of Theonotus, king of Brittany, and his wife Daria, who were both Christians, and had educated their child with the utmost affection, and in the true faith. She understood not only all the Christian doctrines, but much science, history, and poetry. Beautiful and holy, she gave her parents but a single cause for regret,—she rejected matrimony, notwithstanding that many suitors presented themselves. Undeterred by their fate, Conon, the pagan prince of Britain, cast loving eyes on the princess, with whom, had she been an ordinary woman, his chance of success would have been excellent, because he was not only famous for courage, but one of the handsomest men of his time. His father, king Agrippinus, anxious to obtain a suitable bride for Conon, sent ambassadors to Theonotus, who demanded the hand of the princess. Now Agrippinus was a formidable lord, whom no one liked to displease; his demand, therefore, caused much perplexity to the prince of Brittany, who feared that Ursula would not be more tractable in this than in previous cases of the same sort. While he sat pondering what could be done, Ursula, who was divinely inspired with knowledge of the difficult purport of the ambassadors' visit, entered her father's chamber, and addressed him thus,—"Distress not thyself, O my father! I will reply to these gentlemen in the manner which is meet." Theonotus, who was accustomed to rely on the wisdom of his daughter, was particularly glad to be relieved of the difficulty, and gladly consented that she should receive the ambassadors when they came to his council-chamber, on the morrow. They came and found Ursula seated on a throne by the side of her father. She addressed them with perfect grace and ease, saying, "Sirs, thank my good lord the king of Britain for me, and the noble gentleman, his son, whose proffered affection I shall treasure, and will vow never to accept that of another. Three things, however, must be given to me in exchange for the love he asks. Ten noble virgins of England he must grant to me as damsels of honour: on each of these, and on myself, a thousand maidens must wait. Three years he must allow me in honour of my virginity, so that I may visit the shrines of many saints; and all his court must become Christians—and then I will wed his son." One thinks these conditions rather stringent, but the English king was so fascinated by the account given of Ursula by his messengers, that he acceded to them; had himself, son, court and all, baptized, and ordered the eleven thousand virgins to be got together. It is said, they came all glorious in gold and silver vestments, and were sent with the utmost care, as became their dignity and virtues, to Brittany. Ursula assembled them in the meadows outside her father's city, and spoke so sweetly about the true faith that several among them who were not already Christians were baptized in the brook which ran before her seat. Ursula next said to the British prince that her pilgrimage was now to be begun, and that he must come into Brittany and help her father in the government of that kingdom, while she journeyed with the virginal band from shrine to shrine and sought the blessing of the saints and of God—especially in the most holy city of Rome. "If I come not back, good my lord and prince, my inheritance is thine." She and the glorious eleven thousand set sail in ships that had no sailors on board of them, but whose paths across the ocean the loving angels smoothed, while the virgins steered and worked the sails as if they had been born at sea. Divine Providence led them, not by the shortest route to Rome, but to the mouth of the Rhine, and up that river until they reached the wonderful city of Cologne, where they landed for repose, and in order to visit the shrines of the three kings who came to the birth-manger of our Lord, and are called Caspar, King of Tarsus; Melchior, the negro King of Nubia; and Balthasar, King of Seba. At Cologne, an angel appeared in a vision to Ursula, and said that the eleven thousand and she would reach Rome, and on returning attain crowns of martyrdom in the city of the three kings. Thankful for the promise of glory, the princess informed her companions, whereupon they, with eleven thousand and one sweet voices, sang a song of praise to the Lord. Memline's first subject represents the covey of holy ladies landing at Cologne, and gives us the princess in the act of stepping from her barque to the quay, where a damsel, whom we take to belong to the city, receives her. Another lady is standing by the side, who holds a casket containing the relics and precious things which were brought from Brittany. Some of the faces in this little picture justify the fame of Memline by their sweetness and tender beauty as well as by the innocent surprise they exhibit at what is before them of the strange city. Several of the virgins who have already landed are proceeding through the fortified gate of Cologne in order to accomplish the object of their visit at the shrine of the three kings. Upon the walls appear many towers, and beyond them the rich spires of the cathedral. After leaving Cologne, the angel-wafted ships went on until they came to Basle, where the river ceased to be navigable, and this admirable freight was compelled to land in order to cross the Alps on foot. This disembarkation supplies the second subject which is painted on the *châsse;* its composition is, however, totally distinct from that of the first picture, although it again shows Ursula in the act of landing. The city of Basle is represented in the background, together with the Alps and the road that winds along their sides. Upon this road, Memline has shown some of the virgins in the act of ascending the mountains; thus we are led to the third subject. The second picture is as brilliant and tender in its colouring as it is possible to conceive, and not less charming than the first in the variety and delicacy of its expressions.

Preceded by six angels, who bridged the torrents and pitched tents for the virgins, these holy ladies travelled onwards until they reached Rome, where St. Peter and St. Paul are buried. How Pope Cyriacus and his clergy came out to meet them is shown in Memline's third picture, where Ursula and her companions are seen in the act of kneeling to receive the blessing of the holy father. The beauty of some of the faces in this painting is quite indescribable, nor is their variety less astonishing, or the individuality which the artist has so happily given to many of them. With respect to the last-named quality, which is one of the most subtle characteristics of Art, the picture seems inexhaustible; the charmed spectator may sit in front of it for hours while endeavouring to surmise the little history which he feels sure is attached to each holy and lovely face. In nothing are these works more distinct from commonplace artistic representations than in respect to the innocence which is so wonderfully depicted on each face; the virgins are marvellously unconscious of possessing loveliness and piety. When looking at a saint as pictured by Murillo, Guido, or Rubens, one of the last things we find in their faces is this peculiar unconsciousness, this exquisite *naïveté* of the soul; the Madonnas of Raphael also, however charming they may be, fall, with but one or two exceptions, nearly as far short of the unconsciousness of Memline's virgins, as they do of that awful spirituality which characterizes the mother of our Lord as imagined by the great early Italian masters. The countenances of some of the Pope's attendants in the picture before us claim honour for Memline which is hardly less great than that which is due on account of the virgins of whom we have just written; *e.g.*, that of the deacon who bears the cross is unsurpassed by anything of its kind we know. We are not speaking here of expression alone but of actual execution also; these little gems are as perfect in modelling, and brightly true in colour, as those of any painter, let his school be what it may.

While Ursula and her companions were performing the Rhineward journey to the Eternal City, the prince of Britain and many noble companions—moved by love for Christ and admiration of the sweet travellers, a curious mixture of feelings about which the legend is subtly expressive—had undertaken a pilgrimage on their own account, and reached Rome by the sea-route; thus the two parties met on the banks of the Tiber, and the second part of the subject of the third picture is accounted for, wherein we see a number of British youths receiving baptism by immersion from certain monks. The next (fourth) panel has for its subject the re-embarkation at Basle, at which city, by traversing the Alps a second time, the virgins arrived again. Cyriacus and the prince accompanied the convoy notwithstanding the advice and wicked sneers of many who pointed out the impropriety of such a proceeding, and refused to see in the expedition anything that was innocent. His holiness, a cardinal, and a bishop, disregarded these malicious expressions, and, accordingly, we have them before us in the barques. The virgins are in a knot by themselves, some at prayer. *Ethereus* —such was the name the prince-bridegroom of Ursula, received at the hands of Cyriacus in exchange for his British one—appears not in this picture, but does so in the next, which represents the martyrdom. While the pilgrims were in Rome, two great heathen captains, who always oppressed Cyriacus, were angry that so many maidens should go about Europe unharmed, and wrote to the king of the Huns, who was then besieging Cologne, that if he did not destroy them as they passed that city they would marry and produce Christian children; or, if they remained single, would probably convert the whole of Germany. On getting these letters, which also requested him to have Cyriacus slain, the terrible Hunnish king stationed his best archers in the green meadows that are above Cologne and by the river side, and gave them orders to let nothing pass alive. This was hardly done, ere ships which bore the holy convoy came in sight, having on board not only the virgins, but the priests, the pope, and Ethereus. Being very much astonished at the immense number of beautiful ladies thus coming before them, the archers at first hesitated to act as they were bidden; having recovered themselves, however, they shot with might and main, and as the ships came near the bank some of the cruellest soldiers jumped on board, and then stabbed Ethereus, so that he fell dead, a martyr, in the arms of Ursula.* This appears in the fifth picture

---

* The story of St. Ursula has been related in many ways, and many dates have been given to it. A.D. 386 is given by Geoffrey of Monmouth as the true period of the martyrdom; he says that her father was king of Cornwall,

before us, where also is the attack on the other voyagers; two archers are aiming their arrows at the virgins in the boat. After slaying the whole eleven thousand, the Pagans took Ursula out of the ship unhurt, because they were awed by the manner in which she exhorted her friends to die as became noble Christian virgins. They did so, and the army of martyrs was much augmented on that day. The king of the pagans was so much moved by Ursula's beauty and glorious appearance that he said he would marry her himself. High in wrath, the princess defied him; this so exasperated the ruffian that he drew three arrows from his belt, and as she stood there before his tent and among his soldiers, shot her to death. Memline has represented this final incident with wonderful pathos. The saint, fair and holy, stands before the Hun; although her eyes, and with them her mind, seemed fixed on the promised crown and seat in heaven—as depicted in the medallions before described—yet the frail human body shrinks before the coming arrow, so that one shoulder is gently raised and one hand spread to protect her breast.

Memline's other works in the Hospital of St. John need not detain us after we have considered the great triptych and the shrine. It is less necessary to linger before that picture which is next in importance to these, *i.e.*, the triptych of the "Adoration of the Magi," because the Arundel Society has recently published excellent chromo-lithographic copies from the five paintings which are comprised in it. The face of St. Adrian and the colouring of the figure of St. Barbara, in the "Descent from the Cross," are admirable, and should not be overlooked among the many exquisite productions of the great Flemish artist whose works we are considering. In the "Adoration of the Magi," above referred to, there appears a face on

---

brother and successor of Caradoc. Sigebert of Cologne gives the period as 453. However this may be, it is certain that at Cologne there still stands a fine Romanesque church, built in the twelfth century upon a foundation seven hundred years older, and almost entirely lined with bones, which are attributed to the army of virgins. In the Golden Chamber of this church are about 100 reliquaries, some of ancient date and great beauty, of the twelfth, thirteenth, and fourteenth centuries. In honour of the saint, who is patroness of maidens desiring a holy life, the Order of Ursulines was instituted in 1537, and classed under the Augustinian rule in 1572. The day of the company is October 21st. Copies in chromo-lithography from the pictures illustrating the legend of the saint, which are preserved in this church, have been published by Mr. Kellerhoven, with text by M. Dutton, 1860, royal 4to.

the left, as if looking into the chamber, which is said to be a portrait of Memline himself: the tradition which tells us this is not improbable. Among other commendable pictures in the Council-chamber is a capital triptych, by Van Vost, representing the "Descent from the Cross;" on the outer sides are two fine portraits of sisters of the Hospital of St. John.

In Bruges the student will not omit to see the Palais de Justice, which comprises portions of the ancient palace of the counts of Flanders. This edifice originally stood between the Hôtel de Ville and St. Donat's Church, so that the counts could pass on either hand to the one or the other, and by traversing the former gain access to the Chapel of the Holy Blood. The Palais de Justice is chiefly remarkable now-a-days for containing in the Council-room a picturesque chimney-piece, carved to commemorate the Peace of Cambray, 1529, by Gloseucamp, Rasch, and De Smet. Over the shelf is a nearly life-size statue of Charles V. holding the orb and sword, as if claiming the right to rule. The carving extends all along one side of the room; on the left of Charles's statue appear those of Mary of Burgundy and Maximilian, his paternal grandparents; and on the right Ferdinand and Isabella of Castile and Arragon, who held the same relationship to him on the mother's side. The whole is further enriched with medallions, armorials, flowers, pilasters, and other decorations in the fashion of the time in which it was produced. Beneath is represented the story of Susanna, a common subject in municipal council chambers, carved in white marble by G. De Beaugrant of Mechlin. The whole is a striking production, one of the best of its period.

The exterior of this edifice is picturesque if seen from the other side of the curiously black, stinking, and almost stagnant Canal de Mabriers, whence its red-brick *tourelles*, high gables and windows (*c.* 1520) are quaint enough. St. Donat's Church went at the French Revolution; its site contains a statue of Memline, surrounded by trees. In this church took place the atrocious murder of Count Charles I. of Flanders, March 2nd, 1127, a man of most holy life and a great remitter of taxes.* The provocation for this

---

* Count Charles could hardly have distinguished himself in this capacity more than did his relative Edward the Confessor, as we learn from Roger de Hoveden (Annals, 1066). This chronicler tells us "it befell king Edward

crime was Count Charles's unwise interference with trade in Bruges, by ordering all the granaries to be opened, wherein, there being a scarcity, the merchants had stored up corn in hope of profit. Exasperated by this, and refused justice when they demanded it, the provost of St. Donat's, chancellor of Flanders, and some of the injured, associated with many others who were discontented, and came upon the Count while at the very foot of the altar, in the act of reciting the fourth penitential psalm; or, as some say, while extending his hand in almsgiving to a poor widow. He was killed more suddenly and with even greater violence than befel Thomas à Beckett, forty-one years later. After the murder the conspirators proceeded to the house of Thesnard—châtelain of Bourbourg, companion of the Count, whom they had also slain—in order that they

---

that, on a certain day, he was taken, his queen, and Earl Harold, into his treasure chamber at Westminster."

This was the very chamber now standing, that, long after the Confessor's time, "was plundered so strangely of about two millions modern money," when the abbot and forty-eight of his monks were sent to the Tower on suspicion. While we keep the Confessor waiting at its door, the tale of this robbery may be told: it is indirectly connected with Bruges. The chief thief declared that he had been fined at Bruges for the king's (Edward I.) debts, and that while endeavouring to recover his money in the courts at Westminster, he found out the way "into the treasure-chamber of our lord the king" and robbed it, undeterred by the sight of those human skins of former would-be robbers, which were attached to the door. Neither these, nor memory of what the Confessor saw there, warned the plunderer.

Now let the Confessor, the queen, and Earl Harold enter. They went in order to see the treasure which, unknown to the king, had been collected in order that the king might "on the day of the nativity of our Lord purchase clothes for his soldiers and servants." Having entered the treasury, the king beheld the devil seated upon the money, upon which the king said to him, "What dost thou do here?" Whereto the devil answered, "I am keeping guard over my money." Upon this the king said to him, "I conjure thee by the Father and the Son and the Holy Ghost, to tell me how this money is thine!" To this Satan replied, "Because it has been unjustly obtained out of the substance of the poor." No one saw the devil but the king, although they heard him speak; he, however, believed Satan, and commanded the money to be restored to those from whom it had been taken. Let us think how conduct of this sort would disgust a modern Chancellor of the Exchequer. One wonders why the Confessor did not shut the devil up, as St. Evroult served him in the great oven at Echaufour, an act which much dismayed the women of that village when they brought bread to bake. (See *Vitalis* VI. 9.) St. Evroult delivered them from perplexity and, as it would appear, actually used the heat of the fiend's person to bake the loaves. This was turning Satan to account with a vengeance. For the history of the robbery at Westminster, see Mr. Burtt's appendix to "Gleanings from Westminster Abbey," J. H. and J. Parker, 1863.

K

might kill his children; but while on the way there they learnt that Thesnard was still living, so they returned and effectually finished the bloody work; they dragged the châtelain by the feet from the church, down the steps, and flung him into the open street. This fate brought the Count the honour of sainthood and the title of Charles the Good, Martyr.* It was while coming out of this church of St. Donat, that Matilda, daughter of Count Baldwin V. was met by William the Bastard of Normandy, afterwards conqueror of England, then greatly irritated by the long delay of his suit for her hand. It seems that this delay was caused quite as much by the knowledge of the lady's father that William's position was questionable, as by the obstacles which were interposed by the pope in granting her divorce from Gerbod, Advocate of St. Bertin's. William probably thought the lady herself hung back, so, after short remonstrances and complaints, he actually shook her by the shoulders, and it is said, ultimately rolled the young countess in the mud.

No city in Europe contains more antiquities which are intimately connected with its municipal importance than Bruges. A large book might be written about them; indeed, large books have been so devoted. Here, however, we must content ourselves with indicating the most important, in addition to those already referred to. These are the Hôtel de Ville, built by Count Louis de Macle, 1377, originally decorated by statues of counts of Flanders, which, December 30, 1792, were burnt by the revolutionists at the foot of the Belfry. In the Hôtel de Ville is the ancient Council-chamber, with its original coloured decorations, carvings, etc. The exterior, having been badly restored, is not worth noticing. In the Academy of Painting is a noble picture by J. Van Eyck, representing the

---

* This extraordinary affair was mixed up with politics and municipal interests. Count Charles had not only quarrelled with his own chancellor, but was at enmity with Clemence of Burgundy, dowager, widow of Robert of Jerusalem, and mother of Baldwin-a-la-Hache, his predecessor. She supported a pretender to the county in the person of William de Loo, Vicomte of Ypres, issue of a daughter of Philip of Flanders, brother of Robert the Frison, as having a better claim than that of Charles, which was derived through the right of his mother, Adele of Flanders, daughter of Robert the Frison, married to St. Canute of Denmark, of whom we heard before at Jerusalem. It is curious that Charles's father should have been murdered under circumstances resembling those of his own death at Bruges. His bones are in the Church of St. Sauveur in this city.

Virgin and Child with St. Donat and the donor, George van der Paele, canon of St. Donat's (whence this picture came here), with his patron, St. George; also St. Christopher, with Christ on his shoulders in the central panel of a triptych, with SS. Benedict and Giles, and on the wings, the donor, his wife and family, with SS. Adrian and Barbara; on the outside, SS. John the Baptist and George, by Memline, one of his finest works, though damaged by the "restorer." Here are pictures by Pourbus, Van Oost, and Gerard David,—the Baptism of Christ by the last is a very interesting work, sometimes attributed to Roger Van der Weyden.

The Church of Notre Dame was built by St. Boniface, rebuilt by St. Charles of Flanders, *c.* 1120, and enlarged about fifty years later. It has a gigantic brick tower two hundred and thirty-six feet in height, upon which is placed a very beautiful spire, also of brick, rising to four hundred and twenty-two feet; the spire, at about two-thirds of its elevation, pierces a coronet of stone, the whole beautifully proportioned; within, the structure, like Chichester Cathedral, exhibits a nave and four aisles. The nave and the aisles immediately adjoining it were rebuilt in 1180, those beyond at the end of the fifteenth century. The pillars of the nave have fine and characteristic capitals; they are marred by the stupid figures of saints which have been stuck against them and strapped there by iron bands, together with their ugly *rococo* canopies. The arches of the south aisle are Romanesque. The whole of the nave above the triforium is of seventeenth-century work and bad. The crossing is grand in its effect and curious, composed of differing styles of architecture. The church is two hundred and forty feet long, and one hundred and sixty feet wide. There is a marble group of the Virgin and Child, attributed, very ridiculously, to Michael Angelo; the face of the Virgin is foolish in conception, and badly wrought; that of Christ is better. The draperies throughout are preposterously sculptured. In a side chapel is the noble brass monument of Mary of Burgundy, who died March 22, 1482, aged twenty-five. This tomb was finished in 1502, and shows the princess reclining with two dogs at her feet; her face is very gentle-looking, although exhibiting thickish lips; the nose is very clearly cut, the brow good; the hair has been plucked from the front to make the forehead seem high; her hands are clasped together. The monument of Charles the Bold, which stands beside that of his daughter,* was not executed until 1558, and by order of Philip the Second, by J. Jongelincxs and J. Aerts, from the designs of M. Gheeraerds. It represents the duke in full armour but that the head is bare; the helmet is at his feet, which rest on a lion. The hands are bare, the gauntlets are on the side opposite to the helmet. The coronet of Mary is arched in, and on her head; that of Charles is open, like a cap of maintenance. On the sides of both monuments are genealogical trees, showing the descent of the dead. The tomb of Mary is by a great deal the finest piece of workmanship, and really an admirable example of its kind.†

The Cathedral of St. Sauveur was founded by St. Eloy, 646. It is cruciform. The choir and tower date from the twelfth century (1186); the parts between these were, after a fire, rebuilt in 1358: the chapels of the ambulatory are works of the fifteenth and sixteenth centuries (1482—1526). This is the oldest brick building in Belgium, and a very elegant structure, showing some good parts in both architectural and picturesque qualities, among which the chevet and choir-roof are remarkable; the east end has well-formed windows and a triforium arcade; there is no real triforium passage,

---

* Here is the epitaph of Charles the Bold:—
Cy gist tres hault, tres puissant et magnanime prince Charles Duc de Bourg^{ne}, de Lothrycke, de Brabant, de Lembourg, de Luxembourg, et de Gueldres; Conte de Flandres, d'Artois, de Bourg^{ne} Palatin, et de Hanau, de Holland, de Zeeland, de Namur et de Zutphen; Marquis du Sainct Empire; Seigneur de Frise, de Salins, et de Malines; lequelle estant grandement doué de force constance et magnanimité prospera longtemps en haultes entreprinses batailles et victoires tant a Montlheri en Normandie en Arthois en Liege que aultrepart; jusque a ce que fortune lui tournant le doz lopressa la nuict des roys 1476, devant Nancy. Fut depuis par le tres hault, tres puissant et tres victorieux prince Charles, empereur des Romains Vme de ce nom, son petit neveu heritier de son nom victoires et seigneories transporté a Bruges où le roi Philippe de Castille, Leon, Arragon, Navarre, etc., fils dudict empereur Charles la faict, mettre en ce tombeau du coté de sa fille et unique heritiere Marie, femme et espouse de tres hault et tres puissant prince Maximilien archidue d'Austrice depuis roi empereur des Romains—prions Dieu pour son ame. Amen.
The face of Charles is coarse; though bold it is rough, and exactly such as one would attribute to him; there is about the expression a sort of crude pride, which, in a meaner man, would be insolence.

† During the revolution in the last century these tombs were hidden by the beadle and sub-almoner of this church in the house of the latter, who got into trouble by means of this act, for which, however, he was rewarded by Napoleon I. we believe. The remains of Charles were primarily interred at Nancy, next at St. Donat's, Bruges, lastly in this church, 1558. His bones and those of his daughter, says Mr. Weale, lie scattered about the vault beneath the choir here.

but a series of beautiful cusped lancets. The jubé and high altar are hideous. Some of the tracery in the north clerestory is good. The processional path behind the *chevet* and inside the five chapels of the choir is a very noble one. In the Chapel of the Sacrament is a *Mater Dolorosa*, painted on a gold ground, which, whether or not rightly ascribed to John Van Eyck, is wonderful in its expression of intense grief; the long suffering rendered by the forms of the mouth, which are, so to say, set in sorrow, and tremulous with woe, would honour any master. The altar-piece by Pourbus, in the Chapel of the Sacrament, a triptych of the Last Supper, is good of its kind, and shows the influence of Venetian Art. The oak stalls in the choir are admirably carved (c. 1477), and they show artizans at work; among them are a sculptor, a writer on a long scroll, a tiler, and "wasted labour"—two fellows with their feet planted together and pulling in vain against each other. The carvings here are of three periods, the above are the earliest and best, although some couchant lions on the elbows of the stalls are excellent. A fine brass eagle in the choir is dated 1605. The oak screen to the Chapel of the Cordwainers (1470) is very good; in front lies a slab, having a boot incised upon it, and dated 1380. The brasses contained in this church are hardly to be surpassed in interest; among them we find those of Walter Copman, burgess; a "Death," 1387; Martin de Visels and his wife, 1453, a very noble example; Jacques Schelewaerts, 1483, doctor of theology; Walter de Raet, canon of this church, 1510: in the churchwardens' room an ancient crook which is attributed to St. Malo, 565, and formed of ivory bound by strips of gilt copper; also a small crook of Limoges enamel, a work of the twelfth century, and showing St. Valérie delivering her head to St. Martial of Limoges; a questionable tunic of St. Bridget, which is said to be of the sixth century; several MSS. of the fifteenth century; a leaden plate taken from the tomb of Gunhilda, daughter of Earl Godwin, sister of Harold, who found refuge in Bruges, and died 1087; she left some jewels to the Chapter of St. Donat's (which were sold in 1389), and was buried in the cloister of St. Donat. When that church was destroyed the plate was found in the tomb and deposited here. The Church of St. Jacques is well worth seeing on account of its fine cylindrical piers (c. 1400,) and the brasses in the chapels of St. Anne and the Cross, two of which are palimpsests.

The reader will have seen that the people of Bruges were never very respectful to their Counts, and that sometimes they had good reasons for locking them up, and did not fear to do so however much they might have suffered from the bloodthirstiness of these lords when the latter were released. Probably few Counts of Flanders were more popular at Bruges then Baldwin the Ninth, who was styled of Constantinople. Nevertheless it was by no means in his honour that the people assembled one day in the streets here and shouted, " *See! See! there is the Count who married the devil!*" The children ran after his horse's footsteps with this cry, while the rude men laughed and the women grinned spitefully. The Count had no peace with this shout, so he went to Ghent, but was similarly saluted in that city. Now the occasion of this extraordinary cry was as follows—so the people said to those who enquired :—Baldwin had refused to marry Beatrice of France, who was one of the most beautiful princesses of her time in Christendom, although his people desired that he should have heirs in order to carry on the succession, and they did not see how that was to be accomplished without matrimony. The Count, it appears, thought more of hunting than of a wife, so the Lord resolved that he should be punished accordingly, as you will see. Leaving the king of France at Arras, Baldwin rode slowly homewards until he reached his own forest of Ardennes, then thickly inhabited by game of unusual size, and especially by wild boars of wonderful strength and audacity. Arrived, he set all his attendants to work, caused the huntsmen's horns to be blown, and got together several hundred men who were bound to serve him in the forest as in the field. After a day's unfortunate hunting, Baldwin was left almost alone when he came upon a black boar of great strength. This creature outwitted and outran the dogs, killed some of them, and wounded one of the hunters so severely as to exasperate the Count, whereupon he swore by St. Donat's relics never to return until the beast was dead. Onwards went the boar and after him the Count, so that they were soon alone in that part of the thicket where nothing was heard but the voices of the birds. Baldwin's horse failed him, but he still followed the game on foot until the beast turned at bay in a deep nook among rocks, where, after a struggle, it was killed by a stroke of the javelin. Baldwin cut off the monstrous head of the beast—as they always do in hunting the wild boar—after which, being very hot, he sat down to rest and cool himself in the shadow of a beech that grew beside an oak and had strewn the ground for many years with leaves that were red, yellow, or brown, according to the time they had lain on the earth.

The Count soon fell thinking, partly of the boar, partly of Beatrice of France, so that he hardly heard the soft steps of a palfrey which, bearing a lady on its back, came along through the forest. When the lady was near to him, Baldwin looked up and saw that she was the most beautiful but strange-looking maiden his eyes had seen. Uprising from his seat the Count addressed her and said, "Lady, you are welcome to me!" and bent his head in courtesy. To this she returned his own salutation, at first silently, but when he asked why she came there alone, replied in a low and sweet voice, "It is the will of God that I do so. My father is an eastern king and desired to wed me to a man I did not love; then I vowed to God, the God of heaven, that I would marry no one but the richest Count in Christendom, so I came from my father's kingdom with many servants, but I have since sent them all back, lest they should carry me to my father again, and I am going on until I meet the Count of Flanders, the noblest lord in all the west."

At this the Count, who began to love the lady, so beautiful was she, was much delighted, and said in reply, "Fair damsel, I am the Count of Flanders whom you seek, and the richest Count under heaven, for no fewer than fourteen Counts serve me in war, and several wait upon my table: I will, if it please you, take you to wife." So enamoured was Baldwin, and so ardently were his eyes bent upon the lady's face, that he saw no other thing, otherwise he would have known that all could not be right in this matter, for the enormous black boar had disappeared, head and all, and there was not even any blood upon the grass where the lady's palfrey stood. She answered to him again that she would marry him if he proved really what he said. He asked her name and that of her father, to which she replied, "My name is Helius, but my father's name I must not tell, lest he should seek me again." With this the evil spirit had full possession of Baldwin, and he set his horn to his mouth and blew so loud a recall that it was heard for miles through the woods, and even where the miners were at work on the banks of the Meuse. Then there came to him Henry, Count of Valenciennes, Walter of St. Omer, and many more, who asked what sport he had had. Not removing his eyes from the face of sweet Helius, Baldwin replied that he had found the most beautiful damsel, whom God had sent him, and whom he meant, as she agreed, to marry. The Lord of Valenciennes demurred to this, saying he did not deny her beauty, but it would be well to learn her parentage, and whether she might not be had without marriage. This pious suggestion the Count of Flanders rejected, and they set off homewards through the woods, and so onwards until they came to Cambray, where, with a great deal of splendour, the lady and the Count were married. But the people marvelled that no one came to inquire for the lady, beautiful as she was, and richly dressed. In nine months Helius bore a daughter, who was baptized by the name of Jane; and, in due time, another daughter, who was christened Margaret.* Now Helius, as the people saw, would never attend the elevation of the Host at mass, but always left before the bell was rung; and, she was hated, because they attributed to her the many taxes they had to pay. Many years passed and they still complained.

There was a great feast at Wynandael at Easter, 1188; this was given by Helius and Baldwin, and to it came no end of lords and nobles, knights and great folks, but among them was a pilgrim from the east who had brought news of the discomfiture of the emperor of Constantinople, and told how the Sultan of Sura was besieging that city with one hundred thousand Saracens. After he had related this story he asked the Count to let him have food at the lords' table, to which Baldwin, in honour of one who had travelled so far, assented, and ordered all things needful to be placed—so that the pilgrim, who was more than a hundred years old, was soon busily eating. Anon, however, Helius entered with a train of ladies, and sat by the side of Baldwin at the end of the high table; she was as beautiful as ever, although it was fourteen years since the adventure in the forest. When the pilgrim saw her he trembled and stopped eating, while even the Countess grew

---

* These were the true names of Baldwin's daughters. The former married Fernan of Portugal and, afterwards, Thomas of Savoy; she is called the Countess Jane, died 1243, and is buried at Marquettes. Margaret was mother of William de Dampierre, see before.

deadly pale at sight of him; and, turning to the Count, begged that the man might be dismissed, because he knew, she said, so many wiles, and was so cunningly wicked that no one could tell what evil he might do. But the Count would not believe her, and going to the pilgrim bade him eat freely; or, if he would, say what put him in fright. Upon this the old man got up and conjured the people who were about not to leave the hall nor fear that which might happen. He then turned to the Countess Helius and said, "Devil! thou who fillest the body of this woman, depart from it; but, ere thou goest, tell us, in the name of Christ, who drove thee out of Paradise, and by the everlasting might of God, why thou camest here and hast tempted the Count of Flanders into sin? Then go and do no harm!"

Helius, moved by the adjuration and pallid in every feature, said, "I am one of the devils whom God cast out of Paradise, because of pride. We hate the happiness of men, and try to delude them in every way. This Count was too proud to marry the king of France's daughter, so I, seeing that he might be made to perish, entered into the body of a maiden of the East who had died, although she was the fairest under the sun. This body lay alone in the chamber and there was no soul in it, because the soul had gone to its destination as God appointed it to do, so I raised it up and have inhabited it for fourteen years, and tormented the Count and all over whom he had authority, and I should have done more to him but that I had not power, because he crossed himself whenever he lay down and whenever he got up. His daughters are baptized, and I have no hold upon them. Accordingly I shall now take this body to its grave in the east country." So she vanished through a window of the hall and was never heard of any more.*

---

* Some of the learned commentators on the history of Flanders remark that there can be no truth in this story, because the Count married Mary of Champagne, daughter of Henry le Large, and Mary of France, daughter of Louis VII. Our learned friend does not tell us whose was the malicious brain which adapted this picturesque and characteristic version of the story of Lamia to a Flemish political end. With regard to the names of the daughters of Helius we have already shown the portion of truth the story contains; it is also remarkable that Mary of Champagne did go to the east, and died there before her husband. Tieck founded one of his stories on this legend. There is a version of it in Thorpe's "Netherlandish Traditions." Lumley, 1852. Baldwin was not the only noble of whom something similar is related: a

The cry against Baldwin remained, and the story goes on to say it was on this account that he went to the east, where, beyond all doubt, his life ended most remarkably. He is one of the lost rulers; like king Sebastian of Portugal, he went away and returned no more, nor from a battle-field did any message come of the lost Count. As in Sebastian's case, so in that of Baldwin, a pretender appeared in his name and disturbed his subjects. Baldwin was one of those lords who, moved by the eloquence of Foulques of Neuilly, took the Cross as one of the leaders of the Fifth Crusade; his wife Mary, who was sister of Thibault, Count of Champagne, another of the most famous enthusiasts, did likewise. The family of Champagne were crusaders for generations; the father of Mary and Thibault had been distinguished in the second expedition; their elder brother was king of Jerusalem. Such a union, independently of his own ancestral fever, led Baldwin to assume the Cross in St. Donat's Church at Bruges. Before the expedition started, he was appointed one of the six deputies who secured the assistance of the Venetians. Henry Dandolo was Doge; of him they obtained transport, on conditions which did honour to the business-like notions of the Republic. Turning aside from the Holy Land, the soldiers of the Cross captured Zara for the Venetians, and afterwards Constantinople on behalf of Prince Alexius, whose father, Isaac Angelus, was supplanted and imprisoned there by his uncle. In the presence of Dandolo the "crusaders"—as they continued to style themselves—captured the city. Quarrels, plunder, and a second siege, followed these events; three conflagrations of the most extensive sort, ruthless wreckage, sacrilege and destruction of countless works of art,* left Constantinople an

---

certain Count of Anjou, a Plantagenet—whose name, for obvious reasons, one does not mention—had the same bad luck, and lost both his children when their mother took to flight; she tucked them under her arms and disappeared towards Mount Taurus. Temporary possession by Satan was not uncommon in the Middle Ages; see the story told by Vitalis of Hervé, Count of Tours, and his wife, from whose bodies St. Martial expelled a double devil. (*Ord. Vit.* ii. 17.) Satanic paramours were even more common, and no doubt was entertained of the possibility of offspring in such unions. Caliban is an example of the last.

* These included the bronze charioteers of the Hippodrome, the Juno of Samos—so gigantic that it took eight oxen to drag away the head only from among the fragments when they were cast down, and the equestrian Bellerophon on Pegasus, to which the rapid-flowing ignorance of a few ages had already

empire almost devastated for Baldwin to rule when they placed him on the throne. He ruled but a short time. The Bulgarians came against him; they met before Adrianople; in a terrible battle he was overpowered and taken prisoner, and confined, it is said, in the fortress of Terranova; and was never heard of again. A legend avers that the wife of his conqueror fell in love with Baldwin, and proposed to facilitate his escape on condition that he would marry her; the Emperor-Count rejected this, not only because he had a wife living but for religious reasons. Upon this she accused him to her husband, and Baldwin was slain, so they say, at a banquet, and his body cast out upon the rocks at the foot of the castle. It is certain

---

given the name of Joshua commanding the sun to stand still, if indeed the pious fraud of the lovers of Art had not christened the statue as a protection against fanatics. The enormous Hercules of Lysippus, originally from Tarentum, and secondarily from the Roman Capitol; the famous Ass and its driver, wrought for Augustus to commemorate the victory of Actium; the She-wolf of Rome—probably that which Virgil celebrated—the Sphinx, Crocodile, Man fighting with the Lion, Elephant, Scylla; the wonderful eagle bearing off a serpent, said to have been wrought by the magic arts of Apollonius—a testimony to its effectiveness; the Helen, whose beauty, as Nicetas has averred, ought to have moved the conquerors to mercy and to love; the Paris; these, and countless other works of art, were turned into mere bronze, and coined to pay troops unsatiated by the plunder of Constantinople. The only great work in metal which escaped was the famous triple Bronze Serpent of the Hippodrome, which is mentioned by Herodotus himself as standing by Apollo's Altar at Delphi, and bearing the golden tripod dedicated to the god from the spoils of Platea (B.C. 476). This inestimable relic was mentioned by Thucydides, and stood at Delphi until Constantine took it to Byzantium, where it remained safe through many sieges till Mahomet II. broke one of the jaws with his mace; two hundred years later, the Polish ambassador's servants wrenched away the head. Mr. Newton, of the British Museum, recently found the lower folds of the creature still *in situ*, and inscribed upon them the very names of cities referred to by Herodotus and Thucydides as so written. Baldwin retained for himself the Crown of Thorns, and gave Philip Augustus a large piece of the true Cross, which, by some wonderful exercise of faith, was believed to have escaped capture by Saladin at Tiberias. The horses of St. Mark's, Venice, were parts of the spoil. The Golden Dragon was given to the Brugeois, as before noted, from among the spoils of this memorable plundering, which was more destructive of antique art than other acts of barbarism. The conduct of these so-called Crusaders actually justified the reproach that they took the Cross for the sake of pillage. It is to be remembered that their antagonists were Christians. Even the possession of so prodigious a relic as the Crown of Thorns did not secure the Latin Empire of Constantinople against a swift decay. Henry, Count of Namur, brother of Baldwin, succeeded him, and Peter de Courtenay, Richard de Courtenay, John de Brienne, and Baldwin II., came in turn, and the empire ended. The Crown was pledged to the Venetians, and redeemed by St. Louis, who built *La Sainte Chapelle*, in Paris, for its reception.

that a year later the Pope sent an embassy to the Bulgarian king seeking for Baldwin, and got for answer nothing more decisive than a declaration that Baldwin was not alive. The people of Flanders refused to believe the story, so that when, some twenty years afterwards, a man appeared averring that he was their lost Count, they gladly followed and obeyed him. Being defeated in battle, the impostor, by order of the Countess Jane, Baldwin's daughter, was hung, with an old dog on each side of him.

THE HÔTEL DE VILLE, BRUSSELS.

BRUSSELS is a modern city compared with Tournay, Ghent, Louvain, and other Belgian towns. It was a favourite residence of Charles II., Duke of Lower Lorraine. It was not until 1040 that the place was thoroughly and efficiently fortified; some portions of the walls then erected still exist. Louvain was capital of Brabant until 1598, although Brussels had been, as is not uncommon, the real centre of the province. It has a history similar to those of other towns of the Low Countries during the Middle Ages, and had alternately good and evil masters, but, on the whole, suffered less in respect to sieges than some others, its neighbours. Fernan, of Portugal, husband of the Countess Jane, daughter of Baldwin of Constantinople, besieged the place in 1213. After John the Third had been buried in the Abbey of Villers, as we have seen, Brabant passed to Wenceslaus of Luxembourg, but was claimed by the never-resting Louis Maele, who, within sight of Brussels, defeated his rival in 1356, and took possession of the place. He vacated it soon after, and the Duke erected a further line of fortifications which secured Brussels for a time.* The Duke of Alva left his bloody

---

* These were finished in 1379. The only existing portion is a noble round tower, called the Porte de Hal, now containing one of the most interesting collections of antiquities and works of art we know. Here are monumental brasses, enamelled and incised; Limoges enamels, both early and late; Franconian reliquaries, shrines, pyxes, seals of individuals (*secreta*), and those of monastic houses, abbeys, and towns; monumental sculpture, stained glass—some of which is of good quality—and many works in yellow stain, tapestry, brass-work; *Grès-de Flandre* pots, Flemish, German, and Venetian glass of various periods, *faïences*, majolica, Palissy ware, &c.; a very fine collection of armour and weapons, including several ancient and curious attempts at improved construction,—*e. g.*, experimental revolving and breech-loading fire-arms, with barrels turning on pivots, and chambers that are movable on hinges; many swords of beautiful design and superb metal, glaives, pointless executioners' swords with very broad blades; Spanish, English, French, and German weapons; Asiatic armour of mail, and mixed mail and plate; arms and armour

mark upon the capital of Brabant in a manner more signal than elsewhere. On the spot where the group of statues stands above a fountain, and facing the Town Hall, is the view of the Grande Place (which faces p. 144 of this book). Here the Counts Egmont and Horne were beheaded, June 5th, 1568. Alva saw the act from a window in the *Maison du Roi*, which is the house immediately behind the statues, and to which access is gained by the flight of steps where we see the woman talking to her child. Egmont was confined in a room on the second floor of this house during the night before his execution ; here he wrote his last letter to Philip II. The statues represent the victims. This act symbolizes many atrocities committed in Brussels by Alva; the city suffered hardly less by the hands of the Gueux, but with rare fortune it slept again, until the French, under Louis XIV. and Marshal Villeroy, bombarded it so unmercifully that four thousand houses were ruined, and many churches destroyed (1695). The siege did little for the assailant. Within the sixty years last passed, Brussels has more than quadrupled its inhabitants.

With regard to the Hôtel de Ville, M. Schayes, the best authority on the subject, tells us that its foundations were laid in 1401, or 1402. The right wing of the front before us,—*i. e.*, the half of the façade which is nearest the spectator in our view, extending from the tower to the Rue de l'Étuve, and the return façade in that street, were first erected. Later editions to these formed a quadrangle, such as we saw at Bruges behind the belfry, but of larger dimensions than the capital of West Flanders can show. Thus the edifice remained until 1444, when the "*jonghe heer van Sarlot—*" afterwards Charles the Bold, son of Philip the Good, who had come into possession of Brabant by the marriage of his grandfather, Philip *le Hardi*, to Margaret of Brabant, daughter of Duke John IV.—on the 4th of March, laid the foundations of the west wing

---

of northern Indian tribes; Saracenic and German mail; German, French, and English armour, black, engraved, gilded and fluted ; Spanish horse armour; a Roman *milliarium* of the third century, marked with Belgian distances, discovered at Tongres in 1817 ; a twelfth-century font of brass from Tirlemont; an ivory shrine ; tapestry embroidered by Margaret of Austria, 1503 (daughter of Maximilian *cœur d'acier*, aunt of Charles V., and Governess of the Low Countries) ; the cradle of carved wood which was used by Charles V.; the bow, and mantle of red feathers, of Montezuma, sent to Europe by Fernando Cortez, 1520.

which adjoins the spire. The name of the original architect is unknown, but, what is unusual in Gothic buildings, that of the designer of the belfry has survived,—it was Jean Van Ruysbroeck; this portion of the structure was completed in 1454. Roger Van der Weyden was a great friend of Van Ruysbroeck, and probably it was by his influence that the painters got commissions to decorate the interior of the Hôtel de Ville with four large pictures. Some very curious particulars are known concerning the arrangements between the authorities of Brussels, and Roger, their artist; he had the privilege of wearing his cloak over the right shoulder, and that cloak, which was a perquisite, was of finer cloth than that given to the architect. One of the subjects Van der Weyden painted illustrated the course of justice by the legend of Erkembald, a judge of Brussels in the eleventh century, who played the part of Brutus and slew his own son. The wing of the Hôtel de Ville which is in the Rue Tête d'Or was not begun until some time after the above-mentioned portions, and not completed until the end of the fifteenth century. That side of the open square within which is parallel to the front before us was erected in the sixteenth century, and, having been wrecked in Villeroy's bombardment, was reconstructed between 1706 and 1717. In the quadrangle are two fountains; this portion of the edifice has been restored in a barbarous *pseudo*-classic style.

The beautiful spire of the Belfry of Brussels is by far the most elegant and complete of its kind in Belgium, and deserves in Van Ruysbroeck's honour the applause of so many as have seen it. "Monument *inimitable*," as M. De Caumont says with regard to it; it has few equals anywhere. The minaret is forty feet higher than that of the Belfry at Bruges, and, being three hundred and thirty feet in height, is five feet loftier than the vane of the Victoria Tower at Westminster; it is also incomparably more graceful, and a nobler work of art than Sir C. Barry's by no means elegant, grave, or well-proportioned tower, where enormous bulk and huge masses of material, together with infinite ornaments, have failed to produce the impression they might be expected to do. The Belfry at Brussels has been recently restored with much success, so as to present the original appearance of the building; on its summit is a group of St. Michael the Archangel, patron of the city, vanquishing Satan. This was made in 1454, measures thirteen feet in height, and is composed of copper gilt, but so light in its construction as to serve for a vane. A foolish tradition, common in like cases to this, avers that the architect hung himself from the tower because, when it was finished, he discovered it not to be in the centre of the façade. One may say that if Van Ruysbroeck did not discover this before the time stated, he deserved to be hung. He was, however, living about thirty years after the spire was finished. The arcade at the foot of the façade has its caps, on the side removed from us, decorated with humorous carvings; the gallery above the other arcade is styled the *Grande Brétèque*, and was used for proclamations. Opening to this balcony is the Council Chamber, so famous in the history of Brabant; here also is the Salle du Christ, or great Municipal Hall. In the roof of the ancient portion of the façade are thirty-seven dormer windows. The reader will observe that all the windows of the front, except the lower range of the old wing, are square-headed, and enclosed by bold pointed arches; thus the often objected difficulty of adapting flat ceilings to pointed arches is obviated with fine effect, both as regards form, and light and shade, and so that great richness of surface is produced. The dormers in the left wing of the façade are of course fewer in number than those on the other wing. It will be observed that the angle turret cuts the most distant windows in half. In the interior of this edifice are many pictures and tapestries; of the latter is a set which represents Clovis's victory of Tolbiac, his marriage with Clotildis, etc., wrought after designs by Lebrun. The tympan over the principal entrance, at the foot of the Belfry, is carved with figures of SS. Michael, George, Christopher, and Sebastian. Upon the gates is some chiselled iron-work, which, although late, is admirable in execution; it comprises a bold bracket, bearing a group of St. Michael conquering Satan. The chambers of the Hôtel de Ville have been "restored" out of all ancientness.

No Grande Place in Europe equals that of Brussels in quaint and picturesque houses. Besides the Hôtel de Ville, which occupies a large portion of its western side, and the Maison du Roi, or Broodhuis (Bread House) of which we have spoken, it contains the houses of the Brewers' Guild, with a statue of Charles of Lorraine on the apex of its façade,—an outlandish decoration to English eyes: the tailors, butchers, and archers, have their Guild-houses here. The Maison du Roi was erected from the designs of Anthony Keldermans, architect to Charles V., 1515—1525. In the niche which

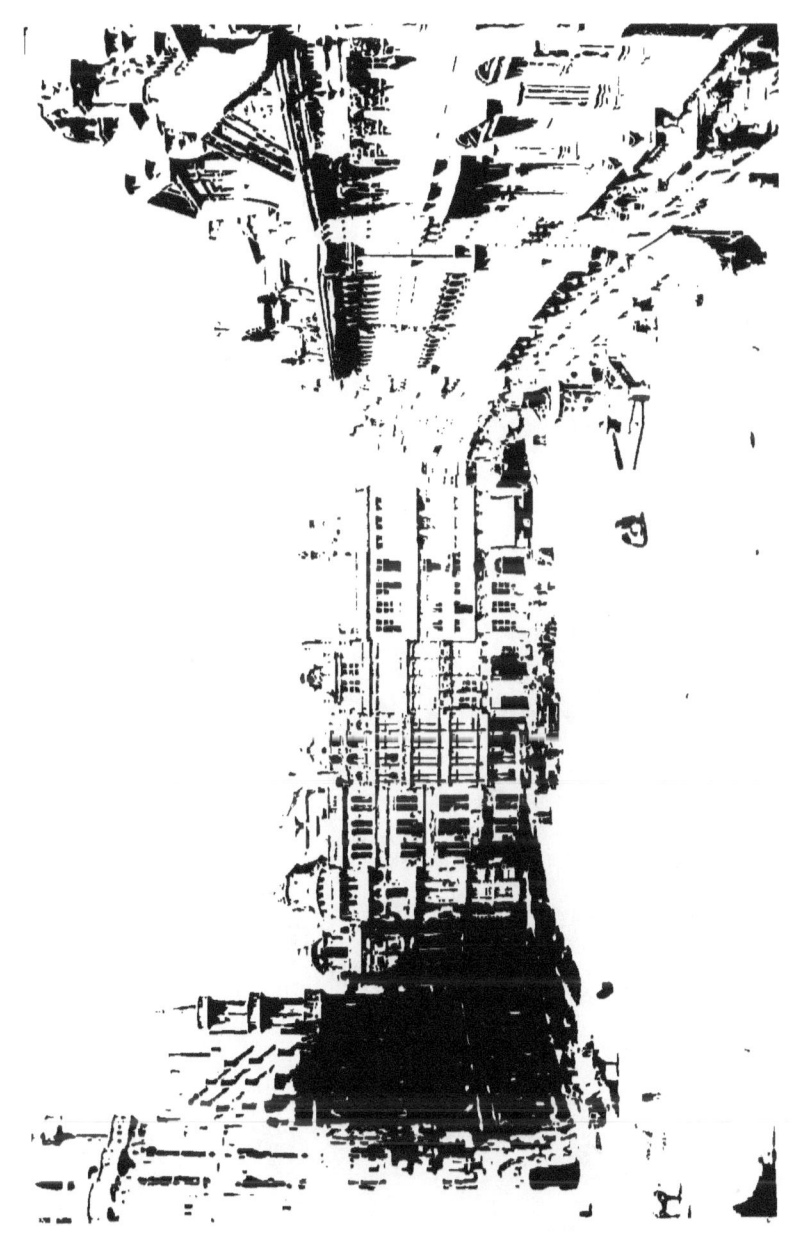

decorates its front is a statue of the Virgin, placed there to commemorate the cessation of a terrible pestilence which devastated the city in 1625. The relief does not seem to have been so effectual as might have been hoped, for in 1627, another hardly less severe pest followed. The lower parts of Brussels have been subject to dreadful attacks of this kind. Isabella, who placed this statue, was soon afterwards reduced to pledge her diamonds in the Mont de Piété, so strenuous were the assaults of the Statholder, Frederic Henry.

The houses on the north side of the Grande Place, which face us in the photograph, were built near the end of the seventeenth century, and are remarkable examples of their kind. Notice one which, with its balconies, suggests the stern of an old-fashioned man of war; this is the second from the Hôtel de Ville. On the Grande Place, in 1428, a great tournament was held by Duke Philip, which lasted for three days, when the Duke of Burgundy was entertained by his cousin and the city of Brussels, and there were between " seven and eight score helmets in the market-place, and crowds of ladies and damsels richly dressed in the fashions of the country; the sword was won by the Lord de Croy."* The chronicler tells us that when the Duke of Burgundy returned into Flanders a few days after this, the weather was very severe, with frost and snow. Such accompaniments are not common in our idea of tournaments.

The picture gallery at Brussels contains many admirable works; 1,—The wings of the triptych, by Hubert and John Van Eyck, in the Church of St. Bavon, Ghent; 2,—the "Adoration of the Magi," by John Van Eyck; 3,—Head of a woman weeping, by Roger Van der Weyden, and others by George Van der Weyden; 4,—A bishop preaching, by Memline; 5,—" Christ at the house of Simon the Pharisee," by Jan de Maubeuge; 6,—" The Virgin and Child," by Quentin Mastys; 7, 8, 9,—Portraits of Queens Elizabeth and Mary, and King Edward IV. of England, of unknown authorship; 10,—Portrait of Sir T. More, by Holbein. Ten paintings by Rubens; also many by Vandyke, Breughel, De Heem, Van der Helst, Ruysdael, Giorgione, Tintoretto, Veronese, and a huge collection of unmitigated rubbish. Of modern paintings none will interest the student so much as M. Leys' " Re-establishment of Roman Catholic

* Monstrelet, Book ii, 54.

Worship at Antwerp." The public library contains many MSS., printed books, and illuminations of great interest. Behind the Hôtel de Ville is a fountain which is surmounted by the *Mannekenpis*, a statue by J. de Quesnoy, which has had the extraordinary fate to be carried away by almost every conqueror of the city, and as often returned to its original place here. There exists a superstition among natives of Brussels that no conqueror will long retain this quaint figure. The history of the *Manneken* justifies the legend ; he has been stolen by the people of Antwerp, by the English after the battle of Fontenoy, by the French under Louis XV., by the English again at a later period, and, we believe, by the Dutch. Each time he has come back to his old place here, where he possesses many honours, and even some estates. Louis XV. made him a knight of St. Louis ; Charles V., the Elector of Bavaria, and Peter the Great, pensioned him, so that he has not only a servant to look after his person, but legal officers who administer his estate. Long may they enjoy their offices, and long may the figure remain in Brussels! Another fountain in the *Marché au Cherbon*, styled *le Cracheur*, is the second remarkable work of the kind in this city, which contains twenty-nine in all.

THE CHURCH OF ST. MICHAEL AND ST. GUDULE, BRUSSELS.

THE situation of this famous church presented advantages which its architects did not neglect. Placed on the side of a hill, and nearly in the middle of the city, its noble twin towers of the west end have great impressiveness, and are aided in their effect by the double flight of steps and platforms from which they arise. Of late the exterior of this edifice has been cleared from those encroaching houses, which, as with other Belgian and French churches, did so much to mar its design. Notwithstanding the opinions of many, and a certain evident picturesqueness which accrues to ancient buildings of this class from the clustering of quaint habitations against their walls, and even between their buttresses, it appears to us absurd to deny that, in general, the gain is great when these dangerous parasites are knocked off. It, doubtless, is true that the mediæval designers did not intend their great intramural works to be seen surrounded by vast spaces, but it is equally plain that such incrustations as we see on nearly all continental churches were not contemplated by architects and founders. In fact the avidity of the ecclesiastical authorities in those countries has been the cause of many noble buildings being smothered in this manner, and afterwards destroyed by fire. The improvement which has been effected by clearing the exterior of the church before us is unquestionably great.

By means of the double flight of steps at its west end, this church has what classic buildings never lacked,—*i. e.*, *podium*, or base; they now return in two flights, but originally had but one slope from each side of the façade, the effect of which could hardly have been so happy as that of the present double flight, which rises in thirty-six stairs and two landings. Some authorities have presumed that the towers, which are 223 feet in height, finished 1518, were originally crowned with spires; there appears to be no evidence in favour of this idea, but, as M. Schayes says, it is probable that they were united by a large flat arch of extreme boldness. If so they resembled in this respect the towers of the Church of Notre Dame at Mantes. In front of each tower is a doorway, opening to the aisles within, and, in the centre of the façade, a double doorway (1518) opens to the nave; all four of these are surmounted by lancet arches, the latter two are coupled, and have above them a rayonnant window; the front is finished by a gable with a beautiful parapet. If ever the west front of Westminster Abbey is relieved of its uncouth additions, here is a model which, if the elements are properly adapted to the style of that edifice, might supply what we are bound to believe Wren intended when he exercised his fine feeling for the picturesque upon such wretched materials and incongruous decorations. The south side of St. Gudule is strikingly picturesque by means of its range of chapels, which with their acute gables, line the side of the edifice, and enrich, with the happiest effect, the lofty church to which they are attached. Each chapel has a gable with crocketted mouldings of elegant character; bold flying buttresses, with well-designed pinnacles and little gargoyles, add to the design. The whole of this view of the church gains by the rich Flamboyant pierced parapet on the wall-plats of the nave, and the enormous expanse of the high-pitched roof, whereon the eye falls with pleasure and finds repose. This portion was finished at a comparatively late period, but in pursuance probably to an earlier design. The front of the south end of the transept (c. 1273) is rather poor, notwithstanding that it has a good porch attached to it, dated 1499. The other end of the transept was completed at the same time as the towers, 1518. The west windows of the choir, and the gravely designed buttresses between them, give great effect to this part of the church (c. 1273), which is severe and fine; the tracery in the windows is of richer character and later date, but good of its kind. The exterior of the east end proper is extremely beautiful, and would be more so but for the hideous little chapel of St. Mary Magdalene (1673), which unhappily protrudes from its extremity. Here are double flying buttresses, crocketted, standing over the roofs of the radiating chapels; the buttresses themselves of this part are surmounted by picturesque little tabernacles, or tomb-canopies, which resemble so many models of a tomb. These are quite new, and probably of the original form. The canopy, or pyramid of tracery, which surmount the heads of the windows, here pierce the parapet, which is comparatively low, and wrought with quatrefoils. There is much good pierced work on the exterior of this edifice. The immense lateral chapels of the choir, before alluded to, are late additions; that on the north, which is dedicated to *St. Sacrement des Miracles*,* displays enormous windows containing, we are sorry to say, much bad stained glass. The chapel on the south side of the choir is dedicated to Our Lady of Deliverance, and was completed in 1653; this displays some good painted glass of its kind, executed by Van Thielden and Baer, of Antwerp, about 1656.

The interior of St. Gudule is wonderfully effective, unspoilt by the common jubé or *rococo* altar-piece. The *chevet* is a fine Gothic work of the best period (*c.* 1273). The triforium is completely developed; that part which is above the choir is remarkable on account of exhibiting something like plate-tracery in the head of each opening of the coupled arches; the shafts which divide the last are thick and rather clumsy, but not unhandsome; the apse is five-sided. The piers, except on one side of the transept, are cylindrical; those of the nave are degraded in architectural character, by statues of the Apostles placed against them and, unfortunately, of larger size than common; the caps of the pillars are decorated with knots of oak-leaves in two rows, backed by a sort of trellis, and are very elegant. The *abaci* are octangular, the bases are unusually low—probably because the floor has been raised, so as to hide a portion of them. The mouldings of the nave arcade are very simple, and do not project beyond the face of the wall. The vaulting shafts, which are clustered and have caps and bases, rest on the *abaci* of the piers. The triforium of the nave is rather clumsy, although of Decorated construction; it is without carving of any sort, and formed by a range of simple, narrow lancets. The clerestory

---

* So dedicated to commemorate the miraculous transactions which followed the theft by a Jew of three wafers of the Host, which were deposited here about 1380. The story is very shocking, whether we take the point of view which is proper to the received character of the wafers,—that which pertains to the transaction in general,—or a merely humane one, which concerns itself with the wretched Jews, who were, whether guilty or not, burnt alive. The story is illustrated by the stained glass of the chapel windows.

comprises six lights with rich and varied Geometrical heads (those before us are restorations, of tracery. This part dates from *c.* 1518. The south end of the transept and part of that on the north, are coeval in date with the choir (1273.) The remainder of the south end appears to have been built at the same time as the nave. The bases of the vaulting in the nave are richer than is usual in Belgium; the roof dates from 1518.

In the choir ambulatory we find Romanesque windows (*c.* 1170). The mass of this portion, which is very fine indeed, dates from a century later. The arcade of the choir has three openings only; the arches of the *chevet*, or extreme east end of the choir, are transitional and almost semi-circular; the Romanesque parts appear to belong to the building of Duke Henry of Lorraine. The church was founded by Lambert, Count of Louvain, in 1047, when the relics of St. Gudule were brought here.*

---

* St. Gudule, to whom, conjointly with St. Michael, this magnificent church is dedicated, is one of the luckiest of saints in that respect, and would be otherwise rather obscure among the saints. She was grand-niece of Pepin of Landen, daughter of St. Amalberga, and educated by St. Gertrude, her god-mother, at Nivelles. She had a habit of rising early in the morning to prayers. One day the lantern which her maid carried before her on the road to church went out by the doing of Satan, and was miraculously relighted at her prayers. She died 712.

HOTEL DE VILLE, LOUVAIN.

THE HÔTEL DE VILLE AT LOUVAIN.

LOUVAIN is one of the oldest towns in the Low Countries. Some say that Julius Cæsar founded it, others declare for a temple of Mars having stood here during the reigns of the late emperors. The fact probably is that the Emperor Arnould having built a castle here, to oppose the Normans, and check their incursions in the country of Lower Lorraine, gave to it the title of the Cæsars' Castle, so that it was the Germanic rather than the Roman Cæsar to whom the origin of the place is due. This emperor, in 891, defeated the Normans who were intrenched here, under their duke Godfrey, and enlarged their camp so as to make that a place of defence which had, ere then, served for the contrary purpose. Thus the tradition is accounted for which gives to Louvain a Roman origin. The first Count of Louvain whose name is known to us died in 985; in 1165 the town was encircled with walls, having forty towers upon them. Long before that time, the Counts had so extended their power, that the whole neighbouring country obeyed them; the title of Duke of Lower Lorraine was given to Godfrey the First, in 1106. The place, like others in this country, was famous for its manufactures of woollens, to which it owed its prosperity, and in some degree, no doubt, its decay. The weavers quarrelled with their counts, their magistrates, with each other, and were ultimately expelled. The castle, which had been for centuries the chief seat of the dukes, was, after the middle of the eleventh century, neglected by them in preference for Brussels as a residence, a choice not hard to be accounted for, when we consider the salubrity of the latter place. In this castle, duke Henry the First was assassinated in 1038,* another good reason for the removal of his successors. Three centuries and a half later Louvain con-

---

* Of this castle a small part still exists near the Mechlin gate of the town, a quarter of Louvain which repays a visit to the enormous earthworks it exhibits. Here resided Edward the First of England, in 1338.

tained more than two hundred thousand persons, so it could not be said to depend greatly on the presence of its lords.

The university of Louvain, which soon become famous throughout Europe, was founded by John the Fourth, last duke of Brabant, in 1426; and about a hundred and fifty years later than this, *i.e.*, in 1578, more than forty-four thousand persons died of the plague in Louvain. Gramaye tells us that in the civil wars of the sixteenth century, about three thousand three hundred houses were burnt here. Among many famous students at the university, probably none is better known, or on the whole more highly esteemed, than Erasmus, who lived and laboured here during the seven years which preceded 1522. In one of his fits of grumbling, this giant of erudition and able thinker declared it was better for a man to cultivate a garden than literature; he did not, because of his grumbling, cease to labour. Charles V. was another noteworthy pupil of Louvain, where he was under the charge of Adrian Boyens (Pope Adrian VI.) Francis Baudoin, the famous civilian, was educated here. Duke John the Fourth conceded to the university the ancient *Halle des Drapiers* of this town, a building which was never finished, because the weavers to whom it belonged were expelled from the city. It is still two hundred feet long and fifty feet in width, and, although the ancient portion is merely a ground floor, still impresses one by its great size. An inscription on one of its angles gives the names of the architects as Jean Stevens, Arnould Hore, and Gort Racs, together with the date 1317[*] as that of the foundation. It remained unused for more than a century, and is said to have been almost in ruins when appropriated to its present use. The university still exists, but can hardly be said to flourish; in its prime, forty-six colleges and about six thousand students were attached to this institution.

The Hôtel de Ville, which is probably the most richly decorated edifice of its class in the world, was begun on the Thursday after Easter, 1448, and finished in 1463. Although it is said to have cost no more than 82,786 florins, this building is exuberant of tourelles, canopies, statues, brackets, tracery, dormers, and other quaint ornaments proper to the style, which we cannot but feel it illustrates rather extravagantly. Recent researches have given the

---

[*] Schayes, Part II.

name of Matthew de Layens as that of the architect; he was a pupil of S. Van Vorst. The interior was finished in 1467. Although so rich, it is probably the smallest building of its class in any of the chief towns of the Low Countries; the dimensions are one hundred and thirteen feet long, forty-one feet wide, and seventy-three feet in height to the parapet. Unfortunately, time, which spares nothing, was peculiarly effective on the elaborate details of this building, so that a few years since it was taken in hand and restored at a vast expense. This operation, never wholly satisfactory, has sufficed to preserve for us the general appearance of the structure, and has not been entirely mischievous to the architectural details: the carvings, however, have, as might be expected, not been so fortunate; they are not now either so full of spirit in design, or of truly admirable execution as of old: this is attested by the ancient fragments preserved in the building. The new work is hard and liney.

It would be difficult to over-estimate the variety of the carvings on this façade; the brackets bearing the statues are decorated with subjects from the Old and New Testaments, which are arranged in chronological order, and begin at the lower stage and are continued in each tier from left to right. It appears that the niches, of which there are two hundred and eighty-two, were never until now filled with statues; the series of those works, as we observe in the photograph, is not yet complete; sculptures with this destination are still in hand. How much they yield of beauty to the front may be seen by comparing the end of the Hôtel de Ville, where no statues are, with the front, which exhibits a large number. Those in the lower tier represent Quentin Mastys, Pope Adrian VI., Stuerbout, Erasmus, Justus Lipsius, De Layens the architect, Pope Martin V., Elzevir the printer, and others. Not only the carving, but the six tourelles, the parapets, gargoyles, and almost all the architectonic works on this exterior, have been replaced. The ancient sculptures display a great deal of that humour or *naïveté* which characterizes works of the period in which they were wrought. The steps by which one enters the building are of the last century, 1709. The old parapet here was of wrought iron, by J. Metsys. The interior of the Hôtel de Ville is well worth seeing, although much of its ancient beauty is gone. The roof of the "Hall of Lost Footsteps" is of oak, resting on the original carved corbels of stone, 1449. The roof of the "Marriage Hall" on the first floor, which is of chesnut wood, is also fine with corbels and basses of New Testament subjects. These are rather later than those just mentioned. Another room shows a roof with beautifully carved pendants, 1468.

In the Grande Place at Louvain, opposite to the Hôtel de Ville, stands the very beautiful Church of St. Peter, which must have been in hand at the same time as its civic neighbour. This church is nearly three hundred feet in length, and seventy-five feet in breadth. It had originally two immense towers at the west end; these are now imperfectly replaced. Of all the Belgian churches this one is most completely inclosed by houses,—the latter leave free no part of the wall which is below the windows, while even the entrances are crowded. This is the more to be lamented, because the structure is homogeneous, and was executed from a single original plan. An ugly wooden bell-turret at the crossing does much to mar the exterior. As in the cathedral at Antwerp, (which see) the Church of St. Peter shows the continuous impost in its piers; the whole of these are apparently of later date than those in the example quoted. The pier mouldings have a rectangular character proper to late work. The triforium resembles that at Mechlin (c. 1452); the tracery is Flamboyant, and much of it very beautiful. The choir has not been disfigured by the black and white marble screen so common in Belgium, but retains its original highly decorated carved jubé (c. 1450) of stone, gilt, and bearing statues of Christ, the Virgin, etc., a superb piece of Flamboyant work which is quite pleasant to see. It displays flat ogee arches in three openings, which are cusped in a florid manner with carvings that seem to ripple along the inner edges, and is crocketted on the outer edges with deeply pierced work of acanthus foliage. Twenty-four statuettes stand on the upper part in niches that are surmounted by tabernacles. The noble rood over this jubé has five statues by its sides; the whole is singularly effective. This screen does not intercept the view of the high-altar; that high altar, although a florid piece of barbarism, is, being smaller, less obstructive than common.* Several of the chapels contain in-

---

* Much of the ancient furniture of this choir has been removed to Oscott, near Birmingham.

teresting aumbries, the iron fittings to which are very good; they comprise locks, hinges, and air-holes,—the last having the form of the Crown of Thorns; these are evidently original, and of fifteenth-century date. One of the money-boxes—that to the Chapel of St. Cornelius—is noteworthy, on account of its rough quaintness. In the Chapel of St. John is a recumbent, woefully restored statue of Duke Henry the First of Brabant, with a sceptre in hand and an *almonière* at his girdle through which pieces of money show themselves. By the side of the high altar is a superb tabernacle for the Host, which is nearly fifty feet high, and was designed by the architect of the Hôtel de Ville. This has brass doors, infinite pinnacles, and carvings in stone of the Passion, statuettes, etc. Before the jubé hangs a fine, twelve-armed chandelier of iron, by J. Metsys. In the south aisle is a large Byzantine crucifix—black, on which the figure wears an ancient robe of red velvet, embroidered with stars and tongues in gold and, in the archaic manner, reaching to the feet, probably a work of the tenth or eleventh century. There is another interesting crucifix on the north side of the nave. In two chapels of the south ambulatory are fine carvings in stone—1. the Trinity. 2. Saints presenting devotees—both fifteenth-century works, full of expression and pathos. We must content ourselves with naming but few of the treasures of this Church, and omit even the names of pictures by Stuerbout, Q. Matsys, Van der Weyden, etc., together with a bronze font, reliquaries, thuribles, embroideries, etc.

THE CATHEDRAL AT MECHLIN.*

HIS is the metropolitan church of Belgium, and, although its magnificent tower is unfinished, is one of the most impressive ecclesiastical buildings in that kingdom. As the traveller approaches the city, this tower is discernible above the trees and across the country for many miles. Unlike many edifices of its class, this one does not lose its effectiveness on near inspection, but, on the contrary, our admiration for its dignity and noble proportions is enhanced by contemplation of its elegance in detail, and mixed with surprise on finding that so fine a work was begun in the middle of the fifteenth century (1452), and still in hand so late as 1583. At the period indicated by the former of these dates, Gothic architecture had greatly declined in France and England, so that we do not recollect any similar structure of that time in those countries which, in stateliness and grace, can compare with the grandest feature of the cathedral at Mechlin.

It is true that the art in question, as was characteristic of a state of decadence, achieved its latest triumphs in building towers, which are pompous rather than serviceable structures, but still the nobility of the vast work before us is remarkable as having been designed

---

* This church is dedicated to St. Rumauld, Rumold, or Rumbold, one of the earliest missionaries in the Low Countries, who was martyred here, June 24th, 775. He succeeded Bishop Walraf in the see by the injunction of an angel who, according to the legend, again appeared and commanded him to resign the dignity. He gave sight to the blind, relieved men of evil spirits which were in possession of their bodies, restored a young nobleman to life, and did other miraculous acts. Having reproved a man who was living in adultery, he was killed by the latter with a hoe; hence that instrument is emblematic of the saint. After his death Rumauld succoured Mechlin when besieged, and restored sight and life to persons who were connected with this city. Not many years since twenty-five paintings of the fourteenth century were found under the whitewash in a chapel of the ambulatory of this cathedral. These works represented the chief events in St. Rumauld's career; they have been whitewashed over again. St. Rumauld's day is the 1st of July.

THE CATHEDRAL, MECHLIN.

after those beautiful perpendicular turrets were erected to adorn the comparatively remote coast of England, and signalize certain parishes by their handsomeness:—the church towers of St. Cuthbert at Wells, and St. Mary at Taunton, are examples in point. The tower at Mechlin is three hundred and nineteen feet in height, but, had the spire, which was designed to complete the work, been added, the vane would have stood no less than four hundred and twenty-three feet in the air. As it is, the climber to the gallery which appears above the skeleton dial may discern on the south, the twin towers of St. Gudule, Brussels, and on the north the soaring spires of the cathedral at Antwerp. The dial is forty-eight feet in diameter; this will give an idea of its distance from the ground, but in examining the photograph, the reader who would obtain a full conception of the altitude of this tower, must remember that part of its base is hidden by trees; the ground-line is, however, discernible between their stems. Enormous as is the mass of masonry forming this part of the cathedral, its base is perforated for the great western entrance, and, until lately, the grand arch which occupies its lower storey within was open to and a part of the interior of the church. Not many years ago an organ gallery was placed under the tower, much to the injury of the effect.

It is needless to describe that which is before the reader in the mass; some account, however, of the details of this remarkable tower may be welcome. The structure is in two stages, to which the spire was destined to form a third.* These are divided by a parapet of pierced work, which marks the place of a platform between the buttresses; a similar parapet which crowns the second stage is placed upon a cornice, and follows the form of the buttresses, so as to constitute a very noble element of the work. The buttresses are marked in stages. The windows have bold, cusped and crocketted hood-mouldings; those in the lower storey are very deeply recessed. The wall above these is marked by blind tracery and mullions of Perpendicular character, as in similar English works; the windows of the upper storey rise from the lower parapet nearly to the cornice, and are divided both longitudinally and trans-

---

* The materials for the spire of Mechlin Cathedral were already on the ground when, in 1583, the work was stopped by order of the Prince of Orange, who transported the stones to Holland, and used them in building the town of Williamstadt.

versely by mullions and transoms; above their heads appear blind-tracery, as below. The whole is enriched by pinnacles and tabernacle work, which, although the details of those parts are florid in character, do not overload the composition.

The church itself is cruciform in plan, and so lofty that, enormous as is the altitude of the tower, from some points of view the latter seems disproportionately small for its huge adjunct. Many parts, including the tower, have been restored; hence a certain hard look of the decorations is apparent even in the photograph. It is difficult to describe where the original work ends and the new begins. The sides of the nave are, at present, very plain: the north end of the transept has been restored, with nine lancets in the gable; that gable is crocketted, and stands between elegant pinnacles. The richest part of the exterior is the east end, which was in hand from 1366 till 1451, when the apse was finished in accordance with the original design. The chapels of the ambulatory, or choir aisle, and those of the east end, project beyond the buttresses, and do not merely fill up the spaces between them, as is most common in Belgium. The whole of this part of the work is rather French in appearance, showing deeply recessed windows, the crocketted pyramids above which pierce the parapet with their carved finials; the parapet is light and elegant. The chapels of the choir aisles show carved and moulded gables, crockets, richly wrought pinnacles, and fine Geometrical tracery in the windows. Much, if not all, of the last is modern; it is, however, carefully varied in design, and adds much to the rich effect of the whole. The buttresses bear high pinnacles, which have statues placed under canopies on their fronts; the gargoyles are quaint, but not too prominent.

The interior of the nave of this cathedral resembles in some respects that of the church of St. Jacques at Antwerp;* it was completed in 1487, *i.e.*, more than a century after the choir. In the base of the tower there are two windows on each of the three closed sides; the fourth, as before stated, is open to the church. The piers are cylindrical, with round bases; the last have a water-holding moulding beneath a fillet, and above a very bold torus. The carving of the caps is rigid, hard, and late in its character. Contrary to the principles of good design, the foliage is not developed from the

---

* See the photograph at p. 170.

form of the vase, but merely attached arbitrarily to it; the caps, which are octangular, are, nevertheless, well and gracefully proportioned to the piers both as respects height and depth. The vaulting shafts rest on the pier capitals, are triple, and have prettily carved caps and bases of their own. The clerestory is rather too low for good proportion. The triforium, or rather wall-passage, is faced by panels of pierced work of Perpendicular character. The vaulting of the church is ribbed and groined throughout.

As was to be expected from the date of its construction, a complete triforium appears in the choir; it is faced by a sort of cage of tracery; the wall-space above the arcade of the choir is panelled, each panel forms a quatrefoil. The continuous impost* appears in the outer columns at the east end of this church. The clustered columns of the crossing and lower walls of the transept are remains of a beautiful church which stood here, and was finished in 1312, and burnt in 1341. The carvings in the spandrels of the wall arcade at the north end of the transept are very lovely, and good examples of the best period of decorative sculpture. There is stained glass of the fifteenth century in the clerestory of this part of the church. The greatest misfortune that has befallen this church is the addition of those statues of saints which have been stuck against the piers of the nave, and still stand, spoiling their fair proportions, ruining the grace of their lines, breaking the vista, and degrading their office to foolishness. A hideous black and white marble screen mars the interior; it does so, however, as regards the choir, in a less degree than is common, because it is interposed between the piers of that part, and is not, as is usual, placed within the space they inclose, so as to hide their outlines and reduce their apparent height. The high altar is a wonderful piece of false classicality. Here, also, are the commonplace and elaborately carved tomb-statues of archbishops and bishops of later days, but not a mediæval monument nor a fragment of old stained glass.

Among all the examples of bad taste we meet with in Belgium, the pulpit in this cathedral is the most astounding; as it is typical

---

* That is, the piers are unbroken by capitals, so that the mouldings of the archivolt descend to the floor, as in Antwerp cathedral; see the photograph at p. 164.

of a multitude of such works, and surpasses them all in extravagance; —let us describe it. The reader who is not familiar with erections of this order, needs to be told that the leading feature of the pulpit in question is a representation of the conversion of St. Paul, produced, not in panelled bas-reliefs and as part of the construction, but in the form of an independent group of figures designed to that end, which appears in front and at the foot of the rostrum, but has, otherwise, nothing to do with it. A great deal more, however, is expressed than this one subject can aim at. The pulpit is mainly a rock (of pine wood) elaborately sculptured with imitative details of the most extraordinary and incongruous kinds ever brought together in an artistic production; the execution throughout is of the most minute order, and must have absorbed a vast amount of time and skill of the mechanical sort. Upon this rock, ivy is seen creeping among its fissures or hanging pendent from its angles; lilies and other flowers are at the foot; long trailing plants appear everywhere; branches of trees of considerable size, all wonderfully wrought with leaves and twigs, enrich, but do not decorate, the surface. Among other extravagances appear a snail, a lizard, two frogs, and a squirrel. In front the (wooden) crag beetles over; at its foot lies St. Paul, as if just cast from his horse; the horse is in the act of struggling to regain its feet. Both statues are of the size of life. In features, costume, and long hair, St. Paul is not unlike a woman; in fact, he very happily represents the sculptural idea of a man at the end of the seventeenth century, the period when this preposterous pulpit was wrought. From the earth, just before the horse's feet, rises a pomegranate tree which is laden with bursting fruit and has ensconced among its branches a pelican busily feeding its young. The preacher appears in a thicket of carven branches. Perched upon a ledge, and at about five feet from the ground on the right-hand, is a group of life-sized statues, comprising (1) Christ upon the Cross, (2) the Virgin in an attitude of declamation, rather than of lamentation—as might have been intended—and (3) Martha weeping at the foot of the Cross. On another ledge, a little higher up, stands Mary Magdalen, also weeping. Close to this group appears the Tree of Life, dead, with the serpent among its branches. The Tree of the Knowledge of Good and Evil, a stout oak, forms, by means of one of its branches, a handrail to a flight of stairs which are wrought in the true tea-garden or "rustic" style to represent roughly-hewn stones; the stairs give access to the embowered pulpit; by their side sits a chubby little angel, busily engaged with a chisel and mallet in carving a coat of arms upon the fractured surface of a bough which pertains to the Tree of the Knowledge of Good and Evil. From one of the steps rises a fig-tree; behind its entangled branches appear Adam and Eve; the latter plucks at the fruit which a serpent, much larger than that before mentioned, bites from its pedicle so that it shall fall into the hand of the mother of mankind. By way of sounding-board there appears, above all this extraordinary mass and "higgledy-piggledy" of carvings and subjects, a gigantic slab or table of rock, the upper surface of which is covered with a forest of bushes growing *en masse*, but elaborated in manner so perfectly imitative that it might drive to despair G. Gibbons and other mere mockers of nature in wood. Above the preacher's head a wooden dove hovers and bears a label in its beak, upon which is inscribed "*Consummatum est!*"

Mechlin contains a considerable number of ancient buildings: among them the most interesting is Les Halles, which stands in the Grande Place, forming one side of the great square shown in the photograph. This was commenced in 1340, but its erection was not at that period carried beyond the first storey, and a fine but not lofty central tower. About 1520 the works were recommenced and, shortly afterwards, again stopped until about eighty years later, when they were resumed for a time, to be suspended as they still remain. The whole forms a very picturesque mass of buildings which are peculiarly mediæval in appearance. On the north side some fine work remains in the upper storey, comprising clustered and deeply cut shafts, with good bases; these have never been finished, and a roof has been placed between them. The lower storey of this front has some late and coarse Flamboyant work in the house-fronts which have been interposed between the more ancient masses that extend for at least one hundred and fifty feet. An arcade, such as was proper to edifices of this class, was doubtless originally intended to go entirely round the base of the structure; some parts of this may have been constructed, as would appear from the traces of very acute lancets which still exist on the walls. At the south-east angle is a high mass of building with turrets and a double-peaked roof. On the north of the cathedral, by the side

M

of the Haes Concordia, appears an ancient house (*c.* 1480), exhibiting a solar with triple lights, which is bracketted out from the wall and has a high pitched roof, the whole having a strange twist, which is due probably to a bad foundation. On the *Zoutwerf (Quai au Sel)*, or Salt-wharf, is a very good and richly decorated Renaissance house, " *In den Grooten Zalmm,*" which bears carved friezes, panelling, bases, pilasters, arcades, etc., together with sculptured sea-deities, fish, and the like emblems. On the Grande Place, the Hôtel de la Grue, and its neighbouring *estaminet*, the latter of which is nearly complete, show fronts of good domestic Gothic design, of Decorated character, enriched by corbels and an arcade of three-centred arches, mouldings, etc. The *Musée* is a nearly perfect structure, less rich, but of the same period as the above, and apparently designed by the architect of Les Halles. Of two old houses on the *Haverwerf (Quai des Avoines)*, or Oat-wharf, one has a wooden front which is full of quaint carvings; the pillars on each side of the door exhibit a boy statuette holding a shield; on the sides of the window of the first stage appear satyrs, and, on the mullion, a faun, all grinning; higher up, on the second tier, appears a series of nine quaint brackets placed between the windows and carved with grotesque figures of warriors, a king, queen, etc. The verge-board shows a seraph at each foot. Next to this quaint structure, which is in a sad state of decay, and at the corner of Kraen Straet, stands a house of later date (*c.* 1610), which is fronted with stone and adorned with sculptures representing Eve tempting Adam, the Expulsion from Paradise, *amorini*, etc. A third house bears a curious carving of God and Christ, and the date, 1669, when the upper part was erected. Near to these houses and by the side of the quay stands one of those gigantic cranes which were once so common in the Low Countries, retaining its enormous tread-wheel of thirty feet in diameter by which the huge bill or arm of the machine is employed to raise goods in and out of craft which lie beside it; a very quaint and now scarce object in Belgium. Of the ancient walls of Mechlin, a grim, high-roofed, fourteenth-century gateway, with two bastions, machicolations, etc., alone remains. No city in Belgium is so rich as Mechlin in quaint buildings; Gothic, Renaissance, and what we call Jacobean houses abound. Although they have plenty of elbow-room, it is fair also to say that the inhabitants of this city appear indifferent to the power and wonderful variety of the stinks which astonish strangers.

Among the treasures which this city boasts is Vandyke's "Crucifixion," which is in the cathedral. The triptych, styled the "Adoration of the Magi," by Rubens, is in the Church of St. John, and shows in its wings the deaths of SS. John the Baptist and the Evangelist; and outside, the former in the desert, and the latter at Patmos. Beneath appears the Crucifixion, which originally had for companions the Adoration of the Shepherds and the Resurrection; the last two remain in Paris, whereto they were removed at the Revolution. Rubens produced the whole of these pictures in eighteen days; they are worthy of the effort. In Notre Dame are more pictures by this artist, comprising eight of his most famous productions; these were wrought in ten days, and intended to represent the Miraculous Draught of Fishes, etc.; of this series part remains at Paris. The statue which is visible in the foreground of the photograph, commemorates Margaret of Austria, and is the work of M. Geefs; though rather heavy in its contours, it is dignified in design and a better work than the same artist's rather melodramatic figure of Rubens, in the Place Verte, Antwerp, and that of Christine de Lalaign, which stands in the Grande Place at Tournay. Even the last-named statue surpasses in artistic value the popular group of Godfrey de Bouillon and his horse, by M. E. Simonis, which is so conspicuous in the Place Royale, Brussels, a production which, although much less rudely executed, is nearly as meretricious in design as Baron Marochetti's theatrical Richard *Cœur de Lion*, which attitudinizes in Palace Yard at Westminster.

THE CATHEDRAL OF NOTRE DAME, AT ANTWERP.

HIS Cathedral, of which one of our views shows the nave, and the other the first aisle on the south side, was begun in 1352, and carried on, probably with intervals of abeyance, until late in the sixteenth century (1541). Broadly speaking, a general plan seems to have been adhered to throughout, so that the whole presents a tolerably uniform aspect; its parts differ in detail, but are nevertheless homogeneous in form. The cathedral is cruciform in plan, and derives no small portion of its reputation from its vast bulk and the extent of space it encloses. One of the largest cathedrals in the world, it measures three hundred and eighty-four feet in length, by two hundred and fourteen feet three inches, at the transept, and is one hundred and seventy feet wide at the nave. The roof is sustained by no fewer than one hundred and twenty-five columns, if columns they can be called which have no capitals and constitute the most numerous aggregation of shafts that exhibit the "continuous impost." This characteristic gives to the interior an appearance which is not wholly pleasing; it must be borne in mind, however, that the actual state of this edifice does not fairly represent the architect's intention, inasmuch as the altitude of the piers before us is less than was originally the case. In the very darkest time of Art, *i.e.*, about the middle of the last century (1745), the floor of Antwerp cathedral was raised no less than two feet, thus the bases of the piers are now hidden; the effect of this barbarous act, which was supposed to be rendered necessary by the growth of the ground outside the building, has been lamentable. Independently of its vastness, this cathedral derives much reputation, and a peculiarly striking aspect, from its having a nave and six aisles,

INTERIOR OF THE CATHEDRAL, ANTWERP.

THE TRIPLE AISLE, ANTWERP CATHEDRAL.

three on each side. Three of the latter, together with a portion of the ambulatory of the choir, one of the choir chapels, and the transept, are displayed in the second photograph.*

---

* The picture which appears on the wall of the transept before us, and has the veil drawn off its surface, is Rubens's masterpiece, the famous triptych, representing in the centre, the " Taking down from the Cross," and in the wings respectively, the " Visitation," of which we see part, and the " Presentation in the Temple." These pictures have been frequently engraved, and need not be criticised here. The Royal Academy of Arts, London, possesses a fine copy of the whole. The President of that Institution, Sir Joshua Reynolds, has written an admirable criticism on this and its companion work, the " Elevation of the Cross," which occupies a similar position in the other limb of the transept. The story is told that at the request of Albert and Isabella, Governors of the Low Countries, Rubens agreed to reside in Antwerp, and built himself a house; doing this, he trenched on land belonging to the Company of Arquebusiers who, in consequence, went to law with the artist. By way of compromising the matter the latter agreed to paint them a picture of St. Christopher, whose name signifies " Bearer of Christ," patron of the Company. He did this after his magnificent fashion, and illustrated the theme in four ways, i. e., by this famous triptych, and the picture which is on its exterior. The latter, even had it been single, would have fulfilled the condition, as it represents the saint carrying our Lord on his shoulders. Rubens nevertheless added—(1) Mary bearing the Saviour in her womb, as appears in the " Visitation " subject—(2) The same in the arms of Simeon, as depicted in the wing of the " Presentation," and—(3) The act of bearing Christ appears in the great central picture which represents the taking down from the Cross. There is no reason to doubt the truth of this story, it accounts for the sequence of the subjects before us in a manner which is thoroughly characteristic of the seventeenth century. It is in connexion with this picture that the story is told of Vandyke having retouched the neck and chin of the Virgin, which were damaged in a studio frolic. It was placed here in 1612. With regard to the " Elevation of the Cross," a work which exhibits in the strongest light some of the salient points of the artist's style, we think the student will be hugely disappointed if, agreeing with traditional criticism, he has estimated it as a work of high art in the noblest sense of the words: he will feel this notwithstanding the fullest recognition of its characteristic *bravura*, a quality, which, however, he may not have been taught to set very high in regard to Christian art, as it is one of peculiarly small value when employed on such a subject as that in question. The figure of Christ is certainly effective, and the management of chiaroscuro is admirable, whereby a great central mass of light is increased in value by the tinting of the flesh of the Saviour so that it comes in perfect tone with the powerful crimson-scarlet of the old man's robe, and with other neighbouring parts. Nothing can be more effective than the technical triumphs of which this is an example. The attitudes, nevertheless, of some of the figures are extravagant beyond measure; see that of the fellow who pushes up the long limb of the cross, and that vulgar reproduction of the *Torso Belvedere* which appears in the design of the contorted figure at the foot of the same. On the other hand, much fine and natural design is apparent in the Virgin and St. John, as depicted in the right wing, a portion of this work which is equal in colour to any of Rubens's productions. Here again, however, the vulgarity of the painter and his school appears by means of an astonishingly coarse woman who holds a great blubbery boy; the

To the eastern limb of this cathedral are attached many chapels; the east end is pentagonal. The date of its commencement we have already stated; the choir-proper was finished by the architect Peter Apelemman in 1411; the ambulatory was completed in 1500, by Herman de Waghemakere. The nave before us was put out of hand in 1460, and is the work of Master Everard. The crossing was covered by the octagon which appears in the photograph, in 1510; externally to this is a peculiarly hideous bulbous copper construction, which is placed by way of spire, and unfortunately conspicuous in all parts of Antwerp. To finish our memoranda of the interior, let us state that the pulpit, which is incomparably less offensive than that at Mechlin, came from the Abbey of St. Bernard-on-the-Scheldt, and represents Europe, Asia, Africa, and America, by statues placed beneath the rostrum. The choir stalls are modern but good. There is no choir screen, a low railing separates the choir from the rest of the church; the rood,—the figure on which is of fine early fifteenth-century work,—is suspended from the roof. The picture which closes the vista by standing above the high-altar, is Rubens's "Assumption of the Virgin;" it was produced by him in the space of sixteen days and for the price of as many thousand florins. This work appears to have been over-restored; at any rate its upper portions are now in a very bad state, the draperies are faded and stained. The finest stained glass here presents itself in the easternmost window of the south exterior aisle, i. e., in the Chapel of the Sacrament (see the second photograph;) this was given by Engelbert of Nassau, c. 1550. There is more of similar character in the fourth and fifth nave clerestory windows, north side.

---

last also is a figure offensive enough to degrade one's ideas of the very subject itself. We cannot overlook a dreadful Magdalen, who poses herself in the neighbourhood. On looking at this picture, a thought of the gulf which lay between the Flanders of Memline and that of Rubens shocks all who know anything about the subject, and consider Art as an exponent of the states of society in ages so diverse as those of the painters. Rubens is himself again in the left wing of the triptych, where appear the brave figures of a rider and a dappled horse, in which, as in others near them, there is much which suggests how the painter, when this part was executed, still profited by what he learnt in Venice. These figures are acceptable to the most fastidious, because it is possible to dissociate them in our minds from anything that concerns the subject, and welcome them as proper to nothing nobler than the "Portrait of a Gentleman." Technically speaking, the workmanship, i. e., handling, modelling, etc., throughout the triptych, are perfect.

On entering the cathedral at Antwerp the effect on the spectator is peculiar; this is derived from the apparently interminable forest of piers which present themselves on either hand, and from the constancy with which the continuous impost has been used. The absence of a choir-screen is remarkable in a country where high jubés are most frequent, and admits here of great freedom of vision. Bare of decorative sculptures as it is, this interior is happily free from the vulgar statues of Apostles that mar so many fine naves in Belgium. The absence of a triforium, and consequent proximity of the arcade and clerestory, give a modern non-Gothic look to the nave before us. Although the continuous imposts of the pillars of the intermediate aisles may enhance that elegance which is due to their slender proportions, the comparatively low roof of the nave, the equal division of its bays into arcade and clerestory, the lack of carvings, capitals, etc., throughout, and above all, the poor forms of the archivolt mouldings, produce an effect which is unworthy of the extent and costliness of the structure we are examining. One sees how art was decayed when this church was erected, and one learns how, at that time, mere size seemed important, and that the spirit of Gothic design was weak when frequent and monotonous repetitions of parts were tolerated in great edifices. In this respect the cathedral at Antwerp resembles the Houses of Parliament at Westminster, and looks as if it had been made by machinery.

The exterior of this cathedral, like those of so many of its class, is almost concealed by thickly clustered houses which cling to its sides in a manner that not only mars the design, but puts the structure in peril of fire. The west front only is open to view; it is here that the most effective portion of the church presents itself in the picturesque and richly-decorated north-west tower. On either side of the portal the architect intended that an extraordinarily lofty spire should rise, surmounting a tower; of these, that on the south-west has been carried only to the level of the roof. Its companion, however, had a happier fate, and, being finished, is four hundred and three feet seven inches in height.* The tower which

---

* From this extraordinary elevation the view is very extensive, including Bruges, Ghent, Mechlin, Louvain, Breda, and other towns in Holland and Belgium. Shortly before his visit to Bruges, before noted, p. 115, our friend Mr. Evelyn ascended this tower. His philosophical reflections and complacency are worth a reference to the " Diary " for 1641.

sustains the spire was begun in 1422, and had, in the first case, a tall flêche with turrets at the angles, a work more strictly Gothic than that which now exists, and which replaced it in 1508. The nature of the alteration then made will suggest itself in the following account of the steeple as it stands. The lower portions of both towers below the level of the clock are undoubtedly parts of the original structure, and exhibit elements of late Decorated, or, more strictly, Perpendicular character; above these, the second stage of the completed (*i. e.*, north-west) tower shows features of decided Decorated aspect, which may be unaltered from the form originally given, and retain that which the part below has lost in restoration. The highest portion is exuberant Flamboyant; indeed, it can hardly be said to be Gothic at all. The richness of this part does not compensate for its lack of purity and severity of form. The work, in fact, is not truly architectural, because it is only superficially formed of stones, that are strung on iron bars, riveted and bolted together to produce an effect which is not genuine, however curious it may be to the uninformed spectator. At the same time it is not to be denied that the result is, even to the educated eye, rich and effective.

Near the foot of the north-west tower stands the famous wrought-iron well-canopy by Quentin Mastys, blacksmith and painter of Antwerp, an example of hammer-work which is so fine in its design that one is almost tempted to say that the artist wrought better at the forge than at the easel. His tombstone was removed from a demolished church and set up at the foot of the tower before us. It is now in the Museum. The place of this slab on the tower is supplied by a copy bearing the inscription of the original,—

"*Conubialis Amor de Muliebre fecit Apellem;*"
and the date, 1629.

The carillons of Antwerp cathedral are hung in the spire just described, and do not equal those of Audenaerde in sweetness or clearness of tone; they comprise ninety-nine bells, and play almost incessantly. The hundredth bell does not belong to the carillons; it weighs nearly seventeen thousand pounds, and is named after Charles V., its godfather (Weale). The steps in the tower are six hundred and twenty-two in number. Besides the pictures just named, this cathedral contains, in addition to many by other painters, a fine triptych by Rubens, which represents the Resurrection, and SS. John the Baptist and Catherine. The interior of the church has suffered greatly from war, fire, and the fanatical Gueux; considering its comparatively recent origin, there is less cause for regret in this instance than in those which are supplied by the great churches of Bruges, Villers, Tournay, Brussels, and Louvain.

THE CHURCH OF ST. JACQUES, ANTWERP.

THIS edifice, notwithstanding that it did not come into existence until the last decade of the fifteenth century, is one of the most beautiful parish churches in the Low Countries. Occupying the site of an earlier building, it was begun in 1491 from the designs of Herman de Waghemakere, one of the architects of the cathedral, whose sons, in 1503, followed him in office and continued the works until about 1530, when their labours were stopped for want of funds. In 1602 the edifice was recommenced; but, to this day, the western tower is unfinished. The nave and transept were begun in 1514, and perfected in 1620; the choir was taken in hand in 1602 and completed in 1652. The apsidal chapels date between 1626 and 1656; the porch on the west front, begun in 1515, was finished in 1694. The dimensions of the church are three hundred and ninety-two feet in length, one hundred and eighty-one feet in width, and, at the greatest height, eighty-seven feet (Weale). The original design for the interior has been carried out without change; the whole has the magnificence of a cathedral, and is in some respects a model of a rich Gothic Low Country church of late date, marred in a less degree than is usual by the multitude and exuberance of its insertions, which comprise statues, pictures, monuments, metal-works, carvings, etc. Of these the screen, stalls, and high-altar, are among the most splendid of their kind produced in the seventeenth century; of course they are out of keeping with the Gothic building, which in style aims at the fashion of a period anterior to that in vogue when it was begun. This style, seriously defective as it is in purity and in that variety of elementary forms which is characteristic of the best Gothic work, has that sort of highly educated expression which does as much for the appearance of men as for buildings, and often gives the pleasant gloss of finish where spirit and strength are wanting. To

THE CHURCH OF ST. JACQUES, ANTWERP.

us the edifice seems exactly such as might result from the genius of a man who had passed through no end of competitive examinations, a person trained to the bone, and master of all that could be taught, but who, if untrained and born at an earlier period, might have produced something really noble.

The plan of the church is cruciform, with seven apsidal chapels, two aisles on the east side of the transept, and a nave with an aisle on each side of it. In the eastern chapel are the tombs of Rubens and his family; that of the painter is marked by a slab of white marble with an inscription which records his interment, qualities, earthly status, and the date of his death, in a vainglorious manner that contrasts painfully with the humility and resignation expressed by the epitaph of Hubert Van Eyck at Ghent. The altarpiece of the chapel is by Rubens, and intended to represent the Virgin and Child with saints; it is one of his finest and most brilliant works. Nearly all the decorations and furniture of this church derive from the sixteenth and seventeenth centuries, and, accordingly, scarcely come under the denomination of "relics." As to the details of the edifice itself, let us say that they are for the most part Flamboyant, and exhibit the rigidity of form which is remarkable in works of that class when executed at a late date and designed by highly trained architects.

The visitor to Antwerp must not forget to examine the fine Church of St. Paul (1540—71) where the ornate Renaissance confessional stalls that line the sides of the nave-aisles are to the highest degree picturesque, however ill they may assort with one's ideas of sculpture-proper. On each side of the seats in these works is a place for the communicant; each front is decorated by two statues of angels, which stand in varied and simple attitudes on either hand, and by nearly life-sized figures of saints. The carving, though late, is fine; the draperies are admirable in disposition and execution, free and faithful in style; the expressions and attitudes have more repose than is generally the case with such works. The backs of these stalls, which line the whole of the walls beneath the windows, are decorated by excellently wrought panels, containing fruit, flowers, etc. The decorative effectiveness of the double range is most striking; the rood-screen, which was of similar character to the stalls, was sold a few years since. The wall-passage, which serves for a triforium, has a fine series of Flamboyant panels in its front; the pulpit is ineffably hideous. The pulpit in the Gothic Church of St. Andrew is a capital specimen of its class. The Church of St. Charles Borromeo is a curious and very instructive example of the degraded condition of building—we cannot say architecture—in the hands of the Jesuits.

The most interesting relics in the *pseudo*-classical Hôtel de Ville* at Antwerp, are the carved chimney-pieces of the Salle des Mariages and the Salle de Justice; both of these works are inferior to that in the Council-chamber of the Hôtel de Ville at Bruges. The exterior of the building is in villanous taste; its statuary is absolutely ludicrous. The remains of the old Exchange of Antwerp, which was built in 1460, continue in much the same state as they were left by the fire of a few years since. In the Milk Market is a very curious house of the fifteenth century; which, although dirty and worn, still retains all the characteristic features of a domestic town-building of its age and class; the front is nearly all glass. The steep gable contains the storehouse originally proper to the shop below, together with the doorway, and the pulley by means of which goods were hoisted in. Between the docks is a huge structure, once the warehouse of the Easterlings, which was built *c*. 1564, and is now nearly deserted; it had originally a look-out tower rising in the middle of the façade, from the summit of which ships entering the river could be observed by a watchman who was stationed to give notice of their approach to the merchants of Antwerp. At present this storehouse compares unfavourably with the like edifices at Nuremberg and Constance; the latter derive from an earlier date than that of the Antwerp building. The Vieille Boucherie (1502), is an oblong brick pile, with octangular turrets surmounted by spires; the heads of the tourelles are bracketted out; the gables have corbie steps; eight bands of stone

---

* A curious anecdote connects this building, which is historically memorable in other respects, with the Hôtel de Ville at Brussels, which we have already examined. It appears that one of the "shrewdest signs and warnings" was given to Count Egmont when riding past the old Hôtel de Ville, by means of two mastiffs, "the which they interpreted to be the Duke of Alva and his son"; these creatures ran between his horse's legs, which caused him to fall, and bruise the shoulder of his master. Egmont, for the time at least, got off better from this accident than did Prince Philip of France, who, in 1131, was killed in the streets of Paris by a fall caused by a pig getting between his horse's legs.

alternate with four of brick to make up its walls. A characteristic old place. St. Julian's Hospital, founded in 1303, gives food and lodging for one night to all poor applicants; many avail themselves of the gifts. Antwerp is one of the richest cities in Europe in old houses, historical associations, and quaint legends. Of the latter, one gives an account of a peculiar fiend which is, or rather was, said to lie in wait for those who traversed the streets after a certain hour at night. He was a relative of Kludde, with whom we met at Villers, and bears the name of the Long Wapper; his habit was to frequent by-streets and, if in a bad humour, to carry off folks, some of whom never returned. He would mock the cries of persons in distress, especially those of children, and sometimes assume the forms of lost babies, to whom charitable mothers, finding them apparently deserted, would give breasts which were of right proper to human infants: when so nourished, the foundling fiend soon grew so intolerably heavy that the good woman would put down her load in amazement, and then learn, to her dismay, that she had nursed the Wapper, who ran off shrieking. He would perform all sorts of tricks, and assume many forms; he would look into church windows in order to gibe at late devotees, and afterwards howl and scream at them as they came out. He would stretch himself to terrible lengths and stand outside the tallest houses so as to see into the upper rooms where people were sitting at night, and alarm them by knocking at the glass, or even by speaking uncouth words in outlandish tongues. He would enter men's houses in the form of a familiar friend, and, while all were talking, suddenly vanish. He would play in the street with boys, and use them roughly, going off with shouts of wild laughter. People were much afraid of him because something was sure to happen to them if they said evil of the Long Wapper. At last it was found that he would never pass an image of the Virgin, whereupon men set to work and placed such things at the corners of every street; this is why there are so many images, and why the Wapper is not now found at Antwerp. He is said to have gone to the sea-coast.*

---

* See Thorpe's "Netherlandish Traditions," Lumley, for a further account of the Long Wapper of Antwerp.

CLOISTERS IN THE PALACE AT LIEGE.

HE palace of the Prince-Bishop of Liège was originally built in 973, but the present edifice dates no further back than 1508; it is the work of Bishop de la Marck, and was completed in 1539. A few years later we find Margaret of Navarre giving an account of this fabric in her memoirs, which may well astonish those who examine the grimy precincts which have replaced the splendid buildings, rich gardens, and many fountains, that so delighted the taste of the queen of Henry IV. Peculiarly obnoxious to fire, it would appear that this building has suffered at least four times from the ravages of that element; this happened last in 1734, when a large portion was consumed. An immense edifice remains, which cannot fail to strike the spectator with what may be called the oddity rather than the quaintness, still less the grace and least of all the dignity, of its parts. For example, the façade which appears in the background of the photograph is good of its kind, while the shafts of the piers which support the cloisters are only less unfortunate in Art than their caps, which last, as the reader will observe, have been wrought in so bungling a fashion as to be actually too narrow for the mouldings of the arcade that rest upon them. The absurdity of this defect is so great that one might almost be tempted to fancy the vaulting of the cloister, and the piers had origins of different periods; the thing would be understood if it were possible that the latter are but makeshifts to support the former in place of better works. This quadrangle is infinitely the least unbeautiful portion of the palace; another and larger quadrangle is completely surrounded by an arcade comprising sixty stumpy pillars of such remarkably hideous form as to be uglier than the so-called "balusters" which so often figure in modern parapets, and have not unhappily been compared to footmen's calves. The arabesques carved on these pillars are not only

COURT OF THE BISHOP'S PALACE, LIEGE.

intensely stupid in conception—which is intolerable in fantastic work—but uncouth to the last degree. How wilfully and needlessly the architecture of this enormous edifice was degraded, may be seen by those who will examine the style of the pretty Hôtel de Ville at Audenaerde, which follows here, and was designed twenty years later than the monstrosity of Liège. The palace of the bishop is now used as a Palais de Justice.

The famous Cathedral of St. Lambert at Liège once stood in front of the palace of the bishop; like the Church of St. Donat at Bruges, it was destroyed in the Revolution at the end of the last century, after having been one of the wealthiest and most splendid churches in Europe. In front of it, the Wild Boar of Ardennes caused the naked body of the Prince-Bishop to be cast (Monstrelet). In the basilica which formerly occupied its site, Grimoald, son of Pepin, was slain; Lothaire II. was crowned there by Pope Innocent II. in 1131, on which occasion St. Bernard was present, and the chapter comprised nine sons of kings, and, of sixty members, but one of ignoble birth. Not a stone remains of the Cathedral of St. Lambert. Many interesting churches are to be found in Liège: among them none surpass that which is dedicated to the Holy Cross (St. Croix), which has a Romanesque western apse and tower (*c*. 1170); the vaulting of the nave (*c*. 1300) is lower than that of the aisles, and borne upon brackets which are attached to the main piers. This church contains a superb reliquary of the eleventh century, enamelled and gilt, in the form of a triptych, with demi-figures of the apostles, and figures of angels, etc. St. Paul's, now the cathedral, is a fine church, begun 1280, finished 1557. The caps of the pillars of the nave arcade are, with great severity of form, extraordinarily beautiful; something like them appears in the Church of Notre Dame at Huy. St. Paul's contains some fine incised slabs, reliquaries (of the eleventh and sixteenth centuries), paintings, etc. St. John's church has a Romanesque tower of the twelfth century, and part of a cloister of Flamboyant work. In St. Denis is a reredos of the fifteenth century. In the tower is the ancient bell named Henry, after the Emperor Henry IV., which was removed from St. Lambert's, and may be styled the "Roland" of Liège. St. Jacques's church is famous for its great size and late Gothic architecture; the latter, in some respects, resembles that once prevalent in Spain; it was rebuilt between

1513 and 1538. There is no southern limb to the transept; the roof is painted with admirable arabesques; the continuous impost appears in the pillars of the nave arcade. Notwithstanding its late origin (1520—40), the stained glass is remarkable for its brilliancy. Copies of this glass have been engraved and published (see Weale's *Quarterly Papers on Architecture*, and other works on stained glass.) In St. Bartholomew's is a handsome brass font, dating from 1112, consisting of a basin supported by ten oxen (there were originally twelve) and decorated with bas-reliefs of scriptural subjects, a most interesting relic. The interior of the Abbey of St. Laurence is well worth seeing. Sir John Mandeville, the English traveller, whose stories have amused so many generations, was buried, 1372, in a grave, now unknown, in the Convent of St. Julian. The city of Liège is one of the most picturesque places in Belgium, a character it owes to the sudden rise of a part of the site above the ordinary level, to the massed buildings on the higher ground, to the churches which are picturesquely grouped, and to the fine quays and occasional large open spaces it exhibits.

The traveller who leaves Liège for the west should do so by the steamers which go by way of the Meuse, and past Huy, to Namur. He will do well to land at Huy and examine its beautiful church of Notre Dame (1311—1377), which is noteworthy on account of its triforium, rose window, nave piers, and carved portal of the thirteenth century. Here may be said to culminate the picturesque scenery of this part of the Meuse. The town, with its houses, churches, bridge, etc., groups admirably with the fortress that crowns the height above. Countless romantic stories are told about the neighbourhood of Huy, concerning its innumerable castles, glens, rocks, caverns, churches, abbeys, and villages. Here Peter the Hermit lived and died; some of his bones are still preserved in the cathedral of Namur, a church in which the relics of him whom Anna Comnena called "Cuckoo Peter" were gathered after they had been dispersed at the Revolution which ruined his famous house of Neumonstier, where they had rested since he died in 1115. The Meuse is remarkable above our English rivers inasmuch that it was long ago, and may be still is, haunted by water-fairies, or Nixen, of whom and of their dealings with mankind there are many legends.

THE LOST NIX-MAIDEN.

If propitiated by gifts of food, the Nixen are said to be good-natured, otherwise they are of uncertain humour and inclined to mischief. It is worthy of note that the upland people of Belgium have innumerable legends, some of which are of highly poetic quality and wholly different from the rather practical spirit of those which are prevalent in the lower provinces. The Meuse is haunted, as they aver, by Nixen; the ruined castles in the valleys are tenanted by ghosts of their former possessors, the abandoned mines swarm with supernatural labourers, and the sound of hammers is often heard where no man shoes a horse or sharpens a plough-share. The pigs of iron or lead which now and then turn up in long deserted spots—left there, as it would appear by the inscriptions they retain, by Roman or Mediæval smelters—are attributed to Kobolds, and grim craftsmen whom enchantments keep at work. Of the Nixen take this legend:—One sunny summer evening the youths of a town were dancing in a meadow which was fringed with trees on three of its sides, and sloped on the fourth towards the margin of the Meuse. Scarcely had the shadows of the trees touched the water and broadened over the field as the sun went down, when nearly a score of ladies appeared upon the bank, whose beauty was wonderful to see; they wore white of the purest hue, were crowned with water-flowers, and had upon their hands long green gloves, which reached nearly to the elbows; they moved so gracefully that none could say whether they walked upon or glided above the earth. After the surprise of the young men was over, and the suspicions of the damsels of the town were calmed by the innocent looks of the new-comers, the two parties united and danced until the moon rose; then they sat where her light fell upon the sward, and some among the ladies sang so sweetly that all who heard them were certain that the visitors were young water-fairies who had left the river for a frolic and meant no harm to any one. The people thought the less of that, because such visits were by no means unheard of. They sang until the moon set, and even for a short time after it became dark. Suddenly their voices ceased, and not more than three favoured men could find the partners who, until a certain moment, were sitting beside them on the grass. The Nixen had gone to their home in the river, and so suddenly had they disappeared that not even the waving of a white robe was distinguishable as the wearers sped over the meadow to the water-side. Three damsels, however, had, while the voices of many were heard in the song, whispered that on the next evening they would return again at the moment when the sun was setting. At that time the youths went to the meadow and waited, but the ladies came not until the moon was high. It was noticed that although they were dressed differently from the manner of the preceding night, yet all three retained the long green gloves which formed so important a part of their first attire. The ladies danced until one of them, heated by the exercise, took off her gloves, and then her partner was sure she belonged to the water-people, for he observed that her fingers were not divided as those of human maidens are, but webbed with thin white skin which held them together, although it did not hinder them being used as fingers should be.

N

Again the companions sang and talked after dancing, when suddenly the clock struck the warning for midnight, and the lady who had taken off her gloves demanded them back from her partner, who, nevertheless, like a cruel fool, refused to give them up, and avowed that he meant to retain them as keepsakes. In vain she begged and threatened, he held fast to his words and the long green gloves. In a few moments, after the sound of the bell was unheard in the woods and its very echo was dead in the mountains, a mystic force seemed to draw the damsels towards the water, for they stepped over the grass and often looked back, joining their entreaties for a return of the gloves. At last the darkness took them all, and silence came where there had been much singing and laughter; the final sound of a voice that reached the youths was, "My gloves! my gloves!" The maidens departed so swiftly that when the lovers ran to the riverside, they saw nothing on its surface, and heard only the usual sound of the ripples. The obstinate youth, fearful of evil, remained on the margin until dawn, but the voice came not again, and nothing more was ever heard or seen except that when the sun was clear of the earth on that morning he saw a large spot of blood suddenly rise from the bottom of the river, and spread and float slowly away. Then he knew that the fierce Nix-man had found out his daughter's absence, and, because she had degraded his people before men by taking off her gloves, it was believed that he had slain at least one of the damsels, and that the blood had risen to the surface of the water to be, as it were, a reproach to the causer of her death. Some persons aver that this story cannot be true because it is well known that all the clocks in Belgium strike the hour thirty minutes before it is due, and that this would give ample time to the Nix-maiden for the recovery of her gloves. We will refuse to credit the tale when it is proved that this irrational habit of the Belgian clocks obtained in the time of the lost Nix.

www.ingramcontent.com/pod-product-compliance
Lightning Source LLC
Chambersburg PA
CBHW032059230426
43662CB00035B/678